Witches'
Spell-A-Day
Almanac

Holiday & Lore   Spells & Recipes
Rituals & Meditations

Editing/Design: Michael Fallon
Cover Design: Lisa Novak; Cover Photo: © PhotoDisk
Interior Art: Claudine Hellmuth (illustrations: pp. 9, 29, 49, 71, 91, 113, 133, 153, 173, 193, 215, 235); Eris Klein (holiday and day icons)

You can order Llewellyn books and annuals from *New Worlds*, Llewellyn's magazine catalog, or online at www.llewellyn.com. Call toll-free 1-877-NEW WRLD to request a free copy of the catalog, or click on "Catalog Request" under the Online Bookstore heading on our website.

ISBN 0-7387-0227-7
Llewellyn Worldwide
PO Box 64383, Dept. 0-7387-0227-7
St. Paul, MN 55164

Table of Contents

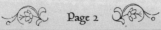

About the Authors

Karri Allrich is an author, artist, and eclectic cook who weaves her Goddess path through all aspects of her life. She shares her Massachusetts home and studio with her husband and their two sons. Her published books include: *Recipes From a Vegetarian Goddess, A Witch's Book of Dreams,* and *Cooking by Moonlight.* Ms. Allrich has also written articles for numerous publications.

Elizabeth Barrette is the managing editor of *PanGaia* and the assistant editor of *SageWoman.* She has been involved in the Pagan community for more than twelve years and lives in central Illinois. Her other writing fields include speculative fiction and gender studies. Visit her website at: http://www.worth-link.net/ysabet/index.html.

Denise Dumars is a member of the Fellowship of Isis who practices with several Isian groups in the southern California area. She teaches college English and has written much about modern myth and magic in such publications as *SageWoman, Fate, The Isis Papers,* and various editions of Llewellyn's annuals.

Karen Follett has been a practicing Witch for thirty years, and was first taught by her great grandmother, a healer and a midwife. Currently a member of the local coven of the Georgian Tradition, she works as a nurse specializing in maternal and child health. In addition, Karen is an empath, medical intuitive, and reiki practitioner. She has been married for twenty years and has two sons.

Therese Francis, Ph.D. is an author, astrologer, folklorist, herbalist, and noted public speaker. Her most recent books are *The Mercury Retrograde Book, 20 herbs to take on a Business Trip,* and *20 Herbs to Take Outdoors* (published by One Spirit). Therese is the author of numerous articles on herbs, astrology, and other New Age topics, and she has written for Llewellyn's annuals for a number of years. An active member of the Sante Fe Astrology Forum, Therese teaches astrology, psychic and intuitive development, self-defense, and the integration of body, mind, heart, and spirit. She currently writes and resides in Sante Fe, New Mexico.

Lily Gardner–Butts is a lifelong student of folklore and mythology. She is a priestess in the Daughters of Gaia coven and a member of the Fat Thursday Writers. Lily lives with her husband, two Corgis, and an ancient cat in Portland, Oregon. She is currently working on a novel.

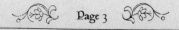

Magenta Griffith has been a Witch for over twenty-five years, an ordained priestess for thirteen years, and was a founding member of the coven Prodea. She leads rituals and workshops in the Midwest, and is librarian for the New Alexandria Library, a Pagan and magical resource center that can be accessed on the web at: http://www.magusbooks.com/newalexandria/.

James Kambos writes and paints at his home in the beautiful hill country of southern Ohio. He has a degree in history and has authored numerous articles on the folkloric traditions of Greece and the Near East and the Appalachian mountain region of the United States.

Jonathan Keyes is a health astrologer who works with herbs, diet, stones, and animal totems to help harmonize planetary influences for health and well-being. He writes a regular "Lunar Health" column for Stariq.com and has written for Mountain Astrologer. He also writes a bimonthly health horoscope that can be found at http://www.astrologicalhealth.com.

Kristin Madden is a homeschooling mom and wildlife rehabilitator. She is the author of *Shamanic Guide to Death and Dying, Pagan Parenting,* and *Mabon: Celebrating the Autumn Equinox.* She was raised in a shamanic home and has explored various Eastern and Western mystic paths since 1972. She sits on the governing board of the Ardantane Project, a Wiccan/Pagan seminary, and is a Druid and tutor in the Order of Bards, Ovates, and Druids.

Robert Place is a visionary artist, and the designer, illustrator, and author of a tarot deck for Llewellyn. He is an expert on Western mysticism and the history of the tarot, and he has taught divination at the New York Open Center, Omega Institute, New York Tarot School, and the World Tarot Congress. He has appeared on Discovery and the Learning Channel, and can be reached through his website at: http://thealchemicalegg.com/.

Laurel Reufner has been a solitary Pagan more than a decade. Currently, she writes articles for various publications, and takes on whatever projects seems too interesting to resist, from her home in southeastern Ohio. Her website can be found at: http://www.spirit-realm.com/Melinda/paganism/html.

Sheri Richerson has more than twenty years experience in newspaper and magazine writing for numerous publications and websites. Her range of writing expertise has included astrology, herbs, aromatheraphy as well as tropical and exotic plants. She is also a lifetime member of the International

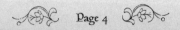

Thespian Society. Her favorite pastimes are riding her motorcycle and her horse, and gardening in her herb and tropical plant gardens.

Jenna Tigerheart is a member of the Covenant of Unitarian Universalist Pagans and the Unitarian Universalist Association. She has practiced witch-craft and an appreciation for our Mother the Earth for many years. She is also a Pagan songwriter and member of the women's chorale group Chantress.

Abby Willowroot is an archetypist, artist, priestess, and mother whose life for the past thirty years has been dedicated to bringing Goddess imagery and consciousness back into contemporary culture. As such, she is founder and director of the Goddess 2000 Project and the Spiral Goddess Grove. Incidentally, nine pieces of Ms. Willowroot's jewelry are in the permanent collections of the Smithsonian Institution in Washington, D.C. Abby's art and articles have appeared in *WomanSpirit, SageWoman,* and *GreenEgg* magazines.

Introduction

A Note on Magic and Spells

The spells in the newly redesigned *Witches' Spell-A-Day Almanac* evoke everyday magic designed to improve our lives and homes. You needn't be an expert on magic to follow these simple rites and spells; as you will see if you use these spells through the year, magic, once mastered, is easy to perform. The only advanced technique required of you is the art of visualization.

Visualization is an act of controlled imagination. If you can call up in your mind a picture of your best friend's face or a flag flapping in the breeze, you can visualize. In magic, visualizations are used to direct and control magical energies. Basically, the spell-caster creates a visual image of the spell's desired goal, whether it be perfect health, a safe house, or a protected pet.

Visualization is the basis of all good spells, and as such it is a tool that should be properly used. Visualization must be real in the mind of the spell-caster so that it allows him or her to raise, concentrate, and send forth energy to accomplish the spell.

Perhaps when visualizing, you'll find that you're doing everything right, but you don't feel anything. This is common, for we haven't been trained to acknowledge—let alone utilize—our magical abilities. Keep practicing, however, for your spells can "take" even if you're not the most experienced natural magician.

You will notice also that many spells in this collection have a somewhat "light" tone. They are seemingly fun and frivolous, filled with rhyme and colloquial speech. This is not to diminish the seriousness of the purpose, but rather to create a relaxed atmosphere for the practitioner. Lightness of spirit helps focus energy; rhyme and common language help the spell-caster remember the words and train the mind where it is needed. The intent of this magic is indeed very serious at times; and magic is never to be trifled with.

Even when your spells are effective, magic won't usually sparkle before your very eyes. The test of magic's success is time, not immediate eye-popping results. But you can feel magic's energy for yourself by rub-

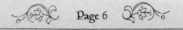

bing your palms together briskly for ten seconds, then holding them a few inches apart. Sense the energy passing through them, the warm tingle in your palms. This is the power raised and used in magic. It comes from within and is perfectly natural.

Among the new features of this year's *Witches' Spell-A-Day Almanac* are: a new, easy-to-read almanac format; new and improved spells specifically tailored for each day of the year (its magical, astrological, and historical energies); and additional tips and lore for various days throughout the year—including color correspondences based on planetary influences, and an incense-of-the-day entry to help you waft magical energies from the ether into your space.

In redesigning this product, we were inspired by the ancient almanac traditions and layout of the "Book of Days," including the nineteenth-century classic example of *Chamber's Book of Days,* which is subtitled: *A Miscellany of Popular Antiquities in connection with the Calendar.* As you will see, our fifteen authors this year made history a theme of their spells, and we hope that by knowing something of the magic of past years we may make our current year all the better. Also, we are enlisting your help, dear reader, for next year's magical lore and historical precedences. Send in your own tidbits of information for days you consider magical, and we may publish it in our 2004 edition of the *Witches' Spell-A-Day Almanac* and send you a free copy of the book. See page 267 for more details.

Enjoy your days, and have a magical year!

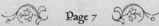

2003
Year of Spells

January

January is the first month of the year of the Gregorian calendar, and a time of beginnings. Its astrological sign is Capricorn, the goat (Dec 20-Jan 20), a cardinal earth sign ruled by Saturn. The name of the month itself comes from the two-faced Roman god Janus, who rules over gates and doorways. This wintry month is marked by icicles, hoarfrost, and snowdrifts, and by the warmth of the home hearth. Traditionally, handicrafts such as wool-spinning were practiced in January, and the spinning wheel has become a symbol of the season. According to Pagan traditions, even in this frozen time there are signs of new life. The days, for instance, are now slowly growing longer, and a few early flowers, such as the paper-white narcissus and white hellebore, begin blooming. The Full Moon of January is called the Storm Moon. The main holiday of the month is of course New Year's Day, a day that calls for safeguards, augurs, and charms. All over the world, people are eager to see what the new year will bring; they kiss strangers, shoot guns in the air, toll bells, and exchange gifts. In Scotland, people watch the threshhold to see what the "firstfooter," or first visitor, augurs for the year. People who make visits on New Year's Day therefore should be sure to bring gifts of herring, bread, and wood for the fire along with them.

January 1
Wednesday

New Year's Day – Kwanzaa ends

4th ♐

☽ → ♑ 6:42 pm

Color of the day: Brown
Incense of the day: Eucalyptus

New Year's Ritual

Fresh starts, all possibilities, a shared vision of hope are in order on New Year's Day. Light candles of many colors, and place them around a bowl of clear water, saying:

> This day is waiting for
> me to choose, if I will
> win or if I will lose.
> The magic I live in the
> coming year, flows from
> the gifts I choose.
>
> The vows I make,
> the chances I take, the
> visions that now fill my
> heart, grow strong with
> intention that is honor—
> able and true.
>
> Magic come and magic
> stay, with me now and
> everyday.
> Creation be alive in me,
> bring light to all I see.
> Fill my heart with peace.
>
> Fill my spirit with the
> universe's light, power,
> justice, and eternal
> might. Open my vision of
> all I see, blessings and
> benevolence are in me.
>
> My powers grow with
> each new insight picked
> from wisdom's tree.
> Magical moments I do
> see, each day beings me
> closer to what I will be.
>
> By the light of these
> candles my illumination
> grows bright,
> By the waters of life
> bring to Earth peace and
> new insight.
> I welcome the new year
> and vow to be valiant,
> kind, and wise.
>
> So mote it be.

Abby Willowroot

Notes:

Holiday lore: New Year's Day calls for safeguards, augurs, charms, and proclamations. All over the world on this day, people kiss strangers, shoot guns into the air, toll bells, and exchange gifts. Preferred gifts are herring, bread, and fuel for the fire.

January 2
Thursday

 4th ♑
New Moon 3:23 pm

Color of the day: Green
Incense of the day: Chrysanthemum

New Year's Resolution Spell

For this spell, choose a few goals that you want to accomplish; these may be related to work or your personal life. Keep them in your mind; with this spell, you will raise spiritual assistance in accomplishing your intentions. To start, you will need to gather four rocks that you've collected from a nearby "special place," perhaps a park or your back yard. You will also need some unrefined salt. After the New Moon has begun, take the four rocks you have gathered and place them outside near your home in an undisturbed part of your yard. Lay down the rocks in a cross, one for each direction. Sprinkle the salt lightly over the four rocks, and toss the rest in the center. Visualize the goals you have set for yourself and say out loud what you hope to accomplish. Leave the rocks out until you have realized your aims.

Jonathan Keyes

Notes:

January 3
Friday

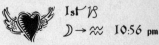 1st ♑
☽ → ♒ 10:56 pm

Color of the day: White
Incense of the day: Nutmeg

Relationship with Your Shadow

Light a candle and place it in the center of a darkened room. Sit or stand with the candle behind you. Watch how a small movement has a large effect on your shadow. Give the shadow shape a name of some trait in yourself that you don't like. Welcome that shadow and play with it. Change the name slightly so it becomes a quality you want in your life. For example, if the shadow is at first arrogance, the new shadow name can be confidence. Then turn and face the candle, realizing that the shadows on the wall are the projections of the shadows within yourself, and, with a little change, they can be qualities that you want in your life.

Therese Francis

Notes:

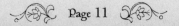

January 4
Saturday

 1st ≈

Color of the day: Gray

Incense of the day: Lavender

Controlling Creativity Spell

Here's a little spell to help you get control of your creativity. Prepare your sacred space as normal, then light two yellow or red candles and call upon your muses. Mix a half cup of sand with three teaspoons vervain in a small bowl. On the sand, focus your intention of being block-free. Suffuse the sand completely with your will. Hold an obsidian stone, ring, or pendant in your cupped hands, seeing it as an empty object ready to absorb the sand's energy. Bury the obsidian in the sand for three days. Keep the stone with you when working, taking it in hand when you feel a creative lapse.

Melinda Fulk

Notes:

January 5
Sunday

 1st ≈

Color of the day: Yellow

Incense of the day: Poplar

Back-to-the-Routine Spell

Way to go—you've survived the winter holidays! Now that you're back into the swing of things, consider your routines. They're the brick and mortar of life, the things you do on a daily basis. For a spell to encourage you to get back to your routine, you need a white candle and a plain ring. First, hold the ring and imagine a typical day. Then light the candle, and say:

> Day in and day out
> Laugh, cry, whisper,
> shout.
> This is what I do
> Show me now what is
> true.

Meditate on what routines mean to you, and how they improve your magical practice. Then blow out the candle; wear or carry the ring with you. As you go through your day, then, think about which routines you appreciate, and which you'd like to change or give up. In the end, honor them all for giving your life some necessary structure.

Elizabeth Barrette

Notes:

Notes:

January 6
Monday

1st ≈

☽ → ♓ 5:57 am

Color of the day: Silver
Incense of the day: Maple

Twelfth Night

A traditional song for the end of the Yule season opens:

> Down with the rosemary
> and bay,
> Down with the mistle-
> toe.

This day is traditionally known as Twelfth Night, the last of the twelve days of Christmas. It's time now to take down your decorations; in fact, many people believe keeping them up after this day will bring bad luck. If you still want some decoration in your living space now, generic winter fare such as plain white lights or greenery will have to do. Extra plants can keep the winter blues away and the air fresh.

Magenta Griffith

Holiday lore: Twelfth Night celebrations in cultures around the world call for cake-baking. In France, the cake is called *Galette des Rois* (the King's Cake); in England, the cake has lucky charms baked inside it, and in Mexico, the cake is crown-shaped.

January 7
Tuesday

1st ♓

Color of the day: Gray
Incense of the day: Gardenia

First Day of Carnival

Yesterday was the Feast of Epiphany, and by the old system of reckoning today is the second day of Carnival. The final day will fall on the eighth Tuesday from today, which is called Mardi Gras (Fat Tuesday). As tarot scholar Gertrude Moakley has pointed out, the festivities associated with Carnival are very likely a source for imagery in the tarot. Today is an excellent day for a tarot reading, especially one

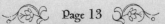

that prepares us for the events of the upcoming year.

Robert Place

Notes:

January 8
Wednesday

1st ♓
☽ → ♈ 4:15 pm

Color of the day: White
Incense of the day: Cedar

The Golden Dawn

Liddel "MacGregor" Mathers was born on January 8, 1854. Mathers founded the Hermetic Order of the Golden Dawn, which handed down a body of literature that forms the basis for many magical lodges today. The Golden Dawn, as it is popularly called, used the Qabala, Rosicrucian ceremony, and ancient Egyptian practices as the basis for a lodge that would help bring back the worship of the Goddess and cement the practices of modern ceremonial magic. Mathers was part of what was called "The Celtic Movement" when he met poet William Butler Yeats in the Reading Room of the British Museum. Yeats joined the Golden Dawn along with several other people famous at the time, including George Bernard Shaw, Florence Farr, Maud Gonne, and Aleister Crowley. Eventually the Golden Dawn broke apart, and the former members founded their own lodges and improvised upon Mathers' teachings. Still, it was Mathers who had set the ball rolling and ushered in a New Age of magical practice.

Denise Dumars

Notes:

January 9
Thursday

1st ♈

Color of the day: Turquoise
Incense of the day: Evergreen

Grow-Your-Money Spell

If you long for more money, prepare your altar with various amounts of currency on either side of a green candle. Inscribe your wish on the candle—scratching, for example "money for monthly bills," right into the wax. Be sure to only request as much as you need and no more.

Light the candle and sprinkle a teaspoon of parsley over the top while saying:

> The money I see is
> growing. The money I
> need will come.
> I release my need into
> the universe.
> This flame brings
> changes into my life.
> I welcome them with
> open arms.

Repeat this three times. Allow the candle to burn down in a safe place until it extinguishes itself.

Sheri Richerson

Notes:

with your coven or like-minded friends. Gather any objects that appear in your dreams from January 1st to the night of your spell. It is believed that if you find the objects in your dreams, good luck will be yours for the year because you have given your soul what it desires. On the night of the January 10, share a potluck feast with your coven. Set the table with a purple cloth for intuition and with a green candle for luck. Have everyone bring the objects they have collected. Share your insights with each other.

Lily Gardner-Butts

Notes:

January 10
Friday

 1st ♈
Second Quarter 8:15 am

Color of the day: Rose
Incense of the day: Ginger

Iroquois Good Luck Spell

The Iroquois celebrate the Feast of Dreams today. They believe our souls communicate to us through our dreams. This spell is best done

January 11
Saturday

 2nd ♈
☽ → ♉ 4:48 am

Color of the day: Brown
Incense of the day: Jasmine

Waking a Sleepy Resolution

Wake a sleepy New Year's resolution by rewording the intent and redirecting the energy toward the goal of your resolution. With this reworded resolution in mind, light a red candle. Focus on your goal and the steps that will get you from point A to point B. Visualize yourself completing the steps and your goal in the present tense. Repeat these or similar words:

This is my inspiration,
Aries' Moon is my moti-
vation. The path to my
goal has now begun.
As my will, this will be
done!

After you have released the energy, you may extinguish the candle. On the next morning, relight your candle and focus on your daily goal each day until the next Full Moon.

Karen Follett

Notes:

tate with them, asking for their blessings and giving thanks for their energies. Light one green and one yellow candle, then hold your hands out over the herbs. Visualize your home and land filled with the healing energy of the Sun. See this merge with Earth energy, creating a bubble that surrounds your home and family. Send this visualization into the herbs through your hands, and say:

Sacred herbs of Earth
and Sun,
Bring health and light to
every one.
Bless our travels and our
hearth,
honored plants of Sun
and Earth.

Bury the mixture at the entrance to your land or at your front and back doors of your home.

Kristin Madden

Notes:

January 12
Sunday

 2nd ♉

Color of the day: Peach
Incense of the day: Cinnamon

Sunday herbal Meditation

Combine bay leaves, cinnamon, cedar, and sagebrush, and medi-

January 13
Monday

 2nd ♉

☽ → ♊ 5:08 pm

Color of the day: Gray
Incense of the day: Lilac

Coven Dedication

When starting up a new coven, have each member bring a sacred tool to bless by saying:

> Great Mother, bless this tool. Let us use it with wisdom on each Full Moon and in the dark of night. With our hearts and our minds, may we work united in this coven that we dedicate ourselves.

After the blessing, light candles and place them in a circle. Focus energy to light the coven's path. Each year on the coven's anniversary, light new candles from the wicks of the old.

Jenna Tigerheart

Notes:

January 14
Tuesday

2nd ♊
Color of the day: White
Incense of the day: Honeysuckle

Minor Injury Spell

When injured, either physically or psychically, immediately rub your hands together briskly until they tingle. Then move your hands in a circular motion over the injured area and several inches on all sides. Imagine that you are filling up the injured area's aura by pulling energy from the surroundings over the "hole." Do this for about three minutes or until the hole feels full and "complete."

Therese Francis

Notes:

January 15
Wednesday

2nd ♊
Color of the day: Yellow
Incense of the day: Maple

A Baby Blessing Spell

Carmentis, a Roman goddess of childbirth, was honored on this day. She had the ability to fortell how long an infant would live. To bless a newborn as she begins life's journey, gather one rattle, a piece of blue paper, a pen with silver ink, a small box, and silver glitter. As the baby sleeps, gently shake the rattle three times; place it in the box. On the blue paper draw with the silver ink an image of a boat; place it in the box. Sprinkle some glitter over the box's contents as you say:

> Little one, your journey
> has begun.
> But the best is still to
> come.
> Live long and live well.
> Let no one break this
> spell.

Keep the box hidden.

James Kambos

Notes:

January 16
Thursday

 2nd ♊
☽ → ♋ 2:56 am

Color of the day: Green
Incense of the day: Vanilla

Skadi, Snowshoe Goddess

Norse mythology tells the tale of wild Skadi, sometimes described as a goddess, other times as a giantess. She is the patroness of woodslore

and winter skills such as snowshoe hiking, skiing, and sledding. She also watches over challenging relationships, so take a close look at yours today. Honor Skadi by wearing white or blue clothing and by reciting these lines:

> Skadi, snowshoe goddess,
> You run with the wolves
> and sing with the winter
> wind.
> Lead us through the
> frozen forest,
> Teach us to rely on
> ourselves,
> and light our way with
> the Northern Lights.
> When all seems dark,
> you remind us we can
> always vote with our
> feet.
> Hail, Skadi!

Elizabeth Barrette

Notes:

January 17
Friday

 2nd ♋
Color of the day: Peach
Incense of the day: Parsley

Remind-Yourself Love Spell

Sometimes we supply our own worst obstacles when attracting love into our lives. This little spell will help. Light a pink candle. Write in red ink on a small piece of parchment five things that you really like about yourself. Charge a handful of rose petals and a piece of rose quartz with your intention of self-love and acceptance, then place them, along with the parchment, into a small bag. Tie everything up, and place the bag somewhere where you'll see it often—a reminder of what's good about you.

Laurel Reufner

Notes:

January 18
Saturday

 2nd ♋
Full Moon 5:48 am
☽ → ♌ 9:29 am

Color of the day: Blue
Incense of the day: Violet

Better Homelife Spell

The home is the place where we relax, recharge, and nourish our health so we can do good work in the outside world. Often it is also where we find important relationships with our friends and family. When our home life is not going well, it is hard to stay grounded and it is harder to feel good in our hearts. During a Cancer Full Moon, we can create a better home environment through magical workings. For this spell, you will need to enlist all of your housemates to make a meal together. Gather a small amount of lemon balm and dill (both Cancer herbs), and a couple of blue candles to put on your dinner table. When cooking the meal, add the spices to the pot and say these words while stirring them in:

I add these spices to the meal,
Let our home mend and heal.
Bring us love and bring us peace,
May our hearts be at ease.

Now sit down for a meal with your housemates, and light your blue candles to symbolize the watery Cancer Moon. Reconnecting over a good meal helps develop a good atmosphere at home.

Jonathan Keyes

Notes:

Notes:

January 19
Sunday

 3rd ♌

Color of the day: Gold

Incense of the day: Sage

Chase-the-Blues Spell

January 19 honors the god Thor who battled the Frost Giants and saved the human race from an eternal winter. This is the time of year when winter's darkness recedes, but winter's cold grows in strength. Ask for Thor's aid as you struggle with low energy, illness, and with depression at this time of year. Adorn your altar with a blue cloth, a blue candle anointed with clove oil, a hammer, and a list of your personal demons of winter. Light the candle and say:

> Mighty Thor, to you I
> pray;
> Keep the winter blues
> away.
> Your strength and
> courage is what I need;
> With your aid I will
> succeed.

Pound your list of winter demons with the hammer.

Lily Gardner-Butts

January 20
Monday

Birthday of Martin Luther King, Jr. (observed)

 3rd ♌

☉ → ≈ 6:53 am

☽ → ♍ 1:32 pm

Color of the day: White

Incense of the day: Coriander

Feast of St. Sebastian

Today is the feast of St. Sebastian. Sebastian was a Roman soldier and Christian. He openly declared his faith before his employer, the Emperor Diocletian, and for this he was sentenced to death by a firing squad of archers. Sebastian was left for dead but miraculously he recovered and again presented himself to the emperor. This time, Diocletian had him clubbed to death and was successful in creating a martyr. Artists in the Renaissance loved to paint St. Sebastian with his body riddled with arrows. It may seem to be an unnecessarily gory subject to

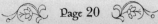

be so popularized in art, but the image of Sebastian's suffering can have an empathetic healing quality for those who are also in pain. In the Middle Ages, the plague was believed to be brought on by Apollo's arrows, and those in danger of the plague prayed to St. Sebastian for protection. If you are suffering from an illness, let St. Sebastian's image help you to experience your pain and frustration fully, accept it, and transform it into health. In Santeria and Voodoo, St. Sebastian is associated with the Orisha named Ochosi, the divine hunter.

Robert Place

Notes:

Auspicious day: Today the Sun moves into Aquarius, the sign of revolution and change, and appropriately we also celebrate the birth of one of America's most revolutionary men, Martin Luther King, Jr. While it does not seem such a strange notion now to dream of a time "when children will not be judged by the color of the skin but by the content of their character," at the time King's "I Have a Dream" speech was something remarkable—and a lesson we can all take to heart on this day.

January 21
Tuesday

 3rd ♍

Color of the day: Black

Incense of the day: Poplar

Celtic Tree Month of Rowan Begins

Also known as the mountain ash, the rowan tree has long enjoyed magical eminence for its protective properties. With the festival of Imbolc just around the corner, today is the perfect day to clear your space of negative energy and make a protection charm for the remaining winter days ahead. Burn a sprig of rosemary to cleanse your home, sweeping the rooms widdershins (counterclockwise) to banish stagnant energy. If possible, find a branch or twig from a rowan tree. Or, if rowan is not available, use a sturdy branch of rosemary. Wind a red ribbon thrice around the branch. With each wrap, say:

> The power of rowan
> protects me and thee.

Hang the branch above your door.

Karri Allrich

Notes:

January 22
Wednesday

 3rd ♏

☽ → ♎ 4:23 pm

Color of the day: Brown
Incense of the day: Pine

Retrograde Communication Spell

If you have been having communication problems lately, it may be because Mercury has been retrograde for the past three weeks. It is a good time to go back over letters, e-mail, and phone calls that didn't quite work out the way you meant them to. Get in touch with people again, this time with a written agenda if necessary, and see if you can't straighten out small misunderstandings. Check to see if your messages got through the first time—letters do get lost in the mail, e-mail does disappear, and answering machines do malfunction. Give people the benefit of the doubt; everyone's communication may have been garbled.

                    Magenta Griffith

Notes:

An explanation: Would your typical Babylonian astrologer have guessed three thousand years ago what effect the dreaded Mercury retrograde would have today? Mercury rules communications, and communications rule the world—so it makes sense that so many people would get worried right about now. But lest you let your worry go overboard—Mercury retrograde does not mean life as we know it is at an end. You just gotta be willing to let go for awhile—about three weeks or so; get off-line and spend time with yourself. There'll be time enough for that e-mail later, to be sure.

January 23
Thursday

 3rd ♎

Color of the day: Violet
Incense of the day: Sandalwood

Seeking Wisdom Spell

The disseminating Moon marks the turn toward completion of the lunar cycle. Wisdom inspired by this Moon phase can lead toward decisive action and the completion of any situational cycle. Write the situation down—describing clearly your needs, options, and desired outcome. "Dress" the paper with peppermint oil to raise the vibrational energy of your petition and your

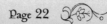

receptivity to the universal wisdom. Keep this paper until your situation is soon resolved. Focus on your situation with care, and say:

> Waning Moon,
> Waning light,
> I seek the shadows of
> darkening night.
> Grant me the guidance
> of your Divine sight.

Release the energy, giving up your situation to the universe. Messages of guidance may begin to arrive very immediately through meditative listening, or they may filter in over a period of time. The universe will provide the wisdom. Listen to the wisdom, and make the decisions of your free will.

Karen Follett

Notes:

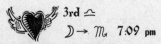

January 24
Friday

3rd ♎
☽ → ♏ 7:09 pm

Color of the day: Pink
Incense of the day: Rose

The Springs of Kupala Spell

Kupala is the Slavic goddess of springs and rivers. Her name means "to bathe," and if you need a new love in the new year, perhaps Kupala can help you. Gather some fragrant flowers, either red or pink in color, and rose or "love" scented bath salts (available at many aromatherapy and metaphysical shops). Fill the bathtub with water and bath salts as directed. Sprinkle some flower petals into the bathwater. While you relax in the bath, recite to yourself:

> Kupala, goddess fragrant,
> dear,
> I ask for love in the new year.
>
> Mountain streams bring
> fresh and free
> Waters rushing to the
> sea.
> As my will, so mote it be.

Scatter the rest of the flower petals into a moving body of water, and the spell is done.

Denise Dumars

Notes:

January 25
Saturday

 3rd ♏
Fourth Quarter 3:33 am

Color of the day: Gray
Incense of the day: Cedar

Catalyst for Change Spell

Holding a piece of clear quartz crystal, or a diamond if you have it, close your eyes and take three deep breaths. Bring to mind all of the restrictions and limitations in your life. Allow yourself to feel any emotion that comes up as a response. Call upon the energy of Saturn, and ask to be shown how best to work with his energy. Visualize these limitations, and see your frustrations transforming. See them become catalysts for change, motivating you to release the past and create a better future. Know that, just as a diamond is formed from coal through intense pressure, your life's pressures and frustrations are working to create a better you. Ask the blessings of Saturn, and carry this crystal with you.

Kristin Madden

Notes:

January 26
Sunday

 4th ♏
☽ → ♐ 10:26 pm

Color of the day: Orange
Incense of the day: Basil

Citrus Spell for Winter Care

During winter months, our bodies need extra care. Citrus fruits give us lots of vitamin C, which helps ward off colds and otherwise keep us healthy. They also represent the warm, bright energy of the Sun and its prosperity and propensity to keep up happy. For this spell, all you need is an orange. Start by holding the fruit in your hands and visualizing it aglow with sunny power. Then, as you eat the orange, silently say this verse:

> The light of the Sun for health,
> The gold of the Sun for wealth.
> You are what you eat.
> The spell is complete.

Save the orange peel for use in potpourri or in a magical sachets.

Elizabeth Barrette

Notes:

January 27
Monday

4th ♐
Color of the day: Lavender
Incense of the day: Myrrh

Angel Protection Ritual

Prepare your altar with three pink candles, one brown candle, and incense of lavender and vanilla. On the first day, light one pink candle; then light one pink candle per day for the remaining two days. On the fourth day, light the brown candle. Each day before lighting the candles, light both incense sticks. Repeat this each time you light a candle:

> Angels, I invite you to
> join me at my altar. I
> ask that you will protect
> me, my family, friends,
> pets, and property. I ask
> that you keep away
> thieves, troublemakers,
> and anyone else with evil
> purposes in mind. I thank
> you truly for your continued
> protection and friendship.

Allow the candles to burn down in a safe place until they extinguish themselves.

Sheri Richerson

Notes:

January 28
Tuesday

4th ♐
Color of the day: Red
Incense of the day: Juniper

A Winter Purification Spell

If winter makes you suffer from cabin fever and the seasonal blahs, let this ritual rid your home of all sorts of negativity. Start by using fragrances associated with January—allspice, ginger, and pine—which are also ruled by Mars, Tuesday's planet. Mix a pinch of allspice and ginger, along with a drop of olive oil in one-quarter cup of water. Then anoint the tips of a small pine branch with this spice mixture. Sprinkle the mixture about your home, using the pine branch as a "wand," repeating at various place around your home:

> Scents of pine, allspice,
> and ginger,
> Clear away negativity
> which may linger.
> Winter skies may be
> dark and drear,

Page 25

> But my home is a haven
> of warmth and cheer.

Sprinkle any remaining spice mixture near windows and doors. Perform as needed on Mondays and Tuesdays throughout the rest of the winter season.

James Kambos

Notes:

January 29
Wednesday

 4th ♐
☽ → ♑ 2:30 am

Color of the day: White
Incense of the day: Neroli

Breaking Writer's Block Spell
Today is the feast day of St. Francis de Sales, patron saint of writers and journalists. On this day, you may do a spell to surmount any creative blocks. To start, hold your arms out to your sides, and turn you head to face your right thumb (if you are right-handed; face your left thumb if you are left-handed). Say out loud:

> I cannot write any more.

Then turn your head to the opposite thumb and say:

> I can write anything at
> any time.

Repeat for both thumbs two more times. With your eyes open and looking forward, see both of your thumbs in your peripheral vision. Take a deep breath. While exhaling, quickly bring your arms in front of you and cross them. You might feel slightly disoriented for a few seconds, but new writing ideas will emerge.

Therese Francis

Notes:

Auspicious day: St. Francis died on this day in 1662. He wrote several books aimed at giving spiritual instruction to ordinary people, and in fact he is best known for teaching that the spiritual life is not just for the religious and the clergy, but for everyone. We can learn from his humble example, for even after his death Francis continued to give of himself. He provided these instructions shortly before he died:

My body be given to the
Theatre of Anatomy to
be dissected; for it will
be a comfort to me if I
can be of any advantage,
when dead, having been
of none, whilst alive.

January 30
Thursday

 4th ♑

Color of the day: Green
Incense of the day: Carnation

Peace Spell

Pax, the goddess of peace, is
honored on this date. With
Concordia and Salus, she represents
the Triple Goddess, Fortuna. Each
of our thoughts and actions today
vibrate through the web that connects
us to the universe and affects the
fortunes of all. A good idea today
would be to use the color blue, a
cornucopia, and an olive branch as
your focus objects. Peace begins with
ourselves, so that will be the focus.
Start by meditating to free your
mind from any undue disturbance,
guilt, and insecurity. Try working
with Concordia; she requires harmony
with others in every area of our
lives—from getting along with our
family to behaving in traffic. This
is particularly difficult sometimes in
contemporary society. Know this,
however: All our acts vibrate along
the web of life. Pray also to Salus,
whose presence means health—health
for ourselves, for our neighbors, and
for the environment. In the end, today
means being conscientious, courteous,
and thoughtful; these are the clearest
ways to peace. I hope you will mark
today as a starting point. Let us all
work for peace all the time.

Lily Gardner-Butts

Notes:

January 31
Friday

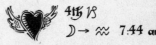 4th ♑
☽ → ♒ 7:44 am

Color of the day: Rose
Incense of the day: Dill

Scrying Spell For Love

Cast a potent spell to see your
true love during the time of
the waxing Moon. You will need a
scrying mirror for this. Also, you
should make a tea using rose hips,
dried orange peel, hibiscus, and
meadowsweet. Drink the tea, then

repeat the names of the herbs until you reach a light state of trance in front of your mirror. Then softly recite this spell:

> Through orange peel,
> Love I feel,
> I wish to know love well.
> Rose, powerful flower of love,
> Tell me of my true love.
> hibiscus flower,
> Sight is your power;
> share your sight with me.
> Meadowsweet,
> Your light I see,
> Show my true love's face to me.

Then look into your scrying mirror. You will see the face of your true love.

Jenna Tigerhart

Notes:

Notes:

February

February is the second month of the Gregorian calendar, and the year's shortest month. Its astrological sign is Aquarius, the water-bearer (Jan 21–Feb 20), a fixed air sign ruled by unpredictable Uranus. The month itself is named for Februa, an ancient festival of purification. As days slowly lengthen, people begin to emerge from their inward state and look outward toward the planting season. There are signs of life as snow begins to recede, buds begin to appear, and some herbs such as thyme and witch hazel begin to grow. February is traditionally a good time for foretelling the future and for purifying oneself. The Full Moon of the month is appropriately called the Chaste Moon. February is also the time for banishing winter, and the main holiday of the month, Imbolc or Candlemas, is a time to gather the greenery used to adorn the house during Yuletide and use it to feed a sabbat fire. A ritual of the season is known as the Bride's Bed, in which a bundle of corn from the harvest is dressed in ribbons and becomes the Corn Bride. At midmonth, we celebrate Valentine's Day, named for the legendary patron saint of love. Images of Cupid, Venus, and the heart are common on this day. Medieval people believed February 14 was the day wild birds chose to couple in order to begin their spring mating.

February 1
Saturday
Chinese New Year

 4th ≈≈
New Moon 5:48 am

Color of the day: Blue
Incense of the day: Patchouli

Community Relations Spell

This New Moon is just a day off from the month's key holiday—Imbolc, also known as Candlemas. It is also the day of new beginnings known as Chinese New Year. Today is a time for celebrating the growing light that now is returning to the Northern Hemisphere. It is also a time to honor our community and our friendships. And since the Moon is in Aquarius, this time is perfect for gathering a group of like-minded people to work a group ritual. Make the gathering a potluck so that everyone can share and connect before making magic. To prepare for this spell you will need to have a place to make a fire, either in a pit outside, or in a fireplace or wood stove. Everyone will also need a piece of paper, and a pencil or pen to write with. For the spell, ask everyone to write down their hopes and wishes for the year on a piece of paper. Ask them to include too some good words about their friends, their neighbors, and their family. When everyone is done, have them speak their words aloud and then toss their paper into the fire one by one. The fire will consume the words and carry them up in the magical smoke. In this way, the group's good intentions will be carried on the air to reach whomever they need to reach.

Jonathan Keyes

Notes:

Holiday lore: The lunar new year traditionally celebrates the Earth's renewed fertility. In China, during the fifteen-day waxing Moon, celebrants eat food, sing and dance, and promote happiness, health, fertility, and fortune for the year. In the spirit of setting things straight, all debts should be paid off now, and houses cleaned and draped with red flowers, banners, and decorations; red is considered lucky and dispels demons. Celebrants also avoid using swearwords during this season, lest they bring ill fortune to themselves, and parents warn children against blurting out such inauspicious words as "death" or "disaster," or anything of similar sentiment.

February 2
Sunday
Imbolc – Groundhog Day – Brigit's Day

 1st ≈

☽ → ♓ 2:55 pm

Color of the day: Yellow
Incense of the day: Coriander

Imbolc Spell

The fires of Brigit were tended by nineteen priestesses at Kildare, Ireland. Today these same sacred fires are tended by nineteen nuns. In the spirit of Brigit's fire, light white, red, or yellow candles to celebrate the return of the light at this time of year. Sing this verse while you light the candles:

> Mighty Brigit, goddess
> of the forge, flying sparks
> and light,
> Mistress who commands
> the strength
> of fire and healing sight.
>
> Patroness of poets, healers,
> and smiths,
> Bring thy blessings and
> gifts.
> Holder who balances the
> delicate forces
> of fire's birth and death.
>
> Transformation come,
> inspiration flow,

> Brigit bless all you know.
> Element of fire, may you
> with Brigit's sacred
> light always warmly
> glow.
>
> Priestess of fire and
> light, open up the forge
> and let creativity flow.
> Visions of magic, muse to
> bards,
> Let the winds of
> imagination blow.
>
> Brigit dance in my life
> and dreams,
> The ancient truths reveal.
> Share your fires of heal-
> ing and vibrant health,
> And keep my spirit well.
>
> Protectress of mothers
> and children be,
> Always watch over me.
> May your fires burn
> bright in my heart,
> And bless each project
> that I start.
>
> Deep in the earth your
> wells of inspiration
> flow abundant and free.
> Come share your over-
> flowing bounty with
> others and with me.
>
> Mighty Brigit, this I
> know.
> Where your magic is,
> So do the wise go.

May I be among your
blessed,
Fill my heart and spirit
with all that is best.

Abby Willowroot

Notes:

 oliday lore: On Imbolc, a bundle of corn from the harvest is dressed in ribbons and becomes the Corn Bride. On February 2, the Corn Bride is placed on the hearth or hung on the door to bring prosperity, fertility, and protection to the home.

February 3
Monday
St. Blaise's Day

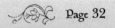

1st ♍

Color of the day: White
Incense of the day: Chrysanthemum

Blessing of the Throats
Signs of spring may be stirring beneath the earth, but our throats still need protection from the ravaging February winds. Make a simple toddy to soothe your scratchy throat and nurture body and spirit. Add

your magical intention as you stir, clockwise, to evoke powers of protection on this cold day.

    1 Irish Breakfast tea bag
    1 cup lemonade
    1 tblsp honey
    1 shot of Irish whiskey
    (optional)

In a small saucepan, gently heat the lemonade on low heat. When it begins to simmer, remove from heat and add the tea bag. Steep for one minute. Spoon honey into your favorite mug, and pour in the lemon tea. (Add a shot of whiskey if desired.) Stir, sip slowly, and enjoy the soothing warmth.

Karri Allrich

Notes:

February 4
Tuesday

1st ♍

Color of the day: Gray
Incense of the day: Poplar

Attuning Your Energy to the Universe
The waxing year and the waxing Moon make this the perfect time for reconnecting with your true ener-

gy; the energy of the universe. To do so, start by sitting in a meditative position. Then, say these words:

Land, sky, and sea,
I reconnect with the
universal energy.

Now, quiet your mind and relax your body. Focus on every layer, one by one, that makes you an individual. Focus on your appearance, your personality, your profession, and so on. Allow these layers to melt away until you become pure energy. Feel your energy blend with the energies of the universe. Focus on having a renewed oneness with the universe, then slowly allow your layers to return to you. Offer daily affirmations that you are one with the universe and her energies.

Karen Follett

Notes:

February 5
Wednesday

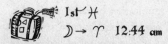

1st ♓
☽ → ♈ 12:44 am

Color of the day: Peach
Incense of the day: Sandalwood

St. Agatha, Soothe My Suffering

Today is the traditional feast day of St. Agatha. It is unlikely that Agatha was an actual historic person, and different variations of her legend exist stil. Like most early female saints, when she became a Christian, she consecrated her virginity to Christ. Therefore, when her beauty aroused a particular Roman senator, she rejected his advances and earned his spite. Ultimately, as punishment her breasts were torn off with pincers and she was thrown into a cell. While in prison, Agatha prayed to St. Peter, who came to her in a vision and restored her breasts. As a result, she is a patron saint of women and is particularly invoked for protection against breast disease. A woman who wants to petition her should lay three pink flowers and light a white candle in front of her image. This is best performed in the morning while reciting the following prayer:

St. Agatha,
You suffered because of your beauty and fidelity,
Yet persevered through your faith.
Please intercede for your humble servant in my hour of need.
Soothe my suffering and deliver me to health and wholeness,
As in turn you were delivered by St. Peter.

When the petitioner feels that she has been helped by Agatha and restored to health, she may thank her by writing a short thank you note on a pink ribbon. In the spring, bury this note under forget-me-nots, and offer your devotions to her.

Robert Place

Notes:

Snow,
snow faster;
Ally-
ally-blaster.

The old woman's
plucking her geese,
Selling the feathers
a penny apiece.

Shake the snow globe and watch the snowflakes whirl around. Visualize snowflakes falling from your window to the ground below. Thank the goddess Holda and close your circle.

Lily Gardner

Notes:

February 6
Thursday

 1st ♈

Color of the day: Turquoise
Incense of the day: Carnation

Winter Goose Spell

Many cultures celebrate February 6 as a snow festival. It is said that when the sky goddess, Holda, shakes her feather quilts it snows. If you're a fan of snow try this charm preserved through the centuries in the stories of Mother Goose. Start by decorating your altar with a white cloth, a white candle, snowflakes made from white or silver paper, a snow globe and quartz crystals. Cast a circle and light the candle, saying:

February 7
Friday

 1st ♓
☽ → ♉ 12:59 pm

Color of the day: Pink
Incense of the day: Thyme

Communicate with a Loved One

This simple spell improves communication between you and a loved one. If desired, anoint two yellow candles with a love oil of your choice, then light the candles. Hold an agate in your hands, and charge it to bring better communication between you and your partner. Lay the stone between the candles, and encircle them with pink or red-colored cord or thread. Allow the candles to burn down before moving the agate, then place the stone on your altar or carry it with you. You might want to charge a second stone and give it to your partner, letting him or her know that it is intended to promote better communication between the two of you.

Laurel Reufner

Notes:

I give thanks for the
rising and setting of the
Sun.
For all good works com-
pleted or begun.
For all the evil thwarted
or undone,
On this day whose sands
are run.

I give thanks for the
passing of the swift
silver Moon,
For all hearts lifted by a
happy tune.
For the good food that
fills the supper spoon,
May more days this
bright come soon.

Elizabeth Barrette

Notes:

February 8
Saturday

1st ♉

Color of the day: Brown
Incense of the day: Lilac

Each Day Is a Gift Spell

Each day comes as a gift, free of charge. It is ours to spend as we see fit. In this busy age, we often rush through without taking time to savor it, let alone give thanks for it. Most spells focus on asking for something. Here is an alternative verse to chant or song when appreciation is due:

Holiday lore: Today is the Buddhist Needle Memorial. On this day, as part of the endless compassion of the Buddhist faith for all sentient and nonsentient beings, are honored all the sewing needles that have been retired during the year. Today, needles are brought to the shrine and placed into a slab of tofu that rests on the second tier of a three-tiered altar.

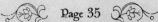

Priests sing sutras to comfort the
needles and heal their injured spirit.

February 9
Sunday

1st ♉
Second Quarter 6:11 am

Color of the day: Peach
Incense of the day: Clove

Finding Truth Spell

Turquoise crystals carry the vibration of the planet Uranus. This
planet's energy is that of the mental
body. Turquoise is frequently used by
those who need to find the courage
to speak the truth, but it can also be
used to find the truth hidden in a
bed of lies. Be sure you are ready for
the truth before using this spell.
Hold the turquoise crystal in your
hand and repeat these words:

> Turquoise, you vibrate
> with truth.
> All lies you do uproot.
> Help me detect all vile
> lies. Keep honesty in my
> spiritual life.

Keep the crystal on your altar as a
reminder to always tell the truth.

Jenna Tigerheart

Notes:

February 10
Monday

2nd ♉
☽ → ♊ 1:45 am

Color of the day: Silver
Incense of the day: Daffodil

The Peaceful Home Spell

Yemaya, the Santería orisha of
the sea who is the patron of
women and the family, can help calm
the troubled waters of one's domicile.
To tap into Yemaya's energy, buy one
blue and one white (Yemaya's colors)
candle. Anoint the candles and yourself with Yemaya oil, or lavender or
violet oil, or with your favorite cologne.
Offer Yemaya a gift of cornbread with
honey and a cup of milk in which a
pearl has been stirred. Close your eyes,
take three deep breaths, and visualize
the problem and its solution—quarrel-
ing kids beginning at long last to play
nicely together, for example. Then
open your eyes, greet Yemaya by saying, "Hekua, Yemaya!" and tell her
your troubles and the proposed solution. Thank her for listening, and
leave the offering overnight. Burn the
candles at least an hour a day until
they have burned down. Hide the

pearl in the room where there is the most chaos, and watch peaceful calm begin its reign.

Denise Dumars

Notes:

Bernadette received the religious habit of the Congregation of the Sisters of Charity, receiving the name Sister Marie-Bernard. She died in 1925, and was cannonized by Pope Pius XI in 1933. Sister Marie-Bernard is now remembered as St. Bernadette. The fountain, meanwhile, has been the site of many miraculous healings. This all just goes to show you: Even today, miracles can and often do happen.

Magenta Griffith

Notes:

February 11
Tuesday

 2nd ♊

Color of the day: White
Incense of the day: Evergreen

On the Nature of Miracles

On this day in 1858 in southern France, Bernadette Soubirous, the fourteen-year-old daughter of a French miller, first had a vision of the Virgin Mary, the mother of Jesus Christ and a central figure in the Catholic religion. Over the next year, the girl saw the Virgin a total of seventeen more times. These visions occurred in the grotto of a rock promontory at Massabielle near Lourdes. Bernadette said that the Virgin Mary asked that a chapel be built on the site of the vision, and that Mary told the girl to drink from a fountain in the grotto, which she subsequently discovered by digging into the earth. In time,

February 12
Wednesday
Lincoln's Birthday

2nd ♊
☽ → ♋ 12:19 pm

Color of the day: Yellow
Incense of the day: Coriander

Divining Success Spell

For divining success, carry an almond with you for one full day before proceeding. Anoint a green or orange candle with lavender oil. Light the candle and visualize the success you seek. See yourself waking up each day with new ideas and the benefits of spirit guidance. Anoint the almond with the lavender oil, chanting three times:

> As I lay me down to
> sleep,
> Dreams and messages I
> will seek.
> Spirit guidance, come to
> me.
> Show me what I need to
> see.

Place the almond under your bed. Each night as you lie down to sleep, hold the intent to remember dreams that will show you the way to success.

Kristin Madden

Notes:

Holiday lore: Lincoln is called the Great Emancipator and is thought of as one of our great presidents. Know this, however: Lincoln was a rather unknown figure until the age of forty, when he first entered the Illinois state legislature. His later assassination threw the country into widespread mourning, inspiring Walt Whitman to write:

> Coffin that passes
> through lanes and street,

Through day and night with the great cloud darkening the land . . . I mourned, and yet shall mourn with ever-returning spring.

February 13
Thursday

 2nd ♋

Color of the day: White

Incense of the day: Geranium

A Dream Spell

Long ago, this day was considered a very magical one. Traditionally, this was believed to be the day when the birds would begin to sing again. It was also known as St. Valentine's Eve. Foods associated with romance were prepared and at night, many people performed rituals to induce prophetic dreams, hoping to see a future lover. The dream spell which follows is very old and perfect for this day. Before going to sleep, place three white-candy coated almonds beneath your pillow. Concentrate as you say:

> Almonds, symbol of love
> and fertility,
> Let me see who my lover
> will be.

Without thinking of anyone specific, go to sleep. Sweet dreams.

James Kambos

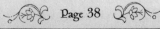

Notes:

meant for me.

Love's great beauty,
Love's great truth
Is in my heart and spirit
too.
Open my heart to the
one for me;
Open my eyes so I can
see.

February 14
Friday
Valentine's Day

 2nd ♊

☽ → ♌ 7:04 pm

Color of the day: Rose

Incense of the day: Sandalwood

Valentine Love Spell

It all starts with two red candles and a small piece of chocolate. Light the candles and eat the chocolate just before reciting this verse:

> Candles glow and love
> grow,
> Fill my heart with sacred
> play.
> Love be near and love be
> clear,
> Open hearts so they can
> hear.
>
> Expressions of love, joy,
> and trust,
> Not confused by want
> and lust,
> Magnify my love to see,
> The heart whose love is

If another heart yet
waits for me,
Reveal my soul mate,
whe'er he may be.
Make me wise to love as
you.
Reveal my soul mate,
loving and true.

Fill my true love's mind
with thoughts of me.
happy, caring, loving,
and free.
Keep me happy, cheerful
and true,
Patiently awaiting my
lover new.

True love will come when
time is right,
May it be this very
night.
If time be right, and I
be prepared,
Speed my love's journey
with no time spared.

So mote it be.

Abby Willowroot

 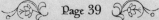

February 15
Saturday

2nd ♌

Color of the day: Gray
Incense of the day: Juniper

Corn Curing Spell

To cure corns, crush a comfrey leaf in your hand until it becomes moist, and then place it over the corn and cover with an old sock. Do this right before bedtime, either outside or near a window where you can see the Moon. In a few days time, the corn will leave your body. For extra healing, while you are rubbing the comfrey leaf over the corn and watching the Moon, repeat this phrase:

> What I see is growing,
> What I rub is going.

As soon as possible after you wake in the morning, bury the crushed comfrey leaf. The leaf will deteriorate into the earth as the corn diminishes.

Sheri Richerson

February 16
Sunday

2nd ♌
Full Moon 6:51 pm
☽ → ♍ 10:22 pm

Color of the day: Gold
Incense of the day: Poplar

Increasing Your Vitality and Creativity Spell

This time of year has been associated with creativity, fire, poetry, and healing. Leo Moons, too, are generally associated with fiery activities and with creativity. This later part of winter of course can sometimes be a time of reduced energy and low vitality in the Northern Hemisphere as we tire of the cold and short day. The time is right now for spellwork that will strengthen our internal fires and help us to feel vibrant, alive, and creative again. Call on the returning light and the Leo Full Moon to help kindle your internal fires. To prepare, you will need a red candle, some red stones such as amber, ruby, and garnet, and a piece of red cloth. In the evening time, put the red cloth out in a special part of your house where you contemplate your space in private (or with a couple of good friends.) Arrange the stones near the candle on the piece of cloth; these will help you energize and ground your creative energies. After you have lit the candles, chant these words aloud several times.

> Fire burn, fire bright,
> help my inner spark to
> light.

Jonathan Keyes

Notes:

crocus *(Crocus sativus)*. On this day, you should hold a crocus flower and repeat the following poem in recognition of the beautiful things that will be coming into your life this spring.

> Welcome, wild
> harbinger of spring!
> To this small nook of
> earth;
> Feeling and fancy fondly
> cling
> Round thoughts which
> owe their birth
> To Thee and to the
> humble spot
> Where chance has fixed
> thy lowly plot.

—Bernard Barton, circa 1775
Therese Francis

Notes:

February 17
Monday
President's Day (observed)

3rd ♍

Color of the day: Gray
Incense of the day: Rose

Celebrate the Coming of Spring

Spring is not far off now; there are signs of its coming appearing everywhere, if you know where to look. Here's a poem written in the 1700s to the first flower of spring, the saffron

February 18
Tuesday

3rd ♍

☉ → ♓ 9:00 pm
☽ → ♎ 11:48 pm

Color of the day: Black
Incense of the day: Sage

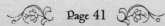 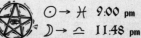

home Protection Spell

Here is a spell to protect your home. Using chalk, draw your house, in outline, on some felt. Add a few protective symbols, then use some floss to embroider your chalk design. When stitching, concentrate on the protective energies that will surround your home. Your stitches can be as simple or complex as you want. Use whatever colors you feel drawn to, but mark the front door in red. Make sure you stitch your home's entire outline, making it more permanent on the felt than a chalk drawing would be. When finished, either hang your artwork out on display or tuck it away somewhere safe.

Laurel Reufner

Notes:

air, fire, water—used in Western traditions. Where these elements meet and interact at their edges, however, they create other energies sometimes called "para-elemental" forces. At the intersection of water and earth, for example, we find the para-elemental energy of ice. You can influence a para-elemental force in much the same way you would work with one of the four elements. To make ice less slippery and more stable, you might coax it to become more like earth. To make it melt and get off your driveway, you could encourage it to move to the water side of its nature. As always, remember to be polite to your elements.

Elizabeth Barrette

Notes:

February 19
Wednesday

 3rd ♎

Color of the day: White
Incense of the day: Eucalyptus

Four Elements Spell

Most magical practitioners understand the four elements—earth,

February 20
Thursday

3rd ♎

Color of the day: Green
Incense of the day: Musk

Find a Job Knot Spell

To find a job in a tough market, light a green candle and wrap a green cord around the base of a candle holder—away from the flame. Send your energy into the candle, and let the cord absorb the energy. Tie seven knots into the green cord while reciting the following statements:

By knot of one, my spell's begun.
By knot of two, my will is true.
By knot of three, a job for me.
By knot of four, an offer in store.
By knot of five, my work thrives.
By knot of six, my spell is fixed.
By knot of seven, the power is given.

Jenna Tigerheart

Notes:

Piscean Water Magic

During a Pisces Sun, a watery meditation invites ancient oceanic energies to inspire your dreams. To take charge of these energies, draw a bath and choose music that evokes the mystical to you. Light candles of sea green and aqua blue, setting them among shells, gull feathers, sea glass, and beach stones. Swirl sea salt into your bath water with your fingers. Immerse your body wholly in the water, and add drops of lavender and jasmine oil. Breathe deeply and surrender to the unknown. Close your eyes now as you float into the mystic seas and drift off along the ancient rhythms of the water. Allow any images and emotions to surface as they will. Let go of the intellect, and forget all your daily conflicts. Banish your inner critic. Shut off the background white noise. Know that Pisces honors the instinct. Breathe and let go. Invite your intuition to reveal a truth.

Karri Allrich

Notes:

February 21
Friday

 3rd ♎
☽ → ♏ 1:09 am

Color of the day: Peach
Incense of the day: Ylang-ylang

February 22
Saturday
Washington's Birthday

3rd ♏

Color of the day: Indigo
Incense of the day: Pine

George Washington, Freemason

The man called "father of our country" was born on this date in 1732. In 1752, he was initiated as a Freemason. He remained a Mason all his life. The Masonic Lodge is often called a secret society, but they are far from secret, they say, and prefer to call themselves "a society with secrets," and a charitable organization "dedicated to freedom, self-improvement, and brotherhood." This hardly seems like the sinister organization some make it out to be. Washington debunked the idea that the Masons practiced the rituals of any occult lodges; he said the Masons did not "propagate diabolical tenets" of any magical orders. Here is Washington's response to criticism of the Masons:

> So far as I am acquainted with the principles and Doctrines of Free Masonry, I conceive them to be founded on benevolence, and to be exercised for the good of mankind.

—Letter to the Grand Lodge of Maryland, 25 September 1798

In any Masonic lodge one can find portraits of George Washington, Teddy Roosevelt, and several other presidents in Masonic regalia. Washington achieved the degree of Master Mason, but was not tremendously active in the organization. Masons call their rituals "plays" these days, and only a small offshoot of the organization—the Esoteric School of Masonry—admits to any occult practices. But oh, to be a fly on the wall at a Masonic ritual attended by the father of our country!

Denise Dumars

Notes:

Holiday lore: We all know the lore about our first president—cherry tree, silver dollar, wooden teeth—but the truth behind this most legendary of American figures is sometimes more entertaining than the folklore. For instance, did you know that once, when young George went for a dip in the Rappahannock, two Fredericksburg women stole his clothes? This story is recorded in the Spotsylvania County records. Picture the young man scampering home flustered and naked, and the icon of the dollar bill becomes just a bit more real.

February 23
Sunday

3rd ♏
☽ → ♐ 3:46 am
Fourth Quarter 11:46 am

Color of the day: Orange
Incense of the day: Cinnamon

Mental and Physical Health Spell

Outside my front door, the yellow-crocus and snowdrops are blooming now. And the wrens are flying to my window box, wondering if it would make a good home; they know, like we do, that February is a time of renewal. Let this period of change inspire you to refresh your mind and your body with a health-boosting ritual. To start, on your altar place a white candle in the center, then light it and say:

I light this candle to
renew my spirit.

To the left, light a yellow candle, then say:

This flame fires my
imagination.

Lastly, light an orange candle on the right while saying:

My body is strong and
healthy.

Thank the candles, and extinguish them. Now you're ready for the season of light to return.

James Kambos

Notes:

February 24
Monday

4th ♐

Color of the day: Lavender
Incense of the day: Frankincense

Peace and Love Ritual

Love and peace are powers greater than we can know, but we can tap into the energies that surround these concepts and bring them into the new week by anointing a rose quartz with gardenia oil today. As you anoint the stone, whisper "peace" and "love" to yourself, magnifying the energy in the stone. Carry the stone with you today and any day you desire peace and love. A few times each day, take a moment to slow and deepen your breathing. Holding the stone in your hand, inhale and say the word "peace" to yourself.

Feel a peaceful sensation fill your body. As you exhale, think the word "love," and see a loving pink light flow through you into the world. Repeat two more times each time you effect the spell. You will not regret it.

Kristin Madden

Notes:

sidered both animal and human, born of a woman and a man. He is male, but can be effeminate in the company of women. He is also thought to be both young and old. But most of all, he was the god of wine and ecstasy. To celebrate Dionysus, toast to him with wine and pour a libation. Ask him to deliver you from the confines of definition and limitation, and seek his wisdom to find the magical place that lies between opposites, a third pole between polarities—the sacred center.

Robert Place

Notes:

February 25
Tuesday

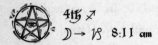

4th ♐
☽ → ♑ 8:11 am

Color of the day: Red
Incense of the day: Musk

Catalyst for Change Spell

In ancient Greece, this day was the central day of Anthesteria, a three-day festival honoring Dionysus. Dionysus was the twice-born son of Zeus and Semele. Snatched from the womb of his dying mother, his fetus was carried to term in the thigh of Zeus. After his birth he was given to Hermes who brought him to the nymphs of Nysa to keep the boy safe. Today, Dionysus is the most elusive of the Greek gods. He was con-

February 26
Wednesday

4th ♑

Color of the day: Brown
Incense of the day: Cedar

Car Protection Spell

To protect your car and its travelers, visually or physically cast a transparent shield around your car

before you set out on any trip. Project the runic aspects of rad (ᚱ) for travel and eolh (ᛉ) for divine protection as you cast, saying:

> Shield of the Goddess,
> surround this car.
> Keep us safe in our travels.

Place rue in the front seat of the car to aid in mental alertness, then say:

> herb of the Goddess
> keep me physically alert
> and mentally clear.
> Keep us safe always in
> our travels.

Always bear in mind the basic principle, "As above, so below." That is to say, divine magic needs to be coupled with mundane common sense.

Karen Follett

Notes:

Pennies Add Up Spell

We've all no doubt spoken the ancient children's rhyme at some point in our lives:

> Find a penny,
> Pick it up,
> All the day you'll have
> good luck.

Truth is, you should always stop to pick up pennies—with your right hand (if you are right-handed) for material gain, or with your left hand for spiritual gain. Or, if you want, you can pick up the penny with your right hand and transfer it to your left hand to let your material energy nourish the spiritual. Conversely, you can also can pick it up with your left hand, and transfer it to your right hand to encourage your spiritual energy to feed your material work. I always save pennies I have found. They only give luck for that day, but they can add up. I use them to save for special items, like new magical tools, or books, or tarot decks.

Magenta Griffith

Notes:

February 27
Thursday

 4th ♑
☽ → ♒ 2:24 pm

Color of the day: Violet
Incense of the day: Jasmine

February 28
Friday

 4th ≈

Color of the day: White
Incense of the day: Nutmeg

Bathing Ritual for Love

Bathing as a ritual is an age-old tradition that has been used to promote beauty and inspire thoughts of love. To ensure love and fidelity as well as to inspire sensuality, try this: Draw a tub of warm water while lighting several strategically placed white candles in the room. Once the desired amount of water is obtained, add a handful of lemon blossoms, fifteen drops of cardamom oil, eight drops of ylang-ylang oil, and ten drops of patchouli oil. Stir the bathwater a couple of times to mix, then dim the lights and submerse yourself in this mixture. Breathe deeply, inhaling the intoxicating scents, and surrender to your higher self.

Sheri Richerson

Notes:

March

March is the third month of the year according to the Gregorian calendar, and the first month of the Roman calendar. Its astrological sign is Pisces, the fish (Feb 21-March 20), a mutable water sign ruled by Neptune. The name of the month itself comes from the Roman god of war, Mars. March heralds the end of winter and coming of spring. It is a transitional time, when warm spring rains and green budding plants return. The robin is a herald of spring, and a symbol of March—along with other migrating birds. Pruning season begins now in the garden, and branches are gathered and bundled together to dry for the coming Beltane Fire on May 1. As trees are still dormant, it is a good time to collect wood for wands now. It is also time to make use of a besom, or a Witches' broom, traditionally made of an ash handle and a bundle of birch twigs. Ritual sweeping is practiced at this time to purify. The main holiday of March is Ostara, or the Vernal Equinox, a time when day and night are equal once again after the dark winter. Seeds saved from the autumn harvest are celebrated and blessed now to ensure a good planting, and the March Full Moon is called the Seed Moon. Eggs are a symbol of the season. They are dyed or painted and used to make talismans, or else they are ritually eaten.

March 1
Saturday

4th ≈

☽ → ♓ 10:26 pm

Color of the day: Gray
Incense of the day: Lavender

Recipe for Good Health

After a long winter, March is a good time to work a spell that will renew your health. As folk wisdom says:

> Eat leeks in March and
> garlic in May;
> And all the year after
> physicians may play.

Peel three potatoes and place them on a green cloth on your kitchen table. Consider three things you can do to improve your health. Carve on each potato symbols or words regarding your intention. Make a potato leek soup with your magical potatoes. Decorate the table in colors of green and white and a bouquet of daffodils.

> Leek Soup
> 4 cups sliced leeks
> 3 cups sliced potatoes
> 6 cups chicken broth
> 1 cup heavy cream
> 3 tblsps sherry
> Chives

Combine potatoes, leeks and broth and cook for 20 minutes. Liquefy in a blender. Add cream, sherry, and chives and cook an additional 5 minutes without boiling, stirring constantly.

Lily Gardner-Butts

Notes:

March 2
Sunday

4th ♓

New Moon 9:35 pm

Color of the day: Peach
Incense of the day: Basil

Psychic Growth Spell

As the winter wanes, the Pisces New Moon symbolizes the deep receptive state that we feel at this time of year. This is a powerful time to get in touch with our psychic strengths and to help augment our spiritual powers. Doing this spell-work will help you to be more aware and in tune with the natural world. It will also help strengthen your spiritual core. Find a tree that you feel is especially powerful, and gather some tobacco or lavender. From the beginning of the New Moon (today) until the Full Moon in two weeks, go outside once a day and stand underneath your tree. Stretch

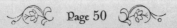

your arms out so that your hands are open flat toward the tree. Send out positive and loving energy through your hands toward the tree. When you feel you are sending a good current, ask the tree for help in strengthening your inner spiritual powers and in tapping into your alliance with the natural world. Feel the currents of energy that the tree is emitting. Draw its strength into all of your chakras, and feel your inner core getting stronger from your communication with the tree. After standing there for a short while (perhaps ten minutes), thank the tree. I like to give trees small offerings of tobacco or lavender after this ritual.

Jonathan Keyes

Notes:

March 3
Monday

1st ♓

Color of the day: White
Incense of the day: Peony

Rest and Introspection Spell

The New Moon offers a time of rest and introspection. The old cycle is complete; the new cycle is beginning anew. During the dark of the Moon, all the stars shine most brightly—just as our own virtues become most evident in times of challenge. For this ritual, you need one black candle, one silver candle, a small black bowl, a pinch of glitter, and some very pure water (preferably rain water, but distilled will do). To start, place the candles on either side of the bowl and light them. Fill the bowl with water to catch the flames' reflection. Sprinkle the glitter into the bowl. As you watch the sparkling water swirling in the bowl, say:

> The Moon, the stars,
> The sable night,
> Together balance dark
> and light.
>
> A time of rest,
> A time of peace,
> A time to dream and to
> release.
>
> Now as the cycles
> Spool and spin,
> Show me the truth that
> lies within.

Let the power of the hidden Moon draw you into itself as you gaze into the bowl. Sit for some time and think about what you accomplished over the last month and what you hope to do in the next. Which projects have you completed and which do you need to start? What satisfies you, and what worries you? See what answers the Moon offers. When you finish, blow out the candles. Pour the water onto the ground, preferably in your garden or in a potted plant, where it will nourish your inspiration through the month to come.

Elizabeth Barrette

Notes:

pleasurable gifts that are present in your life as well as the gifts that you would like to attract into your life. Offer a toast of celebration and honor to these gifts. Bury your paper in the soil, thanking the earth for protecting your present abundance and for the offering future nourishment and abundance. Give the remaining wine as a gift to the earth.

Karen Follett

Notes:

March 4
Tuesday
Mardi Gras

 1st ♓
☽ → ♈ 8:30 am

Color of the day: Red
Incense of the day: Gardenia

Pleasurable Abundance Spell

The early celebrations associated with Mardi Gras honored the abundant, earthly pleasures of Bacchus and Venus. We can celebrate our current pleasures, and as well we can anticipate future pleasures, with this spell. To do so, gather a pen and paper, a glass of wine or juice, and a plot of personal indoor or outdoor earth. On your paper, list the

March 5
Wednesday
Ash Wednesday – Islamic New Year

1st ♈
Color of the day: Brown
Incense of the day: Maple

Al-hijra Spell

Islamic New Year is called al-Hijra. Its date on the Western calendar changes every year, much as do the Jewish New Year and many other New Year celebrations around the world. On this day, you would wish friends in Arabic *"Kul 'aam u antum salimoun."* Also, light a yellow and a dark blue candle, focusing your

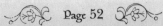

gaze on the energy of each candle's light. Hold up the yellow candle, come close to its flame, and say:

> Dark flows to light,
> Day flows to night,
> As "I" flows into "we",
> And rivers flow to the sea.
>
> Years pass, spirit grows,
> Secrets dance on the wind.
> Begin again, begin anew,
> Spirit in me and spirit in you.
>
> Ancient sands and ancient seas,
> Witness sacred memories,
> In heart and mind,
> Between the two,
> Love and truth are born in you.

Now, hold up the blue candle saying:

> Day flows to night,
> Dark flows to light,
> Dark Moon, New Moon,
> Magic Moon anew.
>
> Silent Moon, subtle Moon,
> Bringer of change and power.
> Lunar blessings flow freely now,
> Carried through night.

> The universe open to us,
> All who seek a balanced way.
> This is a blessed,
> magical day.

Place the candles side by side and breathe their glowing light for a time. Extinguish the candles, and meditate for a moment on possibilities that flow out from the sacred void of darkness.

Abby Willowroot

Notes:

March 6
Thursday

 1st ♈
)) → ♉ 8:36 pm

Color of the day: Turquoise
Incense of the day: Vanilla

Spring's Practical Magic

Stormy March heralds the cleansing winds of spring. Take time out now to clean out the dusty remnants of the winter and to refocus your energy and invite positive change. Become conscious of what you no longer need, and decide which aspects of your life need a brisk cleaning. As you discard items, ideas, attitudes, and other baggage by sweeping, raking, removing, or recycling, visualize the pieces of your life that need releasing. Bless them on their way as you clear away clutter. Making room for the new invites possibility into your life. Finally, gather seeds for the garden or patio pot and set them on your altar; infusing them with the spirit of your fresh goals and aspirations will help them sprout. Plant them during the waxing Moon. As you water, you'll nurture the growth of your dreams along with the fledgling plant.

Karri Allrich

Notes:

March 7
Friday

 1st ♉

Color of the day: Rose
Incense of the day: Ginger

Religious Tolerance Spell

On March 7, 1965 about 525 people began a fifty-four mile march from Selma to Montgomery, in Alabama, demonstrating for the voting rights of the local African-American population. This is a good day to empower our communities with racial and religious tolerance and togetherness. To do so, light seven candles, one in each color of the rainbow (red, orange, yellow, green, blue, indigo, and violet). As you light each candle, say:

> Red, black, yellow, white,
> All are held close by light.
> All religions and their creeds,
> Grow their roots from these seeds.

Place the seven candles in a circle around a gold candle. As you light the gold candle, repeat the above verse, and add the following words as well:

> What we sow we reap times three,
> Let our tolerance set us free.

Jenna Tigerheart

Notes:

March 8
Saturday
International Women's Day

1st ♉

Color of the day: Brown
Incense of the day: Patchouli

Saturn Power Spell

Depending on what system of reckoning is used, Saturday is the sixth or seventh day of the week. The day is named after the god Saturn. Although Saturn came to be identified with the Greek god Cronus, he has certain qualities of his own that do not fit the story of the Greek god of time who devoured his children. Originally Saturn was an agricultural god who ruled over the sowing of seeds. He ruled the earth in the distant past, and his reign was regarded as a golden age of prosperity. To relive that time of joy, the Romans would celebrate the Saturnalia, a seven-day festival in honor of Saturn that began on December 17. During this holiday, the social order was inverted. Slaves were allowed to talk back to their masters, everyone wore casual clothing instead of togas, and time was spent in feasting and drinking instead of working. In a way, ironically enough, modern Americans celebrate a weekly mini-Saturnalia each weekend. In general, Saturn teaches us the importance of breaking routines. Magical power is unleashed when we break patterns and do things in an opposite way from our normal life. Spend this, and part of every weekend, doing things that you normally would never think to do.

Robert Place

Notes:

Holiday lore: While most holidays across the world celebrate the lives and achievement of men, this is one day wholly dedicated to the achievement and work of women. Originally inspired by a pair of mid-nineteenth-century Ladies' Garment Workers strikes, today the holiday is little known in its country of origin; though this day's legacy is clear in March's designation by the U.S. Congress as Women's History Month. Throughout the month, women's groups in American towns hold celebrations and events, concerts, exhibitions, and rituals that recall heroic and gifted women of every stripe.

March 9
Sunday

 1st ♉
☽ → ♊ 9:38 am

Color of the day: Gold
Incense of the day: Parsley

Facing Something New Spell

Today is the birthday of the first person in space, Yuri Gagarin (born 1934). In honor of his courage, light a white candle and sit in a darkened room. Meditate on the candle flame. Envision the flame getting larger and holding you within it. Feel the flame's power giving you courage to do what you want to do. Let the candle burn itself out, knowing the flame stays with you on your new adventure.

Therese Francis

Notes:

Historical note: On 12 April, 1961, Yuri Gagarin piloted the first manned spaceship to leave the pull of our planet's gravity. This achievement is given much less attention than it deserves; part of it is politics, since Gagarin was a cosmonaut for the Soviet Union. Part of it, too, is time; today, space pilots live and work for months aboard space stations, so a simple space flight seems routine. Still, Yuri Gagarin's 108-minute flight in space represented not only a triumph of science and engineering, but also it broke a psychological barrier. It was literally a flight into unknown. "Am I happy to be setting off on a cosmic flight?" said Yuri Gagarin in an interview before the start. "Of course. In all ages and epochs people have experienced the greatest happiness in embarking upon new voyages of discovery. . . I say 'until we meet again' to you, dear friends, as we always say to each other when setting off on a long journey."

March 10
Monday
Tibet Day

 1st ♊

Color of the day: Silver
Incense of the day: Lilac

Spell to Calm Vapors

This simmering potpourri mixture works absolute wonders when the house is tense and the kids are constantly picking at each other. Holding a mixture of one cup cedar shavings, one-quarter cup lavender, and one tablespoon whole cloves in your hand or a small nonmetal bowl, use whatever cleansing method you prefer. Then charge them full of calming and soothing energies. Simmer one-quarter cup of the mixture in a pint of water whenever your house's vibrations need soothing. Try to dispose of the used potpourri outside, letting it take much of the frenetic energy with it.

Laurel Reufner

Notes:

your item it is important to visualize it protecting your home. Either of these items will guard against the intrusion of evil, keep thieves at bay, and, if the item is placed on your door, it will keep envious people away. New homes in particular are protected by these decorations.

Sheri Richerson

Notes:

March 11
Tuesday

 1st ♊
Second Quarter 2:15 am
☽ → ♋ 9:12 pm

Color of the day: White
Incense of the day: Poplar

Garlic Protection
Garlic is an extremely protective herb. If you carry a piece of garlic with you when you travel, it will help protect you against an accident. You can make a protective rope of garlic to hang in your home by simply attaching garlic bulbs to a piece of rope. You can also make a wreath with cloves of garlic on it to hang on your door. When you are crafting

March 12
Wednesday

 2nd ♋
Color of the day: Peach
Incense of the day: Pine

A Wind Spell
The ancient people of the Aegean believed the power of the wind could be harnessed and used to empower their magic. Let the March wind communicate your desires to the unseen realm. To do so, say:

I whisper over the hills
and through the hollows,
For I am the Wind,
come, if you wish to follow;
Speak to me your spells
and magical words,

Or any prayer—all will be
heard;
I will carry your dreams
to Father Sky,
Far beyond where eagles fly.
To send your wish, rise
before dawn;
Facing east before dark-
ness is gone;
Announce each wish, one
at a time;
I will be your messenger
to the divine.

The wind spirit will help you
achieve your goals.

James Kambos

Notes:

of your heart. Take a few deep
breaths to relax and center yourself.
As you chant the following, feel the
intent of your spell flow into the
water.

> I release my limitations
> and strife,
> That money and abun-
> dance will enter my life.
> God and Goddess guide
> me,
> Bless me with prosperity.

Drink all of the water and go about
your day, trusting that the spell is
working its energy in your life.

Kristin Madden

Notes:

March 13
Thursday

2nd ♋

Color of the day: Green
Incense of the day: Sandalwood

Energy of Abundance Spell

For this spell, fill a clean glass
with pure water. For added
power, add a small amount of sage
or nutmeg to the water. Hold it
between both hands and just in front

March 14
Friday

2nd ♋

☽ → ♌ 5:06 am

Color of the day: Pink
Incense of the day: Rose

All You Need Is Love Spell

With the Moon presently waxing
in Cancer, and with lovely
Venus influencing her day—Friday—

this is a good day for a love spell—but not to capture a lover; instead, use today to bring more love into the world. Get a pink candle, and anoint it with rose oil. Light the candle, and burn rose-scented incense. Play appropriate music if you wish, the Beatles' "All You Need Is Love," for example. Say to yourself as you listen:

> Love is everywhere.
> Love is coming to me.
> Love is within me.
> Love surrounds me.
> I send love into the universe,
> Knowing it will come back to me.

Meditate on love for a short while, then blow out the candle. You can relight the candle and repeat this every Friday.

Magenta Griffith

Notes:

Beware the Ides of March

Why is March 15 considered so unlucky? On this date in 226 B.C., an earthquake brought the Colossus of Rhodes—one of the seven wonders of the ancient world—to its knees. But a more famous incident probably accounts for the superstition. Julius Caesar's family may have belonged to the "Peoples' Party," but somewhere along the way he became a tyrant. In February of 44 B.C., Caesar had himself named Dictator Perpetuus—Dictator for Life. Brutus assassinated him on March 15, 44 B.C. Caesar's murder was foretold by soothsayers and even by his wife, Calpurnia, who had a nightmare in which Caesar was being butchered like an animal. Caesar chose to ignore these portents and the rest, of course, is history. As for us, well, the Moon is in Leo today, so lead—but don't dictate—or you may get yourself mauled.

Denise Dumars

Notes:

March 15
Saturday

 2nd ♌

Color of the day: Blue
Incense of the day: Lilac

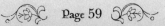

March 16
Sunday

2nd ♌
☽ → ♍ 8:52 am

Color of the day: Yellow
Incense of the day: Cinnamon

Throw Your Worries to the Wind Spell

The Hindus celebrate the festival of Holi by shaking their worries off, dressing in bright colors, and playing. Yes, that's right; they are adults and they play. Hindus in general believe that play is essential to the well-being of humankind (not just children-kind). To prepare yourself for a new attitude toward play, visualize yourself bathed in gold light. Imagine your solar plexus is a cavity filled with your worries. Take some time to examine them and turn them over in your mind. Write each of your worries on a piece of paper, then light the paper and throw it to the winds. Watch your worries fly away on the breezes. Now your solar plexus is empty. What will you fill it with? This is your chance to fill it with things that give you joy, with games and play and frivolous fun. Write down what gives you joy on a piece of paper just as before. Make a promise to make time every week to play.

Lily Gardner

March 17
Monday
St. Patrick's Day

2nd ♍

Color of the day: White
Incense of the day: Chrysanthemum

Paddy's Day Spell

In Scotland's Highlands, this day marks the first day of spring, as well as the feast of St. Patrick. In honor of this day, you should make a soda bread and leave a piece in your garden for the fairies. To do so, preheat oven to 375 degrees, and combine the following ingredients in a bowl:

    2   cups all-purpose flour
    4   tblsps brown sugar
    1   tsp baking powder
    ½   tsp baking soda
    ½   tsp sea salt
    1   egg
    ¼   cup melted butter
    ⅔   cup buttermilk
        A pinch of nutmeg

Stir till moist, then mound the dough into a floured round cake pan. Make

a cross in the center top with a knife (to keep fairies from ruining the bread), and bake for 25 minutes until golden brown. Serve warm with jam, butter, and strong tea. Fairies prefer theirs with milk!

Karri Allrich

Notes:

oliday lore: Much folklore surrounds St. Patrick's Day. Though originally a Catholic holy day, St. Patrick's Day has evolved into more of a secular holiday today. One traditional icon of the day is the shamrock. This stems from an Irish tale that tells how Patrick used the three-leafed shamrock to explain the Trinity of Christian dogma. His followers adopted the custom of wearing a shamrock on his feast day; though why we wear green on this day is less clear. St. Patrick's Day came to America in 1737, the date of the first public celebration of the holiday in Boston.

March 18
Tuesday
Purim

2nd ♍
Full Moon 5:35 am
☽ → ♎ 9:43 am

Color of the day: Gray
Incense of the day: Juniper

A Spell for Clearing and Cleansing

Just a few days before Spring Equinox, the Moon is full in Virgo. This Virgo Moon is a good time to cleanse our altar space and the ritual objects placed there. This is also a good time to cleanse our own body and spirit in preparation for a new turn of the seasons. To prepare, gather a smudge stick of sage or cedar, a clear glass bowl, pure water, and sea salt. To cleanse the objects on your altar, it is good to take them one by one and remember what they are for. Light the sage stick and blow some of the smoke over the object. Call out its name and its power to you. Thank the object for helping you in your ritual and magical work. Ask for the object to retain its power and continue to support your work. Do this for all of the objects on your altar. After you are done, continue to smudge yourself all over your body and ask for help in cleansing and purifying your body, mind, and soul. Then pour pure water into the glass bowl and add a little sea salt to the water. Sprinkle dabs of water all over your body, on your altar, and the area where you do ritual work. While you do this, visualize a cleansing ray of white light enveloping your body and your ritual space and clearing it in preparation for future magical work.

Jonathan Keyes

Notes:

energy for our modern conundrum, find an image of a horse pulling a wheeled conveyance, fasten it to your computer, and say:

> here is my cart,
> here is my horse;
> Mercury, keep us
> straight on course.

This helps Mercury identify the leading edge of his sphere of influence. So you can worry less about becoming roadkill on the infobahn.

Elizabeth Barrette

Notes:

March 19
Wednesday

 3rd ♎

Color of the day: White
Incense of the day: Neroli

Psychic Autobahn Spell

Ruled by fleet-footed Mercury, Wednesday's energy concerns matters of business and travel. Many of us now telecommute to work, but whom can we call for help when the connection breaks down? (There's no Internet goddess yet!) The god Mercury dates from an age when horses, chariots, and the like provided most transportation. So to use his

March 20
Thursday
Ostara – Spring Equinox –
International Astrology Day

3rd ♎
☽ → ♏ 9:38 pm
☉ → ♈ 8:00 pm

Color of the day: Violet
Incense of the day: Carnation

New Beginnings Spell

Now is a time of new beginnings becoming visible, hope and inspiration dancing into being. Take a white and a black candle, and place them in front of you. Light them, and breathe in the glow that comes from the balance of light and dark. Speak this verse as you bask in the glow:

Wakening Earth,
Shake off your slumber
Feel the sunlight.
Kore has returned,
Spring has begun.

All is possible,
Everything awakens.
Pulses quicken,
Rivers flow,
As each and every creature knows.

Excitement fills each brook and stream,
Creatures living in a dream.
Energies bursting from the ground—
Magic,
Prana,
And possibility all around.

Now awakening,
My powers are strong and true.
Surrounded by new life,
New visions are coming through.

Maiden goddesses dance
To each bud's joyous opening.

I am replenished,
Like the baby chick,
I am not finished.

Like the flower bud,
My powers are opening.
I am becoming,
My creative power blossoming.

The promise of life is fulfilled,
Spring has returned,
and we are renewed.
What I initiate now
Grows quickly,
And balance is easy.
So mote it be.

Abby Willowroot

Notes:

March 21
Friday

 3rd ♏

Color of the day: White
Incense of the day: Dill

Balancing Shadow and Light

Just as the balance of dark and light create a complete day, we need to balance the dark and the

 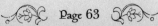

light of ourselves to create a complete person. To do so, first calm and center. Cast a protective circle, and request the guidance of your highest self as you encounter the emotions and behaviors of your shadows. Now, visualize a twilight sky. As the night descends, feel yourself descend deeper into your soul. One by one, ask the shadows to appear to you. Identify and feel the emotions of the shadows. Listen to their messages. Allow them to lead you back to their origins. Are these shadows telling you about your unhealed wounds, unfulfilled needs and wants? Or is there something else? Embrace your shadow, allowing night to give way to sunrise. Listen to the nurturing voice of your higher self as you integrate your shadows and light into balance. Open your circle.

Karen Follett

Notes:

Release Bad habits Spell

To release bad habits today, cook with an onion today. Before beginning, breathe the energy of earth and sky into the knife. As you cut the onion, say to yourself:

> here I see into my core
> and accept myself for all
> that I am, and I release
> that which no longer
> serves me.

If there are specific habits you want to eliminate, visualize them as you cut the onion. Energize the pan as you did the knife. As you cook the onion say:

> heat of fire, heat of life;
> Transform these habits
> before my sight.

Visualize your bad habits transforming and see the patterns you prefer filling the onion and other food. Give thanks for the blessings of change and release as you eat.

Kristin Madden

Notes:

March 22
Saturday

 3rd ♏

☽ → ♐ 10:33 am

Color of the day: Indigo
Incense of the day: Pine

March 23
Sunday

3rd ♐

Color of the day: Orange
Incense of the day: Sage

Soul Journey Spell

The ancient Greeks believed that the soul of each individual entered the world of matter by descending a ladder of seven planets. The word planet is derived from the Greek word *planetai,* which means "wanderer." To the Greeks, the wanderers were the seven celestial bodies, visible to the naked eye, which appeared to move independently from the constellations. They included the Sun, the Moon, Mercury, Venus, Mars, Jupiter, and Saturn. The ancients believed that the Earth was in the center of the cosmos and that the seven planets circled the Earth. Each orbit was thought of as a crystal sphere, one nesting inside the next with the Earth in the center. Encasing the outer most crystal was the eighth sphere of the constellations, and beyond that was the home of the spirit. Pythagoras created the Western musical scale with seven notes to capture the music that these spheres made as the planets circled the Earth. The same theme is reflected in the Biblical account of the seven days of creation. This Jewish tradition divided the month into seven-day weeks, which were adopted by the Roman Empire and received the names of the seven planetary gods. In English, we have substituted the names of equivalent Germanic gods for half of them. As the soul descends from the outer sphere, each planet clothes the soul in qualities—later listed by Christians as the seven virtues and seven vices—as the soul makes its way to becoming a living individual. These planets are soul centers; they are echoed within our bodies as the seven centers commonly called chakras. The journey of the soul can also be conceived of as a journey through inner space. The astrological natal chart is designed to map this process. However, for the mystic the process must be reversed because all life yearns to reunite with what is greater than itself. In a trance state, the mystic ascends this seven-runged ladder and lets go of each quality, until the union with the soul is finally achieved. The ultimate goal to alchemists was not the literal search for gold, but rather it was symbolized by gold and the Sun. As we now proceed through the seven days of the week all these many centuries later, we are in fact reenacting the mystical process described by the Greeks. When Sunday arrives, we have symbolically achieved the goal and should take some time to stop and meditate.

Robert Place

Notes:

the accompanying stone in your cauldron or a special box as a reminder of your progress.

Jenna Tigerheart

Notes:

March 24
Monday

3rd ♐

☽ → ♑ 1:48 pm

Fourth Quarter 8:51 pm

Color of the day: Lavender
Incense of the day: Myrrh

Wild Child Spell

Use this spell when you need to accomplish many brief tasks quickly. Choose a small stone for each task you wish to accomplish. As you hold each one separately, concentrate on your goal and visualize the desired outcome. See yourself accomplishing your tasks. Once the stones are charged, put them in a pocket or pouch to keep with you during the day. When you feel that your focus is wavering, pull out the stones and visualize your goals again while you reconnect with the energy. When you finish each task, place

March 25
Tuesday

4th ♑

Color of the day: Black
Incense of the day: Honeysuckle

Celebrate the Goddess Ritual

Some ancient calendars regarded this date as the Spring Equinox. By some accounts this is the day Attis, the lover of the Mother Goddess, was resurrected. On this day Christians honor the Annunciation of the Virgin Mary. Therefore, on this day of rebirth and feminine power, you should use the following ritual to energize yourself for spring and connect you with the Goddess. On your altar, place spring flowers and light a cream-colored candle. Before these place a small dish of soil, and say:

> Caring Earth Mother,
> guardian of house and home;

I honor you as Maiden,
Mother, and Crone,
As the Earth is plowed
and life begins anew.
I ask for your blessing in
all that I do.

Then, toast the Goddess with sweet white wine or grape juice.

James Kambos

Notes:

the working area. Place your tarot cards within this circle and chant:

The cycle of the Moon
has turned once more.
The power is not gone
for those who seek it.
Show me the new path-
ways I must tread,
Bless me soon,
Lady of the darkened
Moon.

Begin your tarot reading.

Sheri Richerson

Notes:

March 26
Wednesday

 4th ♑
☽→ ♒ 7:51 pm

Color of the day: Yellow
Incense of the day: Coriander

Cybele Oracle Ritual

From the earliest times this has been the time of the dark Moon, and of the festival of Cybele in Antolia, Greece, and Rome. This is a perfect time for divination, illumination, sacred mysteries, and the powers of healing. To ask a question about something in your life, follow this ritual. Take a cleansing bath, and dress in a dark robe. Cast your circle, bless salt, and sprinkle it in

March 27
Thursday

 4th ♒

Color of the day: White
Incense of the day: Evergreen

Change of Luck Spell

To change your luck, if you feel you must, turn your clothing inside out or backward. This is an old gambler's trick to change a losing streak, but it will also work if you are just having a bad day, as so many of us do on occasion. If, on the other hand, you find you already have a piece of clothing on inside out or backward, don't change it unless things are going badly for you. A less obvious alternative, if it is too conspicuous to reverse your clothing, would be to take the contents of your right pocket and put them in your left pocket, and put the contents of your left pocket in your right pocket. Or, if you wear earrings, put your left earring in your right ear, and your right earring in your left ear. And so on and so forth; the possibilities are nearly endless.

Magenta Griffith

Notes:

March 28
Friday

4th ♒

Color of the day: Peach
Incense of the day: Almond

Finding a Mate Spell

It can be difficult to find a mate in this harried age. For a little magical help, write out a list of the traits you want in a mate. Place two

pieces of burning sage or copal inside a wedding vase or pottery bowl. Sitting close to the rising smoke so that your breath commingles with the rising smoke, read your list aloud. Envision your desires rising out into the universe and then returning in the form of the person you are looking for.

Therese Francis

Notes:

March 29
Saturday

4th ♒
☽ → ♓ 4:26 am

Color of the day: Gray
Incense of the day: Lavender

Visions from the Goddess Spell

If you seek divine inspiration or guidance on this day, scatter candles liberally, but safely, around a room. Half-fill a small cauldron or large bowl with water and add some floating candles. Now light all of the candles, leaving the floating ones for last. Ground and center yourself, calling on a particular deity if you so wish. When you feel ready, gaze into the bottom of the cauldron, focusing, yet not focusing, on the flames and the motion of the water. Spend some time afterward meditating upon the vision you receive. You may want to write what you saw, as well as what you think it meant, for future use.

Laurel Reufner

Notes:

bath salts or shower gel. For a stronger effect, also use the oils in a diffuser and place a blue lightbulb in the bathroom. Consecrate the room with salt water before entering the bath. Breathe deeply and ask the undines, or water spirits, to enter the sacred space and help heal your aches and pains. Relax thoroughly, and enjoy your hydrotherapy. Remember to thank and dismiss the undines after the bath.

Denise Dumars

Notes:

March 30
Sunday

 4th ♓

Color of the day: Peach

Incense of the day: Basil

Pisces health Spell

With the Sun and Moon both in Pisces today, this is an excellent time to feel the healing properties of water. You should visit a spa, health club, or other such place today, particularly if it offers hydrotherapy. Or you can do this simple health spell at home. Use blue or green tinted bath salts or a seaweed-based shower gel. Light a blue and a green candle in your bathroom. Anoint your body with lavender, rosemary, and eucalyptus oils. Add a few drops to the

March 31
Monday
The Borrowed Days

 4th ♓

☽ → ♈ 3:04 pm

Color of the day: Silver

Incense of the day: Daffodil

Spring Creeps Softly Spell

By April eve, the first soft stirrings of green emerge with the fairies, delighting us with tiny surprises in damp places. Periwinkle, a glossy evergreen vine, begins sprouting five-petaled flowers—lovely purple stars for the Goddess. Take a solitary walk today and notice small changes in the landscape. Breathe in the mossy scent of early spring, and see the world with fresh new vision. Look upon its small wonders with the eyes of a child. Being a Witch means more than learning to focus energy and power. It also means learning to listen, absorb, and renew through the subtle lessons in nature. So put down this book and take a walk, drinking in the wisdom of the Goddess and the Green Man.

Karri Allrich

Notes:

Holiday lore: According to folk belief, the last three days of March do not rightfully belong to the month. An old Scottish ballad tells how March begged April for a loan of the days. These were then thought to be dangerous days, fraught with taboos and bad weather.

> Ther first o' them was
> wind and wet,
> The second o' them was
> snow and sleet,

The third o' them was such a freeze,
It froze the birds' claws to the trees.

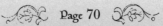

April

April is the fourth month of the year of the Gregorian calendar, and the first month of the astrological calendar. Its astrological sign is Aries, the ram (Mar 21-Apr 20), a cardinal fire sign ruled by Mars. The name of the month comes from the Latin *aprilis,* which derives from *aper,* or "boar," as April was thought to be the month of the boar. April is the month of burgeoning life force, sunshine, and life returned to the forests. Birds are building nests now; lambs are romping on greening hillsides. Apricot trees are blossoming, and herb gardens are filling out. Now is the time to plant your garden. Potatoes, onions, lettuce, and tomatoes are sacred to various divinities now. It is a good time to create a circle for meditation outside, either of stones or shrubberies. The four cardinal directions should be marked in the circle, and connected by a cross quarter cross. Cut mazes and labyrinths now in turf or in fields. Plant tree saplings too—maples, hawthorn, and holly are sacred in April. Bunnies and hares are symbols of fertility at this time of year, associated with rites of spring. The Full Moon in April is called the Hare Moon. Holidays in April include April Fools' Day, which comes from Roman celebrations of the New Year rebirth. Earth Day on April 22 celebrates the bounty of the planet. April 30 is called May Eve and is celebrated with revels and bonfires.

April 1

Tuesday

April Fools' Day

 4th ♈

New Moon 2:19 pm

Color of the day: Red
Incense of the day: Musk

The Sacred Magic of Play

Like the Fool of the tarot, the energy of this day is a signal of the amazing possibilities for those who dare to take a few risks. To do so, place paper, pen, a red candle and holder, glitter, crayons, and other childlike toys before you. Then say:

> This spell I work in early morn,
> Ready this day for magic born.
>
> I am here, and I am not,
> The magic must find me before I am caught.
>
> I write my spell upon this paper,
> I light this tall red candle taper.
>
> I am the Fool open to wisdom,
> I am the wise soul at play.
>
> Magic can be spun from light,
> and sound and colors bright.

> Visions linger,
> And laughter rises.
> Messages come as happy surprises.
>
> Magic dance in my heart
> And banish all worry and woe.
>
> On this magical day the universe reveals,
> A glimpse of secrets to me.
>
> Secrets that less playful souls,
> Can never know or see.
> So mote it be.

Abby Willowroot

Notes:

 New Moon Energizing and Vitalizing Spell

The sign of Aries is associated with initiation, energy, and vitality. You can take advantage of this time by doing spellwork to boost yourself. If you have been feeling lethargic and heavy through the long winter months, this is a perfect time to charge your batteries and fire yourself up. Start by collecting two red peppers, a clove of garlic, and some ginger. You will also need a small pot filled with dried sticks and paper along with some matches. To work the spell, wake up before dawn and go outside to a place where you can view the rising Sun. Place your pot of sticks and paper before the Sun, then lay out the peppers, garlic, and ginger as offerings. When the Sun peaks over the horizon, light the fire in the pot, and meditate on the flames until the fire burns out. Say these words as you watch the fire:

> Spirit of the flame, spirit
> of the Sun;
> I give thanks for your
> heat and warmth.
> Help my inner fires grow
> and glow brightly.
> Bring me renewed
> strength, energy, and
> vitality.

Jonathan Keyes

Notes:

Holiday lore: April Fools' Day originated because the Romans celebrated their New Year on this day. In fact, their eight-day New Year festival of rebirth and renewal that was so popular that it persisted well into the Middle Ages, until the new Gregorian calendar was adopted. Some believe the day's current tradition of mean-spirited pranks come from a lingering confusion and resentment at the loss of the old festival.

April 2
Wednesday

1st ♈

Color of the day: Peach
Incense of the day: Sandalwood

Leo the Lion and Hercules the Hero Invocation

If you look up at the southern sky tonight in the early evening, the most prominent constellation that can be seen from anywhere in North America is Leo the lion. You can find it on the ecliptic with Cancer to your right and Virgo to your left. Leo will appear directly beneath Ursa Major. Therefore, the easiest way to find it is to first find the Big Dipper and look for the next bright group of stars below the pan of the Dipper. Leo is composed of a group of stars that form a question mark with a bright star, Regulus, at its base. This represents the head and neck of the lion, and Regulus is its heart. Behind this group are three stars forming a triangle. This is the

hind section of the lion's body. The Christian veneration of the saints derives from the pre-Christian veneration of heroes in the classical world. Classical Pagans would pray to and ask favors of the heroes in the same way that Christians pray to saints. Chief among the venerated heroes was Hercules, and the constellation Leo commemorates the first of his twelve labors, the slaying of the Nemean lion. Hera had sent the lion to terrorize Nemea, and Hercules was assigned the task of protecting the people of the region. The lion's skin was impenetrable, and Hercules could not use any weapon against it. He resorted to strangling it to death. Afterward, he skinned it and used its hide as an impenetrable armor. Besides commemorating the battle with the lion, the constellation Leo is Hercules' armor. We can make use of it for our protection as well. If you are in need of protection, hold your hands up to Leo and repeat these words:

> Hercules, who loved and
> protected your people,
> I call on you for protec-
> tion now.
> Clothe me in you armor,
> which repels all danger.
> Shield me from harm,
> and lead me to victory.

Now visualize the light from the stars in Leo coming down and encircling your body.

Robert Place

Notes:

April 3
Thursday

 1st ♈
☽ → ♉ 3:20 am

Color of the day: Turquoise
Incense of the day: Carnation

Casting for Fast Cash Spell

Use this spell when you need to find a quick source of income or cash. Start by charging a green or gold candle with your intent. Visualize your need and the money that is necessary to fill that need. Visualize the money being yours and the need being fulfilled, and say:

> Money needed,
> Plenty fast,
> Money revealed
> when this spell is cast.

Repeat these words, and feel the energy rise. When you cannot contain the energy any longer, release it to the universe; then ground the remaining energy back into the earth, and spend some time meditating. Open your mind to the universe and its guidance. Keep your eyes, ears, and mind open to any income opportunities that the universe will provide in upcoming days.

Karen Follett

Notes:

On Friday night I go
backwards to bed,
I sleep with my petticoat
under my head,

To dream of the living
and not of the dead,
To dream of the man
that I am to wed.

Lily Gardner-Butts

Notes:

April 4
Friday

 1st ♉

Color of the day: Rose
Incense of the day: Thyme

Mother Goose Love Charm

April is dedicated to Aphrodite, the goddess of love. During the current waxing Moon, a love spell on Friday is sure to work. Try this charm from Mother Goose. Focus on what you want in a lover. Build a fire in your fireplace or in your cauldron. Throw a pinch of sea salt in the flames and say:

> It is not this salt
> I wish to burn,
> But my lover's heart
> that I wish to turn,
>
> So that he may not rest
> nor happy be,
> Until he comes to me.

April 5
Saturday

 1st ♉
☽ → ♊ 4:24 pm

Color of the day: Brown
Incense of the day: Jasmine

Good Fortune of Your Own Spell

Aloe vera is thought by the people of Africa to bring good luck to those who possess it. As luck may have it, today is also the day the ancient Romans celebrated the Festival for Good Luck to honor the goddess Fortuna. To create some good fortune of your own on this auspicious day, place an aloe vera plant on your altar. Place pieces of agate in

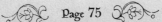

various places around the aloe plant, and place a yellow candle in front of the plant. Inscribe the words "To bring good luck" on the candle, and repeat the following verse while lighting the candle:

> My home is a garden,
> Surrounded by a wall of
> luck,
> And made on peculiar
> ground.
> This is a spot enclosed by
> grace,
> Out of the reach of the
> world's negativity
> And surrounded by
> fortune's flame.

Allow the candle to burn in a safe place until it extinguishes itself.

Sheri Richerson

Notes:

Balance Spell

Daylight Saving Time begins today; now Spring is truly here. To achieve balance and prepare yourself for the active months ahead this spell may help. To start, light a gray candle, and place before it the Chariot card from the tarot. Take a good look at the card. The charioteer is strong, determined, but above all he is balanced. Now write a list of the things you wish to improve in your life so you may achieve balance—a better diet, financial control, better relationships, and so on. Each time you read your list say the words of power below, and soon you'll gain control over your life:

> West, east, south and
> north,
> As the Chariot I go forth;
> Careful in thought,
> word, and deed,
> I have the strength to
> succeed.

James Kambos

Notes:

April 6
Sunday
Daylight Saving Time Begins 2 am

1st ♊

Color of the day: Yellow
Incense of the day: Coriander

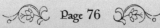

April 7
Monday

1st ♊

Color of the day: White
Incense of the day: Rose

Find a New Coven or Circle Spell

To find a new coven or circle, use an onyx crystal. Onyx crystals hold an energy that is perfect for locating things and for information gathering. To work the spell, hold the crystal between your palms and feel the energy. Hold the crystal up toward the light, and say:

> Onyx crystal, you hold
> the energy of informa-
> tion. help me find my
> spirit home, a circle of
> like-minded friends,
> with whom I can wor-
> ship and learn as one.

Keep the crystal with you until you find your new circle or coven. For extra power this spell can be cast during the New Moon.

Jenna Tigerheart

Notes:

April 8
Tuesday
Buddha's Birthday

1st ♊

☽ → ♋ 4:36 am

Color of the day: Gray
Incense of the day: Gardenia

Symbol of Protection Spell

For a dose of protection, sit in the center of your home or room and breathe deeply. Enter a meditative state and visualize yourself in the center of a glowing pentagram. See a protective circle surrounding you and your home; then, surround this circle with an energy box. Visualize the box charging with red energy, then orange, yellow, blue, green, and purple. Ask your guides or deities to send you a symbol of protection and wait for an image, feeling, or sound to come to you. See this symbol surround and fill your energy box and protective circle. Feel a bit of this energy fill your personal protective circle. Thank your guides or deities for their blessings and go about your day.

Elizabeth Barrette

Notes:

April 9
Wednesday

1st ♋

Second Quarter 6:40 pm

Color of the day: White
Incense of the day: Eucalyptus

Celebrate New Growth Spell

Today is the first day of the Cerealia festival of ancient Rome, which celebrated the return of the six vegetative months. To do this yourself, fill several small clay or plastic pots with potting soil to about two-thirds full. Hold a few tomato seeds in your hands. Pass your hands over a candle flame, saying:

Fire for strength.

Breathe on the seeds, saying:

Air for strength.

Put your hands into a bowl of water, saying:

Water for strength.

Then place the seeds in the potting soil, saying:

Earth for strength.

Cover the seeds, water them, and place the pots in sunlight. In about four to six weeks, the seedlings will grow to about six inches in height—ready to transplant into your garden or into larger pots.

Therese Francis

Notes:

April 10
Thursday

2nd ♋

☽ → ♌ 1:54 pm

Color of the day: Green
Incense of the day: Geranium

Wishing Well Spell

I heard this from a friend who is devoted to the Irish goddess Brigid. In the old days, a well was an open pool that formed around a spring. They were holy places, where water came magically from the earth. The custom developed of offering the spirit of the well a coin, with the spirit granting a wish to the gift-giver in return. Today, you can toss a coin in a fountain or a creek or stream. Just make a wish beforehand, and always leave without looking back.

Magenta Griffith

Notes:

April 11
Friday

 2nd ♌

Color of the day: Pink
Incense of the day: Ylang-ylang

Lucky in Love Spell

Love spells can be fun. Start this one by calling on Ops, Fortuna, and Thoth for good fortune in love. Since any love is a gamble, we will use gambling imagery in this ritual. Wear your loudest, luckiest Las Vegas or Mardi Gras-style outfit. Invite friends over for a "Casino Night," and serve champagne, cheese, apples, and nuts. Have party favors such as Mardi Gras beads or doubloons, and play cards or roulette. Tell you guests that you are betting that you will be lucky in love. Do not wager or accept any money during the games, even if others do. Ask your guests to wish you luck when it comes to love in your life. Be aware what cards you draw or what numbers come up on the wheel. Write them down. These will provide clues to potential suitors. Good luck!

Denise Dumars

Notes:

April 12
Saturday

 2nd ♌
☽ → ♏ 7:07 pm

Color of the day: Indigo
Incense of the day: Violet

Getting Accepted Spell

This spell is for those of you trying to get into a particular college or program of study. Hold a yellow candle in your hands and visualize yourself getting an acceptance letter. Set the candle, in a holder, on top of a book. Choose a book dealing with the area you want to study. Circle the candle with either a stick of cinnamon or a slice of ginger. Light the candle and let it burn for half an hour. Do this everyday for a week. On the last day, dip one of the cinnamon sticks in the melted candle wax and either carry it with you or place it where you will see it often.

Laurel Reufner

Notes:

April 13
Sunday
Thai New Year – Palm Sunday

2nd ♏

Color of the day: Peach
Incense of the day: Clove

Water Meditation

Today is the annual Buddhist water festival. Water that bathed the Buddha statues is saved and thrown on the faithful to cleanse them of evil spirits. Take a small box of baking soda and two cups of sea salt, and add them to warm bath water. Play meditation or temple bell music, and burn a new white candle. As you slip into the bath, let the warm water engulf you. Visualize your worries, your guilt and self-criticism, and all your frustrations fall away from you into the water. Feel how much lighter and freer you feel as the water gently laps around you. Stay in the bath as long as you feel comfortable.

Lily Gardner-Butts

Notes:

April 14
Monday

2nd ♏

☽ → ♎ 8:42 pm

Color of the day: Gray
Incense of the day: Frankincense

Power of I Am Spell

The Sun in Aries kindles the fire of the solar plexus and asserts inwardly, "I am." Today, light candles of yellow and sunny orange. Wear the arousing scents of ginger, cinnamon, and lemon. Take time to breathe from your abdomen, and imagine the core of your very self as a flame. With each breath, the flame grows brighter and more intense. This is the flame of desire, the fire of your focus. Today is the day to ask yourself: Are you defining your needs and fulfilling them? Are you giving yourself the care and consideration you so freely offer to others? Be present and centered in your body as you breathe and move through your normal day today. Open yourself to rebirth and renewal and all possibilities. Be ready to embody the divine spark in this season of awakenings.

Karri Allrich

Notes:

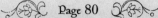

April 15
Tuesday

2nd ♎

Color of the day: White

Incense of the day: Ginger

Corn Curing Spell

Spring comes at different times to different parts of the country. Today, when spring is so close, take a few minutes to walk through the woods, or perhaps a park, to look for signs of spring in your area. Do you see swelling buds or tiny new leaves on the bushes? Are tulips blooming underfoot? Do the trees seem a little more alert than they did last week? As you walk, call out:

> Wake up, Apple!
> Wake up, Oak!
> The spell of winter has broken.
> Wake up, Maple!
> Wake up, Pine!
> See reborn the light divine.

Help rouse the world from its wintry slumber, and rejoice in the spring.

Elizabeth Barrette

Notes:

April 16
Wednesday

2nd ♎

☽ → ♏ 8:16 pm

Full Moon 2:36 pm

Color of the day: Yellow

Incense of the day: Cedar

Finding a Partner or Strengthening a Relationship Spell

Libra Moons are associated with partnership in general, making this a good time to find a partner or to strengthen the bonds of the relationship we are already in. A good partner will help us to feel nourished, respected, and loved. Finding the right partner means knowing what is good for our hearts. This spell helps us to find a good partner or to strengthen the bonds we already have within our relationship. To start, gather a small mirror, a white candle, and two red roses in a vase. Place the mirror against a wall near your altar so you can look at yourself. Place the vase of roses in front of the mirror and the candle in front of the roses. Then light the candle and stare into the mirror. Look deeply into your own eyes and at the reflection that the candlelight makes in your face. If you are in a relationship that you want to stay in, visualize the two of you becoming closer and more in love. Offer thanks for the gifts your partner gives you and the things she brings out in you. Speak these things out loud. If you are looking for a relationship, visualize the attributes you want most from a partner and then speak these things out loud. Also speak the things that you will bring to a partnership and how you will love, honor, and cherish a new partner. When you are finished, take the roses out of the vase and allow them to dry on your altar. These two roses will symbolize, and will help to bring, new love or a growing connection between you and your partner.

Jonathan Keyes

Notes:

April 17
Thursday
Passover Begins

 3rd ♏

Color of the day: Violet

Incense of the day: Musk

Passover Protection Spell

Speak these words to evoke the ancient protection of the Passover holiday:

Starry nights and
brilliant days,

Protection bless us,
And fill this space.

May those we love
gather in strength,
And unify at times of
strife.

We call upon the Cosmos
of which we are a part,
May we flow with you
and make a start.

Winds of night,
Blow softly and upon all
beneath.
Waters of the sea,
Protect us as we bathe
in your healing deep.

Fires of the earth,
Warm us without harm.
Bring energy and not
disaster.

Earth beneath our feet,
Stay solid and true,
As we move upon your
ground.

May we be granted
The blessings of long life.
May the heavens smile
upon us,
Every day of our long, full
lives.

May the wisdom of the
ancients,
Visit us in our dreams,
And fill our waking time.

By the power of the bear,
May there be strength in
our actions.

By the vision of the
hawk,
May our sight be ever
sharp.

By the grace of the cat,
May our bodies and
spirits be lithe.

These things be granted,
So mote it be.

Abby Willowroot

Notes:

keep your mate faithful. No doubt the Wise Ones who once walked the hills of Appalachia where I now live gathered violets on the edge of the woodland to use in spells such as this:

To ensure your love
remains true;
Pick six violets, all must
be blue.
Put them in water that
you have blessed;
Place them where your
lover's head shall rest.

After you do these things, take three ribbons—pink, yellow, and white—and wait until the darkness of night. Tie them around the branch of a tree, and say:

We are now bound,
So mote it be.

James Kambos

Notes:

April 18
Friday
Good Friday

3rd ♏
☽ → ♐ 7:51 pm

Color of the day: White
Incense of the day: Nutmeg

A Violet Love Charm
Violets are symbols of loyalty, and in April they are plentiful. They carpet our lawns like a blue mist. You can use them in spells to

April 19
Saturday

3rd ♐

Color of the day: Blue
Incense of the day: Patchouli

Four Elements Spell

This is the final day of Cerialia, the Greek festival held to honor the virgin goddess, Artemis. Artemis is the goddess of animals and the hunt, and in her earliest images she is depicted with an animal on each side. This image is known as the Mistress of the Animals. In Rome, Artemis was identified with Diana. The root of Diana's name is *Ana,* an ancient goddess name related to the Latin word *anima,* which means "soul" and which is the root of the word "animal." Artemis is also the goddess of the Moon, and she is said to be the protector of women. All should honor her on this day by wearing silver jewelry that depicts her in some way—either as a stag, a hound, through her bow, or the Moon. It is especially important for any women who are going through a major life change, such as marriage, pregnancy, or a change of career, to honor and draw on the protection of Artemis and Diana.

Robert Place

Notes:

April 20
Sunday
Easter

3rd ♐

☉ → ♉ 7:03 am

☽ → ♑ 9:20 pm

Color of the day: Gold
Incense of the day: Poplar

Spell for Easter

Today is a day of opening, of change and transformation. Focus today on the things you wish to transform in your life. For Christians this is the highest of holy days. In Christian belief Jesus emerged from the cave after three days in the realm of the dead, and he walked among humans before ascending back into heaven. In Greek tradition, the maiden goddess Persephone returned from the realm of the dead in spring to walk again on earth. Whatever your belief system, this is a time of sacred transformation and reverence for life and rebirth. It is a time when the energy of millions of people is focused on gratitude, joy, and celebrating life's mysteries. It is a good time to focus on strengthening spirit and community by saying:

> Air, fire, water, earth
> Bless this day of rebirth.
> Transform all that I see
> Into truth, freedom,
> clarity.

Sharpen my focus
And strengthen my will.
Give my heart compassion
toward any and all.

Banish all separateness,
And replace it with joy.
Let me hear music clear,
In a diversity of voices.

Bring success in all things,
and gratitude for the gift.
May I walk in wisdom,
And understand the
truth.

So mote it be.

Abby Willowroot

Notes:

the mood. Start by lighting some incense. As the smoke begins to curl up into the room, open all the doors and windows that you would have open on a nice day. Smudge each room in your house by carrying the incense and waving it around, making sure to waft smoke out open doors and windows. Let your other house members follow behind you with bells, maracas, or other noisemakers. After the incense and charcoal burn out, sprinkle the ashes outside your doors.

Laurel Reufner

Notes:

April 21
Monday

3rd ⅤⅢ
Color of the day: Silver
Incense of the day: Peony

Family Housecleaning Ritual

While this spell isn't intended for a serious house cleansing, it will be sufficient for helping to air out your home a bit and to lighten

April 22
Tuesday
Earth Day

3rd ⅤⅢ
Color of the day: Black
Incense of the day: Pine

Earth Day Ritual

The original Earth Day was celebrated on the Vernal Equinox in 1969. Now April 22 is celebrated as Earth Day by various groups and communities around the world. Begin the day with this ritual, and then go out and do something for the environment.

> The Earth is your home,
> It needs your care.
> The environment begs:
> Take care, take care.

> Nurture me and clean
> my rivers,
> Clean my land and sea.
> I give you life and food to eat:
> I give you shelter and
> spirit relief.

> Be gentle with me,
> Take care what you do,
> Or I will die,
> And so will you.

> Dedicate yourself to be,
> A healing force for
> what's given to you.
> Your course is set, my
> duty clear,
> Recycle and reuse all the
> year.

> I am the Earth,
> Bearer of generations yet
> to be.
> Bless my body by plant—
> ing a tree,
> I promise it will nourish
> thee.

> I bless all creatures
> With water pure.
> Cease your pollution,
> so all may endure.

> Bless my environment
> with your love and will,
> I can be healthy still.

> Each Day I give life to
> thee,
> So dedicate this day to
> healing me.
> So mote it be.

Abby Willowroot

Notes:

April 23
Wednesday
Passover Ends

3rd ♑
☽ → ♒ 1:58 am
Fourth Quarter 7:18 am

Color of the day: Brown
Incense of the day: Maple

New Beginnings Spell

To create new beginnings for yourself, and to do away with negativity, set up two white candles on your altar. Dress in white and place a five-pointed star in the center of the altar between the candles. Place a drop of lotus oil on the forefinger of your power hand, and anoint each chakra in order while chanting:

> All negative habits and
> influences are removed.
> I am now renewed in
> strength and spirit.
> Open my mind, give me
> balance, and show me
> the spiritual path I must
> follow. Unfold the lotus
> blossom now so that I
> may give and receive
> blessings.

Sheri Richerson

Notes:

become our master and make us lose sight of what is truly important in our lives. To do so, gather a lighter, a fireproof container, some powdered ginger, and a dollar bill. Focus for a moment on your relationship with money. Trace this relationship back to its origins. Ignite the dollar bill, and place it in the container, repeating:

> I am not my money.
> Money is my servant.

Charge the ginger with your personal power. Sprinkle the ginger over the burning dollar. Verbally assert:

> I am master over my
> money.

Release the energy to the universe.

Karen Follett

Notes:

April 24
Thursday

 4th ♒

Color of the day: White
Incense of the day: Sage

Mastery over Money Spell

We place an extraordinary amount of value on money, especially when it's in short supply. Yet our happiness is not really dependent on money. We should in general strive to make sure that money does not

April 25
Friday
Orthodox Good Friday

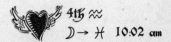 4th ♒
☽ → ♓ 10:02 am

Color of the day: Peach
Incense of the day: Ginger

Parable of the Tiger and the Lion

Once upon a time, the gods assigned different animals to be guardians of humans, to guide them and demonstrate the traits necessary so that humans might attain godhood. These animals were placed in the zodiac to honor their sacred duties. One of these animals was the lion, physical protector of humans and representative of courage. The lion was basically a lazy fellow; he preferred to sleep rather than do his job. Seeing that the humans were left unguarded, and that they did not have teeth or claws to protect themselves, the tiger often stepped in to help. After many years, the gods noticed that the tiger was doing the work of the lion, so they stripped the lion of his powers and removed him from the zodiac. In honor of the service the tiger, the gods gave to him the duty of protecting the humans. When you feel depressed or overwhelmed, call on the powers of the tiger by freely giving service to others.

Therese Francis

Notes:

April 26
Saturday

 4th ♓

Color of the day: Gray
Incense of the day: Lilac

Motivation Spell

Sometimes we need a good kick in the pants to get things done. Use this spell when you know what you need to do, but need a dose of motivation. To start, gather a tourmaline stone for initiative, an oak leaf for potency, and ginger tea for energy. Place the stone in the place of fire on your altar. Drink the tea. Place the oak leaf in the place of earth on your altar. With one hand on the oak leaf and one on the tourmaline, say:

> Tourmaline, you vibrate
> with power of the leaf
> and of the flower. Your
> motivation is what I
> need, send your finishing
> power to me.

Jenna Tigerheart

Notes:

April 27
Sunday
Orthodox Easter

 4th ♓
☽ → ♈ 8:54 pm

Color of the day: Orange
Incense of the day: Cinnamon

home Abundance Spell

Take a fresh egg and wash it with witch hazel. Hold it in both hands and say:

> I bless this egg with the
> energy of life and love.
> May this home be blessed
> with an abundance of all
> that we may need.

Dig a hole on your land or in the dirt of a houseplant. Poke a hole in each end of the egg. Use a long needle to break the yolk. Blow the insides out into the hole and cover with dirt. Rinse the inner egg with chamomile tea, and let it dry. Decorate with symbols of health, family, and prosperity and keep it in a special place in your home.

Kristin Madden

Notes:

April 28
Monday

 4th ♈

Color of the day: Lavender
Incense of the day: Lavender

Finding the Perfect Pet Spell

To find a new pet, first think of the type of pet you want. Then go through a magazine, looking for images and words that describe your perfect pet. Cut them out and attach them to some construction paper. Visualize your perfect pet living and interacting with you. Be open to the many ways it is possible for your pet to arrive. If you get an urge to go to the animal shelter or to tell a specific person you are looking for a pet, follow through on it.

Therese Francis

Notes:

April 29
Tuesday

 4th ♈

Color of the day: Red
Incense of the day: Juniper

Pagans in the Military Protection

Today is author Ed Fitch's birthday. As a Wiccan minister and serviceman, Fitch was instrumental in starting the mentoring program for Pagans in the military. If you know someone in the service, use this spell to send energy directly to him or her. If not, send protection to all soldiers. Put a picture of the flag, an eagle, and winged Isis on your altar. Burn a white candle for protection, and blue and red ones if you wish. Take three deep breaths, close your eyes. Envision the eagle flying to the troops, its wings transforming into thos of Isis and forming a protective light. Take three deep breaths and open your eyes. Burn the candle each day until it burns down.

Denise Dumars

Notes:

May Eve Spell

Tonight's twilight begins the Bright Fire, or the Celtic festival of Beltane. May's warm Sun inspires in all thoughts of love and pairing. The longing for merging with our opposite is strong. On this eve of the return of summer's pleasures, take a moment to honor your own integrity. Prepare a candlelit bath scented with lavender and rose. Scent your hair with rosemary oil and soothe your skin with lotions. As you care for your body, revel in its gifts and natural beauty. See yourself through a lover's eyes. Nurture and love yourself. For if you do not love yourself, how can you expect another to truly love you? Self-worth is the gift the Goddess brings to you this night.

Karri Allrich

Notes:

April 30
Wednesday
May Eve

 4th ♈
)→ ♉ 9:26 am

Color of the day: Yellow
Incense of the day: Pine

May

May is the fifth month of the year. Its astrological sign is Taurus, the Bull (April 21-May 20), a fixed earth sign ruled by Venus. The month is named for Maia, a Roman goddess and mother of the god Hermes (the word is from the Greek for "mother"). May is a month of full-blown growth and colors of every sort. The main holiday of the month—May Day, or Beltane (May 1)—is a celebration of color and flowers. A traditional part of the May Day celebration is the Maypole, which traditionally was cut from a fir tree on May Eve (April 30) by the unmarried men of the village. All its branches, except for the topmost, were removed and then adorned with ribbons and placed in the village square. On May Day, dancers hold the ends of the ribbons attached to the top of the Maypole—girls going one way, boys another. As the ribbons wind and shorten, the dance becomes a spiral, symbolizing death and resurrection. Making and exchanging wreaths of flowers is an old tradition in May. In some traditions, the Sacred Marriage— between the May Queen and the May King, also known as Jack-of-the-Green—is important on May Day to ensure a vigorous growth in the crops. The Full Moon of May is called the Dyad Moon, the time when the two become one and all things meet in perfect balance and harmony.

May 1
Thursday
May Day — Beltane

 4th ♉
New Moon 7:15 am

Color of the day: Green
Incense of the day: Jasmine

Beltane Spell

May day is a good time to promote love and happiness in your life. To do so, use pastel-colored candles, as many as possible, and a large bowl of fresh water with flower petals floating in it. Adorn your ritual space with flowers and new leaves, and sing the following verse to the spirits of the holiday:

> Queen of the May,
> Jack-of-the-Green,
> A more joyous time has
> never been.
>
> Flowers bloom
> and children sing,
> Fairies bless each river
> and sacred spring.
>
> All life is joyous
> and we revel,
> In being healthy, happy,
> and alive.
>
> The Morris Dancers
> Stomp the Earth,
> Wakening Gaia with
> blissful mirth.

> Petals abound
> in vibrant hue,
> Signaling all Earth's life
> is born anew.
>
> Blessings flow
> all around,
> Magic springs underfoot
> from the ground.
>
> Love and passions
> fill the air,
> Celebration and revelry
> is everywhere.
>
> On this day,
> My true love come to me;
> Let us share our hearts
> in festivity.
>
> Dancers prance
> the Maypole round,
> Laughter and music
> freely abound.
>
> Joyousness and reverence
> mix together now,
> Blessing virgin, bird, and
> cow.
>
> Danu's Fairy Folk now
> draw near,
> Their laughter and
> magic is growing clear.
>
> I share this day
> with those I love,
> healing Sun streams
> from above.
>
> Flowers crown
> the Queen of the May,

So blessed be this sacred day.

So mote it be.

Abby Willowroot

Notes:

 New Moon Gaining Money Spell

Taurus Moons are associated with the material plane and wealth and money in general. Many of us have problems at times being able to pay the bills, to buy what we need, and still save a little money each month. Now is a good time to do spellwork to help attract money. To start, gather one dollar bill, a small picture of yourself, a small piece of brown or green cloth, a small shovel or spade. For this spell, place the picture of yourself inside the dollar bill and then wrap the two of them into the piece of cloth. Go outside and dig a small hole near a favorite tree or plant, and bury everything in the ground in the dark of night. As you bury the cloth, say these words:

Money sack,
I lay you down,
I bury you in the ground.

When I come dig up the sack,
I'll have more money to bring back.

Wait a while, perhaps two to four weeks, and see if your spell worked.

Jonathan Keyes

Notes:

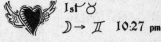

May 2
Friday

1st ♉
☽ → ♊ 10:27 pm

Color of the day: Peach
Incense of the day: Rose

Seeking May Love Spell

So, you didn't find the love of your dreams at the Beltane ritual. With the Moon waxing in Taurus, however, and on a Friday yet, this is an excellent time for a love spell. Be careful, though, since Mercury is retrograde now, and this means you must plan carefully and not expect immediate results. This love spell is very simple, but takes preparation. Spend some time thinking about what you seek in a mate, and write down a list of qualities in two columns—one of what you want in another person, and another column of what you have to offer. Cast a circle, light two candles to light your love's way to you. Recite the list of qualities, alternating the two columns, moving the two candles closer as you speak. End by blowing out the candles.

Magenta Griffith

Notes:

myself to my mother the Earth. As this image returns to the earth, this aspect of my personality dissolves into my psyche and is transformed into new capabilities.

Robert Place

Notes:

May 3
Saturday

 1st ♊

Color of the day: Gray
Incense of the day: Juniper

Bury Your Old Self Spell

If you are bothered by an aspect of your personality that you would like to let go of, then take a new potato and a knife and carve the potato into an image that represents the aspect. At midnight, take the carving out into a forest or field and bury it in the ground. As you do, repeat these words:

With this image, I
consign this aspect of

May 4
Sunday

 1st ♊

Color of the day: Yellow
Incense of the day: Sage

Remembrance Day Spell

Today is Remembrance Day and a perfect time to honor those who have gone before us. To do this, set up a special altar in your home specifically for your ancestors. Carefully choose a spot that will not be disturbed for at least a week. On this altar place photos of deceased loved ones. Burn lavender or rose incense, and light a white candle daily. Spend some time speaking to each loved one, asking for advice or help and meditating until you receive some sort of answer. When the week is over be sure to remember that you can call upon these ancestors when you need their assistance throughout the remainder of the year.

Sheri Richerson

Notes:

May 5
Monday
Cinco de Mayo

 1st ♊
☽ → ♋ 10:42 am

Color of the day: Gray
Incense of the day: Coriander

Cinco de Mayo Independence Spell
Celebrate this Mexican holiday by doing something unexpected and free today. As you set off, sing the following verse to yourself and contemplate your personal freedom:

> Soaring Eagle with
> vision true
> see all that is below,
> Notice what is new.
>
> King of the air,
> Sacred bird of the Spirits,

Wise and strong and
seldom seen aloft,
Lend me your vision so I
may see what is true.

Strength fills your
mighty talons,
Courage fills your spirit
and beats in your heart.
Your mighty wings
spread wide and shadow
all that lies below.

Great Eagle,
Symbol of victory and
might,
I call on your independ—
ence,
And the courage of your
heart.

Moving with the speed
of your sacred feathers,
Eagle lend me your eyes.
Make my vision keen
and true;
Make my spirit to soar.

Open my mind
to your many visions.
Strengthen my grip to
the tenacity
of your steely talons.

Spirit of wisdom,
fill me with guidance on
my eagle flight.
Independence grows in
me daily, tempered with
respect.

Courage grows in me
daily, tempered with
judgment.
Keen sight fills my eyes,
tempered with discern-
ment.
Strength fills my body,
tempered with restraint.

I fly free with brother
eagle.
So mote it be.

Abby Willowroot

Notes:

Holiday lore: Don't confuse Cinco de Mayo with Mexican Independence Day on September 16. Cinco de Mayo marks the victory of the Mexican Army over the French at the Battle of Puebla. Although the Mexican army was evetually defeated, the *Batalla de Puebla* became a symbol of Mexican unity and patriotism. With this victory, Mexico demonstrated to the world that Mexico and all of Latin America were willing to defend themselves against any foreign or imperialist intervention.

May 6
Tuesday

 1st ♌

Color of the day: White
Incense of the day: Honeysuckle

A Green Man Ritual

The Green Man is a forest deity who is depicted as a human face surrounded by foliage. He controls all green and growing things and ensures that crops grow and pastures are lush. Request his aid to protect your garden during the current waxing Moon in spring. To start, form a human figure from garden material. Immerse the figure in a bowl or body of water. Place the figure among your garden plants, and recite this charm:

Father of green leaves,
Bringer of rain,
Bring forth the flowers,
herbs, and grain.
Protect soil and plants
from all pests.
Let this garden be
blessed.

Sprinkle some water around the garden.

James Kambos

Notes:

May 7
Wednesday

 1st ♋

☽ → ♌ 8:46 pm

Color of the day: Peach
Incense of the day: Neroli

Traveling the Rainbow Spell

Now is an ideal time for travel. There is good weather in many places, and it is early enough to beat the summer rush. Make your trip happier by tapping into the positive power of the rainbow. Find a rainbow suncatcher or decal, and hang it in the window of the room where you make your travel plans. Open the drapes and allow the Sun to bring the rainbow into the room. Or place a rainbow sticker on the computer if you make your travel plans over the Internet. Afterward, do a chakra meditation using the brilliant colors of the rainbow: red for the base chakra, then orange, yellow, green, blue, indigo, and violet. Close your eyes and breathe in each color. Do this again as a protection spell before traveling.

Denise Dumars

Notes:

March 8
Thursday

 1st ♌

Color of the day: Turquoise
Incense of the day: Vanilla

Honoring the Green Man Ritual

The spirit of the forest green is celebrated today in Cornwall, England. He is known by many names—Lord of the Greenwood, Robin Hood, and today as the Green Man. Whatever his name, his spirit embodies the push of new vegetation, the rising sap and coming lushness. He is the life force returning; honor him today by taking time to walk in the woods or city park. Revel in the new growth, and bring along a picnic supper for two. A fresh salad of spring greens, garlicky olives, soft goat cheese, sliced cooked eggs with a loaf of crusty bread, and a bottle of fruity aromatic wine is perfect. Eat with your fingers!

Karri Allrich

Notes:

May 9
Friday

 1st ♌
Second Quarter 6:53 am

Color of the day: Rose
Incense of the day: Dill

Loving Relationship Spell

As the saying goes: "Like attracts alike." A beacon of emotional neediness can attract those who may either mirror or take advantage of your needs. Instead of requesting love, you should focus your intent on a more loving relationship—with yourself or with the divine, for instance. Focus your intent today on a red candle. Anoint the candle with rose oil and inscribe with the rune gyfu (✕), which is for love, equality, and balance. Light the candle and say:

> By the power of land,
> sky, and sea, I accept the
> love that the universe
> sends to me.

Snuff the candle, and repeat the ritual daily until the Full Moon.

Karen Follett

Notes:

May 10
Saturday

 2nd ♌
☽ → ♏ 3:31 am

Color of the day: Indigo
Incense of the day: Pine

Unity Spell

In 1869 on this day, officials and workers of the Union Pacific and the Central Pacific railways met on Promontory Summit, in the Utah Territory, to drive in the golden spike. This object symbolized completion of the first transcontinental railroad, an event which joined the nation from coast to coast and reduced a journey of four months to just one week. To build unity today, take a note card, and write down a blessing or wish for someone close to you. Mail the card to that person. (To cast this spell in a coven or circle meeting, put the note cards into a basket and let everyone draw a card.) As each person opens the card and reads the blessings, the ties between you are strengthened.

Jenna Tigerheart

Notes:

May 11
Sunday
Mother's Day

2nd ♍

Color of the day: Gold
Incense of the day: Basil

Ancient Mother's Wisdom Ritual

Of course today is a good day to give thanks for the blessings of your mother. You can also tap into the wisdom of all your female ancestors today by lighting a single candle and focusing on the flame. Place before you a rock, a twig, a piece of string, a leaf, and any pictures you may have of your mother or other female ancestors.

Ancient mothers,
Cave mothers,
Foremothers of all—

I am of your blood,
I am of your bone,
I am you incarnate.

You live in me,
In my mother,
And in my mother's
mother.

You are alive
in each cell and bone,
In every part of me.

I call to you now,
Seeking your wisdom
and your ancient knowing.

Calling to you,
Reaching out,
past millennia of change.

Hear me now,
Grandmother of my
clan,
I seek your ancient
wisdom.

You who are,
She who was first,
Giver of life to
generations.

Your children have lived
For thousands of years.
Each one of them is you.

Each of your daughters
carries within her,
Your memories and your
skills.

Help me now,
Great Clan Mother,
To know your powerful
wisdom.

Bring visions to me
from the depths of my
bloodline,
And bring glimpses of
their lives.

Help me to know
and celebrate now,
The ancient power of
my great and loving
bloodline.

help me to live
always in your knowledge.
So mote it be.

Abby Willowroot

Notes:

Holiday lore: The earliest Mother's Day celebrations can be traced back to the spring celebrations of ancient Greece in honor of Rhea, the mother of the gods. During the 1600s, the English celebrated Mothering Sunday on the fourth Sunday of Lent. In the United States Mother's Day was first suggested in 1872 by Julia Ward Howe (who wrote the words to the "Battle Hymn of the Republic"). President Woodrow Wilson, in 1914, officially proclaimed Mother's Day a national holiday to be held each year on the second Sunday of May.

May 12
Monday

2nd ♍

☽ → ♎ 6:42 am

Color of the day: White
Incense of the day: Chrysanthemum

Ring of Balance Spell

It can be difficult finding balance today. Being able to come home to a nurturing environment is a necessary luxury, vital to good mental health. To do so, try following these helpful magical herbal tips. Honeysuckle has a calming energy, making it perfect for what we most need in our daily lives. For this spell, form vines of honeysuckle into a small wreath, focusing on having a balanced home. Decorate the wreath with objects, herbs, or flowers representing things you need to bring into your home in order for the energy to feel more balanced. Hang the wreath in your home for a week, and afterward leave it as an offering outside where you think its energy is needed.

Laurel Reufner

Notes:

May 13
Tuesday

2nd ♎

Color of the day: Gray
Incense of the day: Evergreen

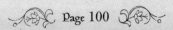

Abundance Spell

On this date, the Romans honored Ceres, the goddess of grains. To tap into this energy, make a magical porridge for abundance being mindful of what each ingredient represents. Your intention will make it so.

> 1 ½ cups whole-grain wheat (for abundance)
> ½ tsp salt, to manifest the spell
> ½ cup honey, for happiness
> ¼ cup walnuts (intelligence)
> ¼ cup almonds (well-being)
> 1 tsp cinnamon (abundance)
> ½ cup raisins, for dreams

Soak the grain in water for twenty-four hours, then drain and rinse it. In a heavy pot, add 4 cups boiling water to the grain. Simmer for 5 hours until the wheat is tender. Make sure the cereal doesn't cook dry; add water if necessary. When tender, drain excess water and add salt. Add honey and cook on low heat until the honey is incorporated. Add nuts, cinnamon, and raisins. Cook until heated.

Lily Gardner-Butts

Notes:

May 14
Wednesday

 2nd ♎︎

☽ → ♏︎ 7:14 am

Color of the day: Yellow
Incense of the day: Eucalyptus

Ease of Mercury Spell

Mix together celery seed, fennel, and lemongrass. Place them in a small, light-blue cloth circle, and tie with a white string. Feel your sacred circle around you, and visualize Mercury fringed in golden light with winged helmet and shoes. Say:

> Hermes, thrice blessed,
> I thank you for your
> presence in my life.
> Grant me ease of travel
> and communications.
> Help me to be quick and
> clear of mind and speech.

See him reach out and touch your bag, imparting some of his golden light to it before flying off. Carry the bag with you throughout the day.

Kristin Madden

Notes:

May 15
Thursday

 2nd ♏
Full Moon 10:36 pm

Color of the day: White
Incense of the day: Sandalwood

Ides of May Spell

Today is the Ides of May. In the original Roman lunar calendar, the Ides marked the center of the month, the time of the Full Moon. However, when the Romans switched to a solar calendar, the Ides fell out of sync with the Moon. Today is magical because it is the Full Moon and the Ides, and therefore the two calendars are back in sync for a day. From the earliest times in Rome, the Ides of May marked the celebration of Mercury, the god of travel, luck, skill, wealth, and magic, who was worshiped in every culture by a different name. For example, Julius Caesar said Mercury was the chief god of the Celts, and as can be seen in the English name for his day of the week, he was equated with Woden, the chief god of the Germanic people. On this day in 495 B.C., Mercury's temple in Rome was dedicated. The entire month of May, in fact, was dedicated to Mercury's mother, Maia, which is why it was named after her, and the Ides of each month is sacred to Mercury's father, Jupiter. In the Buddhist calendar, the Full Moon in May is called *Wesak*. It is the most sacred day of the year. On Wesak Buddha was born, on Wesak he achieved enlightenment, and on Wesak he died and passed into Nirvana. Like Mercury, Buddha was a teacher of spiritual wisdom and interestingly his mother had the same name as Mercury's, Maia. The magic of this day should not be ignored. Take the day off, and go for a hike in the woods. When you come to a crossroads in the path, offer a gift to Mercury. He likes coins. First hold it up to the east and say:

> To Hermes, the messenger
> of Zeus.

Turn to the south and say:

> To Thoth, the teacher of
> magic.

Turn to the west and say:

> To Mercurius, the
> bringer of wealth.

Turn to the north and say:

> To Woden, the source of
> wisdom.

Now, bury the coin in the center of the crossroads and say:

> To Mercury Artaios, the
> master of all the arts, I
> offer this gift.

Mercury Artaios was the god's name in Celtic France. Artaios is related to the Celtic word for "bear." During the day, you may receive a gift from

Mercury in the form of a windfall. I myself once found a beautiful five-pointed white antler on this day. A gift from Mercury can be used as a ritual tool, or as a talisman.

Robert Place

Notes:

pour some of the infusion around your newly growing plants. Do this regularly, and when you eat herbs and food from the garden, you will increase your own virility and personal magnetism with each bite.

Jonathan Keyes

Notes:

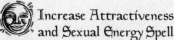

Increase Attractiveness and Sexual Energy Spell

The Full Moon in Scorpio is a time of increased fertility and sexual energy. Plants start to grow strong during this time, and flowers start to blossom, their odor permeating the air. Take advantage of this time by increasing your own magnetism, charisma, and sexual energy. Of course, take care, for you may draw unwanted attention. For this spell you need an ounce of nettle leaves and a piece of rose quartz. Boil a half gallon of spring water. While the water is boiling place the nettles in a sealable container with the piece of rose quartz. When the water is boiled, pour it over the nettles and the rose quartz. Steep this infusion for twelve hours until the water has cooled, then strain into another container. Walk around your garden, and

May 16
Friday

 3rd ♏

☽ → ♐ 6:43 am

Color of the day: Pink
Incense of the day: Thyme

Moon Rise Spell

Have you ever watched the Full Moon rise, from its first glow on the horizon until it fully arrives in the sky—a queen resplendent in her glory? Tonight would be a good night, weather permitting, to do so. Though the Full Moon was actually last night, she will still be nearly as big and full as she can be tonight. Moonrise will be after sunset, so it will be dark enough to be impressive. You'll have to find out the time of moonrise in an almanac or in your

local paper, since it varies depending on time zone and latitude; you could always call the local public library and ask them too. This would also be a good activity for a group of friends, a coven, or a study group. Take chairs outside, and spend time watching the beautiful Moon.

Magenta Griffith

Notes:

card past-present-future layout. A high number card (6 through 10) indicates you should choose a more complex layout, like the Celtic Cross. A court card means people are at the core of the question, while the Major Arcana means higher forces are at work. For these, choose a comprehensive layout.

Elizabeth Barrette

Notes:

May 17
Saturday

 3rd ♐

Color of the day: Brown
Incense of the day: Lavender

Precision Tarot Divination

The tarot is a sophisticated divinatory tool capable of giving very precise information. But where do you start? Some situations or questions are so complex, they make it difficult to decide on the right kind of reading. You can begin by drawing just one card from the deck. A low number card from the Minor Arcana (1 through 5) suggests the matter is simpler than it seems, and you should use a basic layout such as the three-

May 18
Sunday

 3rd ♐
☽ → ♑ 7:03 am

Color of the day: Peach
Incense of the day: Coriander

Mother Goose Remembrance Spell

Today is the anniversary of the death in 1703 of Charles Perrault, the man who wrote the Mother Goose stories. Celebrate this day by gathering a storytelling circle that brings a group together with the magic of laughter. To start the gathering, sit in a circle. One person takes a sip from a cup of water or wine, and says:

> One day on the way
> home from (insert a

place), I spied a (insert an animal) doing (insert a verb).

The person then passes the cup to the next person in the circle. That person takes a sip and continues the story. Each person adds one line after taking a sip, with the intention of making the story as extremely unbelievable as possible. Keep going around the circle, until the story is finished or everyone is laughing too hard to keep going.

Therese Francis

Notes:

with the Moon, focus on your goal, and speak these words three times:

> Mother Moon,
> I call on thee.
> Hear my voice tonight.
> The stars shine around you
> like jewels very bright.
> My path has grown misty
> and it's hard to see my way.
> Help me, Mother,
> to find my path,
> So I see what will be.
> Shine upon me
> with the light that I extol.
> Light my path,
> and show the way
> to my goal.

Jenna Tigerheart

Notes:

May 19
Monday

3rd ♑

Color of the day: Silver
Incense of the day: Myrrh

Mother Luna's Guidance Spell
To reach a goal when the path is hard to find, use this potent spell to draw upon Mother Luna's guidance. The Moon can often be the way to clarity through reflection and ritual. To start, look at the Moon and focus on her energy. After you are in touch

May 20
Tuesday

3rd ♑
☽ → ≈ 10:01 am

Color of the day: Black
Incense of the day: Sage

Planning Your Garden Spell

As days grow warmer and the Earth becomes fertile, our focus turns toward our summer gardens, window boxes, and patio pots. As you purchase your herbs and vegetables for planting, infuse each with magical energy. Herbs contain practical and magical properties; enhance these with your intention. Plant during the waxing Moon to support growth and invite the power of each herb to flourish and expand as you tenderly give it a new home. Add a coin or two to the soil to invite plenty and to honor the earth element of pentacles. Plants nurture us and support our growth, both physical and spiritual. By recognizing the mystery within this green gift from Nature, we become a more intimate part of life's cycle.

Karri Allrich

Notes:

Home or Business Protection Spell

To bless your home or business, place a bowl of candy, herbs, or stones by your front entrance. Bless the bowl's contents by speaking the following verse:

As all who enter here
are children of the Great
Mother,
May those who pass
always walk safely in
her steps.

May they feel the guid-
ance of her hand,
And know she is always
with us,
From the time we meet
till we meet again.

Invite visitors to take an offering.

Karen Follett

Notes:

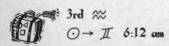

May 21
Wednesday

3rd ♒
☉ → ♊ 6:12 am

Color of the day: White
Incense of the day: Cedar

May 22
Thursday

3rd ♒
☽ → ♓ 4:41 pm
Fourth Quarter 7:31 pm

Color of the day: Violet
Incense of the day: Dill

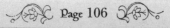

A Prosperity Spell

Prosperity is important in our culture; do not be ashamed if you are among the many who wish to bring money into your life. Instead, do this: On a piece of virgin white paper, using gold ink, write your need and the amount of money (within reason) it would take to purchase this item. Place the paper in an envelope along with an oak leaf and a pinch of sage or nutmeg. Seal the envelope. Bind the envelope with gold and dark-blue ribbons. Hide it and forget about it. Repeat the spell in one lunar month only if needed. When your request manifests itself, give thanks by burning the envelope and its contents. Scatter the ashes on the ground and press a coin into the soil. It is done.

James Kambos

Notes:

Purify Your Relationship Spell

Today is a great time to cleanse and purify everything that is around you. On a Friday such as this, include your relationships. Place a cauldron in the center of your altar with a red candle on the right, a black one on the left, and a white one at the back of the altar. Draw an unbroken circle around the altar with pieces of elder blossoms, rose petals, marjoram, mint, and rue. Inside the cauldron place a vial of oils containing clove, frankincense, lavender, and jasmine. Then await the Full Moon. When the Full Moon arrives, light the candles, anoint your chakras with oil, and move throughout your home allowing the smoke to fill all corners and descend over you. Once this is done, give thanks and extinguish the candles.

Sheri Richerson

Notes:

May 23
Friday

4th ♓

Color of the day: Rose
Incense of the day: Ylang-ylang

May 24
Saturday

4th ♓

Color of the day: Blue
Incense of the day: Jasmine

Calling the Rusalki Spell

The *Rusalki* (singular, *Rusalka*) were sensuous sirens in Russian mythology. To attract their bounteous power for love and protection (of you or of waterways), read this poem at a river, lake, or seashore.

Rusalka

> We wrapped ourselves
> in your silken waves.
> We clouded men's eyes
> with our colors, our
> patterns,
> The blues and greens
> that blend river water,
> Green banks, and leaden
> sky as one.
>
> We flashed
> our eyes, spume-green,
> sea-blue, and drew
> the power of the wind
> within us.
>
> And when they called
> your beauty forth,
> All the seawalls
> in the world
> could not contain it;
> We laughed and danced
> the joy of otters,
> undines, mermaids,
> Manatees.
>
> In your aqua world
> made flesh.

Denise Dumars

Notes:

May 25
Sunday

 4th ♓
D → ♈ 2:59 am

Color of the day: Orange
Incense of the day: Parsley

Gypsy Travel Spell

The gypsies honor their patron, St. Sarah, on this day. Say this charm to St. Sarah when you are going on a long journey, and she will protect you as she has protected the gypsies for centuries. To start, in a yellow bag place bells, an agate, and a sprig of rue. As you leave home, say:

> Traveler, Tartar, Tinker,
> St. Sarah, don't you sink
> her;
> Keep me safe in a car;
> Please let me fly far.
> Traveler, Tinker, Tartar.

When you return home safely, bury the rue and thank St. Sarah for keeping you from harm.

Lily Gardner-Butts

Notes:

love, and peace to all those that have gone before. Keep the flowers for seven days and return them to the earth.

Kristin Madden

Notes:

May 26
Monday
Memorial Day

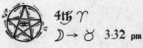 4th ♈

Color of the day: Lavender
Incense of the day: Daffodil

home Remembrance Meditation

Today is a good day to remember, of course; you can do so by placing a vase of poppies, or gardenias and eucalyptus, in a place of honor in your home. On a small pink card, write in black ink:

> For those that have gone before, thank you.

Attach it to the vase for the day. That night, burn myrrh incense and set up sacred space as usual. Place the vase in your circle along with matches and a fireproof container. Spend a few moments meditating on your ancestors, departed loved ones, and all who have given their lives to protect others or defend freedom. Burn the pink card in the container, and send blessings of thanks,

May 27
Tuesday

4th ♈
☽ → ♉ 3:32 pm

Color of the day: Red
Incense of the day: Musk

Courage for Leadership Spell

Mars rules the sphere of conflict and leadership, and the day Tuesday. Here you can find energy for courage or protection. This is a good day to make a Mars talisman. Start with a suitable emblem, such as a Mars sign pendant or a red stone like carnelian. Light a red candle and say:

> Champion of Olympus,
> Lend me your sword and shield;
> Strengthen my spirit when I must take the field.

Concentrate on imbuing the talisman with Mars' energy. Let the candle burn out on its own. Whenever you need extra support, wear or carry the talisman. You can also repeat the charm before entering a conflict.

Elizabeth Barrette

Notes:

Blessed be the earth.

Toss the salt in the bath water, stir it three times clockwise. Light the candle, hold it over the bath and say:

Blessed be the fire.

Lastly, light the incense, and say:

Blessed be the air.

Put the candle and incense in some safe place in the bathroom, get in the tub, and enjoy.

Magenta Griffith

Notes:

May 28
Wednesday

 4th ♉

      Color of the day: Brown
Incense of the day: Maple

Magical Bath Ritual

A magical bath is perfect for the stress of today. To take one, you will need a candle, incense and an incense burner or tray, and some salt (preferably sea salt). Give your tub a quick rinse, and start filling it with warm water. When the tub is as full as you like it, touch the surface of the water and say:

Blessed be the water.

Then put a little salt in your hand, touch the salt with your other hand, saying:

May 29
Thursday

 4th ♉

      Color of the day: Green
Incense of the day: Carnation

Pinning Down Your Finances

Want to gain control of your finances? Try this: Light a green candle and set it nearby. Sort through some play money, pulling out the larger bills. Holding the money in your hands, visualize real money in its place. Think what it will feel like to have such money.

Place the stack down on a small board and use a hammer to nail it in place. Take care not to drive the nail all the way through the board. Let the candle burn completely down, and wait.

Laurel Reufner

Notes:

May 30
Friday

 4th ♉
☽ → ♊ 4:32 am
New Moon 11:20 pm

Color of the day: White
Incense of the day: Almond

Strengthen Your Ability to Express Yourself Spell

Sometimes it can be difficult to express ourselves through words. We may be shy or feel our words are not important or will not be valued. This Gemini New Moon is a good time to develop the powerful resource of speaking and expressing oneself. To prepare for this spell you will need the flower essence of trumpet vine (you can find this at most health-food stores). Trumpet vine helps to draw forth our power to communicate and express. You will also need to gather or buy some fennel, thyme, and peppermint. On the night of the New Moon, make a tea with the herbs. Sip the tea and then take four drops of the flower essence under your tongue. Visualize your throat chakra opening and gently flowing. Continue to do this twice a day until the Full Moon. You may want to visualize the color red in this area as well; this can help to generate vitality and energy in your throat chakra, and will help you to communicate and express yourself more directly and clearly.

Jonathan Keyes

Notes:

May 31
Saturday

 4th ♊

Color of the day: Gray
Incense of the day: Violet

Feeling Overwhelmed Spell

If you are feeling overwhelmed right about now, here are some tips to help you fell better:

1. Turn off the telephone, TV, radio, and any other distraction.

2. Sit in a comfortable chair, with your eyes closed.

3. Breathe in as slowly as you can and then exhale quickly. Do this four times to get centered.

4. Say the following mantra at least thirteen times:

> So much time, so few
> things to do.

It doesn't matter that you know there's too much to do right now, just repeat the mantra and breathe in as slowly as you can.

5. If you can, sit for a few minutes more and let your thoughts drift past your mind. Do not actively attempt to do any problem solving. Many times, solutions will appear.

Therese Francis

Notes:

Notes:

June is the sixth month of the year. Its astrological sign is Gemini, the twins (May 21-Jan 20), a mutable air sign ruled by Mercury. It is named for Juno, the principal goddess of the Roman pantheon, wife of Jupiter the king of the gods; she is the patroness primarily of marriage and the well-being of women. The warm dry breezes dry the fields now, and the hay is mown. The air is perfumed with the fragrance of honeysuckle and wild rose and filled with the birdsong. Fireflies dance in tall meadow grass. Toads are common in wet areas. Fuchsia, foxglove, and lavender blossom, attracting bees and birds. Culinary herbs are ready for harvesting. Squirrels and chipmunks bicker in the garden over prized plants. Birds are busy feeding hatchlings now. Broken birdshells are to be found cast away from nests under the trees; finding a hatched eggshell is a sign of great fortune and favor. Birds are also molting their old feathers now, which can be used in magic. By mid-June, the weather moves into the full heat of summer. The June Full Moon is the Mead Moon, named for the fermented drink made from honey. June is considered the best month for marriage. The main holiday in June is the Summer Solstice, which marks the time of year when the waxing Sun reaches its zenith and days will begin to shorten again.

June 1
Sunday

1st ♊
☽ → ♋ 4:27 pm

Color of the day: Yellow
Incense of the day: Clove

Fairy Attraction Spell

In June my garden is an oasis of color and fragrance—I hope yours is too. Now is a good time to attract the fairy folk to your garden. First, mark off the area with a mixture of water and olive oil, sprinkling it here and there with your fingers, and say:

> Water, olive oil, bind and
> protect the soil I call mine.

Beneath ferns and foxgloves, and near rocks and the base of trees, sprinkle a few grains of clear glitter. Then say:

> I welcome you spirits of
> tree and vine.

Ground your energy when done. Perform this spell during a waxing Moon outdoors, at that breathless moment just before sunset.

James Kambos

Notes:

June 2
Monday

1st ♊

Color of the day: Silver
Incense of the day: Rose

Birthday of Mother Shipton

On this date in 1488, seer Ursula Sontheis (later known as Mother Shipton) was born. Around the same time as Nostradamus, she received prophecies that she set down in verse. Many came true in her lifetime, and some say that her prophecies are still coming true today. Shipton became famous and incurred the ire of important people who were the recipients of unflattering prophecies. Several of her predictions about Cardinal Woolsey came true, and he vowed to have her burnt at the stake. Fortunately, she never was—perhaps kept safe by her popularity. While she did never become quite as famous as her rival Nostradamus, Mother Shipton did predict many things to come, for instance:

> Carriages without horses
> will go,
> and accidents fill the
> world with woe.

And:

> When pictures look alive
> with movements free,
> And ships like fishes sail
> beneath the sea.

Fortunately for us, Mother Shipton's predictions were not always correct. After all, she predicted that the world would end in 1881.

Denise Dumars

Notes:

unneeded energy back to the universe. Thank the deity and honor your connection with her.

Karen Follett

Notes:

June 3
Tuesday

1st ♋

Color of the day: White
Incense of the day: Gardenia

Goddess Energy Spell

The strength and the energy of the Goddess is within us. Cancer's crescent Moon creates a waxing bond between our goddess-within energy and the energy of the Great Goddess. To tap into this bond, sit in the light of the crescent Moon. Relax your body and mind. Visualize a silver energy radiating from the Moon to the top of your head. Take a deep breath, inviting in the energy into your crown chakra. Feel the energy move through you with each breath. Feel your energy meld with the energy of the Goddess. Become one with her. Release any

June 4
Wednesday

1st ♋
☽ → ♌ 2:25 am

Color of the day: Peach
Incense of the day: Pine

Relationship Charm Spell

June is a fitting time to contemplate your relationship with a loved one. Whether actively involved or living alone, this charm helps focus love energy in a positive manner. On the night of a waxing Moon gather a pink candle, two rose petals, lavender oil, and a china plate. Cast a circle, and light the candle. Contemplate the flame as a symbol of love's light. Place the rose petals on the plate, and add three drops of oil, saying:

Love's truth burns
bright,
I welcome my soulmate
on this night.

Tip the candle to drip wax onto the petals, enough to form a coin-sized token, and mold the wax and petals together. Keep this token safe for six Moons, then bury it beneath a rose bush.

Karri Allrich

Notes:

Earth; any little thing will help. When you are finished with your visualization go outdoors and put into action what you have visualized.

Lily Gardner-Butts

Notes:

June 5
Thursday

 1st ♌

Color of the day: Turquoise
Incense of the day: Geranium

World Environment Day Ritual

The planet is a living organism. To send your protective energies out to the environment, decorate your altar with a green cloth, plants, and tree branches today. Burn a green candle that has been anointed with myrrh and vetiver. Center yourself, and know that each of us is connected to every animal and plant and stone on this planet. Imagine Mother Gaia whole and healed. Breathe in the green scent from the candle, and consider what you could do this day to promote the health of Mother

June 6
Friday
Shavuot

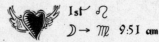 1st ♌
☽ → ♍ 9:51 am

Color of the day: Rose
Incense of the day: Nutmeg

Shavuot Ritual

Shavuot is the Jewish celebration of the harvest in Israel and of the giving of the Ten Commandments on Mount Sinai. To celebrate the energy of this day, decorate your altar with spring greenery, a candle, and the first fruit of the season. Cut the fruit in half. Raise some energy and empower the fruit with the energy of harvest, plenty, appreciation, and lawfulness. After the fruit is empowered, offer half of the fruit up to the divine with thanks for the gift of divine word. Light the candle and offer up the rest of the fruit to the divine in celebration of the harvest. After the offering, feast on milk and cheese. Leave the candle burning for the remainder of the day.

Jenna Tigerheart

Notes:

oliday lore: Shavuot, the Feast of the Weeks, celebrates the harvest season. The name of the holiday, which means "weeks," refers to the timing of the festival (seven weeks after Passover). Shavuot also commemorates the giving of the Ten Commandments to Moses at Mount Sinai. According to tradition the Israelites were thought to have overslept on this morning. To compensate for this negligence, Jews hold a vigil on the eve of Shavuot.

June 7
Saturday

 1st ♏
Second Quarter 3:28 pm

Color of the day: Brown
Incense of the day: Cedar

honoring Vesta Ritual

On the Roman calendar, this date originally marked the festival of Vestalia, a feast held to honor the goddess Vesta. Vesta is the goddess of fire and the hearth. It is unusual for this goddess to appear in any sort of icon, because her image is of fire itself. On this day, women and bakers should be honored. It is an excellent day to bake. If you do so, be sure to leave some cake or bread on the fireplace or stove afterward as an offering to the fiery spirit of the goddess Vesta. Note: She also likes violets.

Robert Place

Notes:

June 8
Sunday
Pentecost

 2nd ♏
☽ → ♎ 2:30 pm

Color of the day: Peach
Incense of the day: Cinnamon

Every Day a Picnic Spell

Everybody loves a picnic, including ants. Those of us who walk on two legs generally prefer not to share a meal with those who walk on six. You don't need to resort to chemicals in order to find a little picnic peace; instead, just ask:

> For our goodies you may yearn—
> Sister Ant, please wait your turn.
>
> Don't rush in to steal our food,
> There's no need to be rude.
>
> We won't eat up every crumb,
> If you're patient you'll get some.
>
> We will leave them when we're through;
> We'll leave a picnic just for you.

It's that easy to gain insect cooperation.

Elizabeth Barrette

Notes:

Summer Sacred Space Ritual

ap into the summer spirit for setting up your own sacred space. Start by gathering sea salt and lemon juice. Set up your space in your usual manner. Have a bowl of warm water on the altar and burn sandalwood incense. Add the sea salt and lemon juice to the water. Hold the bowl up to the Goddess, and ask that this liquid be blessed with the powers of purification and protection. Starting in the north, go around your home, sprinkling the water in each room. Be sure to include all doorways, windows, closets, and vents. Say as you go:

> May this house be blessed
> by the Goddess, so that
> only the most beneficial
> energies might enter.

Kristin Madden

Notes:

June 9
Monday

2nd ♎

Color of the day: Peach
Incense of the day: Clove

June 10
Tuesday

2nd ♎
☽ → ♏ 4:39 pm

Color of the day: Black
Incense of the day: Ginger

Protection Wreath Spell

To create a protection wreath perfect for this day, tie sprigs of dill, garlic, and pieces of ginger root on to a wreath. To give this decoration a fancier look, accessorize with dried flowers, good luck or protection tokens or amulets, and streaming ribbons. You can attach this to the outside of your home or to your front door, or you can use it as a decorative home accessory. Be sure to burn a white candle while you are constructing your wreath. Once it is finished, hang it up and chant:

> herbs of the earth,
> Spirits above,
> I request your powers
> To protect this property.

Allow the candle to burn out on its own.

Sheri Richerson

Notes:

Get Your Career Moving Spell

You can get things moving in your chosen career today. Just sit down and get comfortable. Holding a small die-cast toy car in your hand, spend some time focusing on your career and on where you'd like to see it go. Actually see yourself doing the career-related things that you really want to be doing. See your boss or supervisor noticing your good work and then thanking and rewarding you for it. Pour as many of these thoughts into the little car as you can. Take the car to work and set it on your desk, or stash it in a locker or drawer. Look on it once a day or so and recall your visualizations. See the car getting you there.

Laurel Reufner

Notes:

June 12
Thursday

2nd ♏

☽ → ♐ 5:12 pm

Color of the day: Violet
Incense of the day: Musk

June 11
Wednesday

2nd ♏

Color of the day: Brown
Incense of the day: Neroli

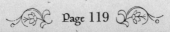

Lottery Spell

If you buy lottery tickets, use this spell. Every time you buy a ticket, think to yourself that you are doing it as an act of magic. Say to yourself:

> I am open to wealth
> coming to me,
> I am open to good fortune
> coming to me,
> I am open to my luck.

Assemble a prosperity altar, and put the lottery tickets on it. Surround them with symbols of good luck—a four-leafed clover, rabbit's foot, and so on. You might want to add a small container of cinnamon, or to burn cinnamon incense. Put any money you find on this altar as well—pennies you find on the street, change from vending machines, and so on. Like will attract like, and money will attract money.

Magenta Griffith

Notes:

Turning Knowledge to Wisdom Spell

Books are wonderful tools. In them, words turn into knowledge. For instance, the words of witchcraft, once veiled and hidden, can now be found in abundance at any local bookstore. However, witchcraft is the craft of the wise, not the craft of the well-read. Under the layers of conscious knowledge lies the soul of wisdom. Today, using any device to promote meditation—such as a candle, smudgebundle, and so on—relax your body and open your mind. Choose and read a passage from any desired book. Focus on the passage. Ask the divinity to guide you to the wisdom behind the words. Feel yourself transcend through the layers of conscious thinking and subconscious processing. Connect with your higher self within the collective inner conscious and listen for the wisdom of the soul.

Karen Follett

Notes:

June 13
Friday

 2nd ♐

Color of the day: Rose
Incense of the day: Pink

June 14
Saturday
Flag Day

2nd ♐
Full Moon 6:16 am
☽ → ♑ 5:38 pm

Color of the day: Rose
Incense of the day: Sandalwood

Charge Magical Objects Spell

Sagittarius is a fire sign, and one of the best things we can do during a fiery Moon is to charge and energize the various magical objects we work with a small fire ritual. By charging each magical tool, we ensure that they are vital and full of life when we work with them. To prepare, gather any magical objects you wish to have vitalized and energized, along with a red candle. For this spell, go outside under the Full Moon with your magical objects and the candle. Light the candle and one by one draw each object over the flame and say these words:

> With this flame, consecrate.
> With this flame, generate.
> With this flame, energize.
> With this flame, vitalize.

Each time you draw an object over the flame, recall to your self the purpose of the object and the source its power. Perhaps, too, you may want to say a few words about the meaning of that object out loud. Then, when you have contemplated the nature of each object fully, give thanks and return your sacred objects to the altar from where they came.

Jonathan Keyes

Notes:

June 15
Sunday
Father's Day

3rd ♑

Color of the day: Gold
Incense of the day: Basil

Father's Day Spell

To celebrate this holiday of our fathers, gather one blue, one red, and one green candle, and light all three of them. Place the red candle in the center of the three. Take a piece of string that is thirteen inches long, and tie a knot in the string after you speak each of the following lines:

> Father,
> Ancient hunter,
> Protector of clans and
> kin,

Ancient warrior
And keeper of fire,
Protector of the hearth.

Powerful presence
whose courage is mani-
fest in compassion and
loyalty.

Father, son,
Uncle, brother,
Loyal as the mighty
Bear.

Teacher of the ways
of sacred nature,
Listener of the winds,
rider of the waves,

Tiller of the earth,
Spirit free,
Dancer of the ancient
hunts.

Father.

Wind whisper your
secrets from the ancients.
Water flow through him
with your healing
secrets.
Fire of the cosmos fill his
life force with thy spark.
Earth speak to him
through thy animals,
rocks, and sea.
Let thy trees whisper in
his ears.

Shamans of old,
Chieftains and fathers,

Guide his spirit
with wisdom and
courage.
Bring ancient lessons
of the alpha wolf,
Protector of the pack.

Strength, courage,
wisdom, insight.
Father of many gifts,
Radiant as the Sun.

Ancestor, protector,
Companion, healer,
Teacher, and friend.

Father.

The strength and fidelity
of the fathers is held fast
in these knots of truth.
So mote it be.

Abby Willowroot

Notes:

Holiday lore: The first Father's
Day was observed on June 19, 1910
in Spokane, Washington. At about
the same time in various towns and
cities across American other people
were beginning to celebrate a father's
day as a balance to the more well-
known Mother's Day holiday. In

1924, President Calvin Coolidge supported the idea of a national Father's Day. It wasn't until 1966 that President Lyndon Johnson signed a presidential proclamation declaring the third Sunday of June as Father's Day. It's a good day to honor the wisdom of the elder males in your family.

June 16
Monday

3rd ♑

☽ → ♒ 7:41 pm

Color of the day: Silver
Incense of the day: Peony

Household Protection Spell

To protect your home today, hang a potted rosemary plant near the back door. This will prevent evil from entering the house. You might also choose to hang a sprig of garlic cloves for the same purposes. Also, you can use the garlic or rosemary for cooking while they are protecting the house. Just replace the garlic sprig before using the last piece.

Therese Francis

Notes:

June 17
Tuesday

3rd ♒

Color of the day: Gray
Incense of the day: Poplar

Lily Spell for Protection

On this day in the Shinto faith, people adorn their houses and villages with lilies to protect them from disaster. Here in the West, it was believed that the first lily sprang from the breast milk of the goddess Juno, for whom the month of June was named. To use the powers of lilies for protection, steep lily blossoms in alcohol for seven days. Strain the infusion into a white vial. Sprinkle it on the window and door sills in all the rooms of your house, saying:

> Mother Juno, protect
> this home from travail.

Arrange a bouquet of lilies on your kitchen table and burn a new white candle.

Lily Gardner-Butts

Notes:

June 18
Wednesday

 3rd ♏︎
☽ → ♎︎ 11:48 pm

Color of the day: White
Incense of the day: Coriander

A Knot Spell for Travel

Use a sky blue cord or ribbon for a safe driving spell. With each phrase below, tie a knot in the cord:

> By knot of one,
> My spell's begun.
> By knot of two,
> Destination is true.
> By knot of three,
> My route I see.
> By knot of four,
> My safety is sure.
> By knot of five,
> I safely drive.
> By knot of six,
> My spell is fixed.
> By knot of seven,
> The power is given.

Hang the cord from your rear-view mirror while driving.

> Jenna Tigerheart

Notes:

June 19
Thursday

 3rd ♒︎
☽ → ♓︎ 12:57 am

Color of the day: Green
Incense of the day: Sage

Meditation on the Night Sky

The Egyptian goddesses Isis, Ma'at, and Taueret are used for their symbolism in this poetic meditation on the starry sky.

> Taueret,
> O hippo mother,
> Crocodilian on your back
> like a shawl
> as you walk across the
> zodiac.
>
> Belly large,
> Teeth like fenceposts,
> horned and hooved
> And feared by canid
> and Selkit scorpion
> alike.
>
> Blue in the night sky,
> Pillar of the gods,
> As Isis rules the day
> and Antares,
> Satio Isidis,
> Rules the night.
>
> O Taueret,
> Mother of stars,
> Gifting,
> Domained,

Encapsuled of starlight,
Eater of the Pole Star.

Deathless caiman of
obsidian, lapis, dark,
Swallower of souls
that we shoot into the
sky in obsolete iron.
Judged on Ma'at's feather,
Whether or not
to return.

Denise Dumars

Notes:

ble, place four candles of appropriate color, one for each season, in a circle. In the center place a gold candle, for the Sun. Light the seasonal candles saying:

> Seasons must turn,
> Let the Sun return.

Light the Sun candle and say:

> Shining One,
> Charge me with passion,
> Turn my words into
> action.
> It must be!

End this rite with a love spell, or some form of divination.

James Kambos

Notes:

June 20
Friday

 3rd ♓

Color of the day: Peach
Incense of the day: Dill

Ring of Fire Spell

This spell is based on a little-known solar ritual from the Aegean islands. Long ago on this evening before the Summer Solstice, hoops were set ablaze, and villagers would guide the Sun's return by jumping through these rings of fire. You can create your own ring of fire with this spell. At dusk, outdoors if possi-

June 21
Saturday
Litha – Summer Solstice

 3rd ♓
Fourth Quarter 9:45 am
☽ → ♈ 10:06 am
☉ → ♋ 2:10 pm

Color of the day: Indigo
Incense of the day: Maple

Summer Solstice Spell

Today is one of the holiest days of the year. At first light, take a tall white or yellow candle and a short black candle outside; light them to symbolize the longest day and shortest night of the year. A flower-scented incense is good to burn while you intone the words below:

Brother Sun and Mother
Moon,
Day is longest now.

Energies of the brilliant
Sun
Aid all at work
Or having fun.

Longest day,
A blessing is,
From rise to set supreme
is the Sun.

Fueling growth and
passions bright,
Strong and true is the
solar light.

Bounty grows
And river flows,
As Earth is warmed and
lighted.

Creative energy reaches
zenith
on this day of shortest
night.

Crops grow high and
excitement grows,

with each new ray of
Sun.

Every day,
All creatures play
and hail the mighty Sun.

Ancient solstice,
Fires burning,
honor the Sun and feed
the light.

Druid, Indian, Norse,
and Celt all danced
on Summer Solstice,
joyously felt.

Solar winds
and solar flares
Wash away our hunger
and our cares.

Mighty Sun,
King of warmth,
Makes humans to frolic
and bees to swarm.

Keep this day
In memory bright,
To warm you on long
winter nights.

May the rays of solstice
keep us warm,
All through the year.

The Sun has kissed
Flower field and tree,
The Sun is supreme.
So mote it be.

Abby Willowroot

Notes:

Notes:

June 22
Sunday

 4th ♈

Color of the day: Orange

Incense of the day: Parsley

health-Charging Spell

If you have an indoor basil plant that needs repotting, you can charge the basil to aid in your good health and digestive maintenance. To do so, set the pot on a sunny windowsill where you will be able to remember to care for it. Begin the spell by grounding and centering. Focus on the basil as a means to good health. Now, put some gravel on the bottom of your new pot and add some potting soil on top, leaving room for the basil. Carefully tap the plant out of its current container. Put it in the new pot, adding more soil around it. Give the plant a drink of water and finish by adding a yellow stone, preferably agate (for good digestion) on top of the soil. You might charge the stone ahead of time.

Laurel Reufner

June 23
Monday

 4th ♈

☽ → ♉ 10:15 pm

Color of the day: White

Incense of the day: Lavender

Weed the Garden Ritual

Time to weed the garden? With the Moon waning, you can weed and do magic at the same time. Start by thinking about what you want to get rid of in your life, and perhaps in the world. Then, go into your garden, equipped to weed with kneepads, hoe, fork, and the like. As you pull each weed, name it, and say these words:

> I remove hate,
> I remove poverty.
>
> I remove my anger at my boss.

And so on. Be creative in your designs. Afterward, be sure to dispose of the weeds carefully. Either bag them and put them into the garbage immediately, knowing they are going away, or if you compost, ask the Earth to transform them as they rot.

Magenta Griffith

Notes:

waning Sun, and paves the way for its rebirth. As patron of Midsummer, St. John has absorbed all the Pagan magical practices associated with this period. For example, the Celtic Midsummer bonfires came to be called "the Fires of St. John." This is the time to gather the Midsummer magical herb called St. John's wort, also known to Voodoo practitioners as High John the Conqueror.

Robert Place

Notes:

June 24
Tuesday

 4♄ ☿

Color of the day: Lavender
Incense of the day: Frankincense

Rituals for the Baptist

Today is the feast day of St. John the Baptist. John was the cousin of Jesus. He paved the way for his cousin by living in the wilderness where he preached and prophesied that a savior greater than he would soon come. John is the one who was said to be "crying in the wilderness." Unlike most other saints his feast day does not mark his day of death but his birthday. As the feast of Christ is celebrated near the Winter Solstice to align Christ with the symbol of the waxing Sun, St. John the Baptist's feast comes just after the Summer Solstice. He rules over the

June 25
Wednesday

4♄ ☿

Color of the day: Yellow
Incense of the day: Sandalwood

Full Bloom Spell

Now summer is in full bloom. And wouldn't you know it, fairies just love a flower garden! Their favorite plants include foxglove, bluebell, marigold, cowslip, snapdragon, and morning glory. You can attract them with ornaments that jingle or sparkle, too, such as wind chimes or

suncatchers. Those big glass gazing balls are definite fairy magnets. All the better if your garden includes moving water, such as a fountain or sprinkler, and a place to hide, such as a ceramic "toad abode" or a rock pile. When you work outside, you can also sing:

> Now I've made a sacred space,
> Fairies welcome in this place.
> I won't peek, and I won't tell.
> You can stay here safe and well.

Elizabeth Barrette

Notes:

according to legend and lore, invented the great American game of baseball. This a good day for group activities, such as this large group ritual to raise energy for a common goal. To start, stand in a circle holding hands, your right hand facing down over the neighbor's left hand. The leader clearly states the purpose of the energy raising—such as providing healing energy for Joe, or some other purpose. The leader then says "Zoom." The next person to the right repeats the word, and so on around the circle as quickly as possible. As the energy builds, everyone raises their hands, envisioning the energy vortex rising up and then going out into the universe with the declared purpose.

Therese Francis

Notes:

June 26
Thursday

 4th ♉
☽ → ♊ 11:13 am

Color of the day: White
Incense of the day: Carnation

Zoom Spell for Energy
Today is the birthday, in 1819, of Abner Doubleday, the guy who,

June 27
Friday

 4th ♊

Color of the day: Pink
Incense of the day: Thyme

Sweet Dreams Spell

Now that Midsummer has passed, it is the perfect time to gather fresh herbs and rose petals for creating a dream sachet. To enhance peaceful dreams, make a blend of equal parts rose petals, lavender flowers, mugwort, rosemary, and lemon balm. Store the mixture in a sealed plastic bag for three days to allow the scents to mingle. Scoop one-half cup of the mixture into the center of a pretty square handkerchief or clean cloth napkin. Gather then corners and tie it with a sky-blue ribbon. As you tie up the sachet, say:

> Herbs and blossoms
> bring me delight,
> Sweeten my dreams
> with deeper insight.

Tuck the sachet into your pillowcase. You can make a few extras for your restless friends.

Karri Allrich

Notes:

June 28
Saturday

 4th ♊
☽ → ♋ 10:52 pm

Color of the day: Gray
Incense of the day: Lilac

God Within You Ritual

To connect to the presence of the divine within yourself, close your eyes and allow yourself to feel its presence. Then visualize yourself connecting to the mind of a chosen god or goddess. You will see this as a beautiful light surrounding your head. Think of the information you wish to obtain, and then visualize the information instantly flowing into your mind from the light. As you relax and enjoy the light, say softly to yourself:

> I am alert and expect to receive the information within the next couple of days.

Imagine yourself overtaken by the peace that comes with the knowledge that all the information you need is easily accessible. It will come to you through the divine mind of your favorite god or goddess. Combine these images with the joy of your restful heart, and release these feelings into the universe.

Sheri Richerson

Notes:

Then make additional bundles so that you have enough for each door of your house that leads to the outside. In the evening, tie the small bundle to the door handles on the inside of the house. As you do so speak these words:

> I tie the bundles to the door. No harm will come here any more.

Jonathan Keyes

Notes:

June 29
Sunday

 4th ♋
New Moon 1:39 pm

Color of the day: Peach
Incense of the day: Cinnamon

Increase Security and Serenity Spell

Sometimes even our own home can feel unsafe to us. Perhaps we've been robbed, or maybe there is simple disharmony within the house due to personality conflicts. A Cancer New Moon is a good time to bring safety and security to a home setting. To prepare for this, gather an ounce each of willow bark and lemon balm at an herb or natural foods store. Also gather a few tiny moonstones from a gem store, a few small pieces of blue cloth, and a few pieces of string to wrap up the cloth. To begin your spellwork, on the night of the actual New Moon in Cancer, place a small bit of the herbs and a moonstone in a piece of cloth, and wrap the bundle up with string.

June 30
Monday

1st ♋

Color of the day: Lavender
Incense of the day: Chrysanthemum

June Meal Blessing

For this last day of June, enjoy a special meal tonight and honor yourself, your friends, and your family. As you sit down to eat, offer this meal blessing.

> Great Spirit, source of all life,
> Thank you for this food.

Thank you for your
guidance and protection.
Thank you for my home
and my loved ones.

May those who gave
their lives and energies
to bring us this meal be
blessed with peace, love,
and release.

May we each be ever
grateful for all that we
have,
And may we extend
those blessings into the
world.

As we receive so do we
give back,
So mote it be.

Kristin Madden

Notes:

Notes:

July

July is the seventh month of the year. Its astrological sign is Cancer, the crab (June 21-July 20), a cardinal water sign ruled by the Moon. The month is named for Julius Caesar. The heat of July is oppressive, only occasionally interrupted by sudden summer storms. Leaves wilt on trees and plants suffer in the parched fields. July is the traditional month for visiting the seashore or other body of water as an escape. Sand and seawater are useful in magical rituals at this time; as are shells, particularly cowries, which resemble and symbolize the sexual organs of the Goddess. Snails and shellfish, such as mussels and clams, have magical resonance. A visit to the beach is a perfect time to perform magic; an incoming tide (and waxing Moon) is a time to cast spells of increase, prosperity, and fertility. An outgoing tide (and waning Moon) is a time for spells of banishment. One of the most magical objects you can find on the beach is a stone or pebble with a natural hole in it. July harvest time begins with cabbage, from which one makes sauerkraut for the winter months, followed by all the herbs of the garden. The Full Moon of July is called the Wort Moon; *wort* is old Anglo-Saxon for "herb." Use a white-handled ritual knife to harvest herbs for magical purposes. Give thanks to the spirits that dwell in the herb garden.

July 1
Tuesday

 1st ♋
☽ → ♌ 8:13 am

Color of the day: White
Incense of the day: Honeysuckle

Object Cleansing Ritual

For a magical cleansing, gather any unclean objects on the day after a Full Moon, wrap them in a red cloth with some sea salt, and bury then in an area of the yard that you do not use for any purpose. After a month has passed, remove the object, bury the salt in the earth where the object was, and burn the cloth.

Therese Francis

Notes:

light a red candle to release negativity. Then prepare your altar with seven green candles that will burn for five to seven days. These candles should be rubbed with pulverized nutmeg, allspice, and poppy seeds. Inscribe your specific wish on the side of each candle. Afterward, on each day for the next seven days you should light one green candle, and allow it to continue to burn itself out. On each of these days, once the candle has been lit spend some time meditating on your request. This is a very powerful and demanding spell, and you should consider carefully before you embark on it.

Sheri Richerson

Notes:

July 2
Wednesday

1st ♌

 Color of the day: Yellow
Incense of the day: Eucalyptus

Business Project Spell

This is a great time for advancing your business prospects. First

July 3
Thursday

 1st ♌
☽ → ♍ 3:16 pm

Color of the day: Turquoise
Incense of the day: Geranium

July Protection from harm Spell

This spell can be used when you need protection from a person who is harming you in some way. It is imperative that this spell be performed with goodwill toward your adversary, or else the spell can lash back at you. To start, sew together a poppet in the likeness of your adversary. As you construct the poppet, hold the image of your adversary in your mind. When the poppet is finished, place it in a box with food and a toy. Remember, you want this person to enjoy life elsewhere and leave you alone. During a waning Moon, particularly while the Moon is in Scorpio, bury the box in a spot away from your home and business where it won't be disturbed.

Lily Gardner-Butts

Notes:

July 4
Friday
Independence Day

 1st ♍

Color of the day: Pink
Incense of the day: Sandalwood

Freedom Spell

Today is a day of freedom, of celebration and sharing, and of unlimited possibility. To tap into this energy with a freedom spell, you will need some cinnamon, salt, sugar, pepper, and three candles, preferably one red, blue, and white. Place the three candles on a plain green cloth before you in a circle. Leave space in the center for small piles of cinnamon, salt, sugar, and pepper. Light the candles, and pick up a pinch of each substance as you speak its name, then speak the following verse:

> I claim freedom
> whose blessings are
> many and bountiful.
> Life sustaining as salt,
> Comforting as cinnamon,
> Sweet as sugar,
> Sharp as pepper.
>
> I claim freedom by my
> actions and my spirit,
> I honor the freedom of
> others.
>
> I claim justice
> Whose practice begins
> with me and flows
> through all things.
> Sharp as salt,
> Rare as cinnamon,
> Nourishing as sugar,
> Grounding as pepper.
>
> I claim justice
> by my granting of justice
> to others.
> I claim justice in the
> ways.

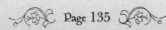

I respect the rights of those I disagree with, I claim justice by all that is magical.

I claim the freedoms of belief, association, speech, education, to follow my dreams, to live in peace. I claim these things by my daily actions and beliefs.

I claim freedom. By being a part of a community, I am free. So mote it be.

> Abby Willowroot

Notes:

ʜoliday notes: On July 4, 1776, the Second Continental Congress adopted the Declaration of Independence. Philadelphians were first to mark the anniversary of American independence with a celebration, but Independence Day became commonplace only after the War of 1812. By the 1870s, the Fourth of July was the most important secular holiday in the country, celebrated even in far-flung communities on the western frontier of the country.

July 5
Saturday

1st ♍

☽ → ♎ 8:20 pm

Color of the day: Brown
Incense of the day: Juniper

Old Midsummer's Day Divination

ɪn ancient times this date was considered Midsummer, and worshippers held festivals and plays today. Now, this day seems an ideal time to continue celebrations left over from July 4. We can also add the time-honored method of card divination as part of the festivities. To do so, get your favorite tarot deck. The person you will read for should shuffle the deck and then cut it with his or her left hand. Pull four cards. These represent summer, fall, winter, and spring for the person seeking the reading. Each card should give clues about particular moods, events, and potentials for each season in the coming year.

> Denise Dumars

Notes:

July 6
Sunday

 1st ♎

Second Quarter 9:32 am

Color of the day: Yellow
Incense of the day: Sage

Sun in Your heart Spell

This is the third Sunday after the Summer Solstice. It is a perfect day to welcome the Sun into your heart. Start by getting up before sunrise, which will be at about 4:30 am in New York and at 4:45 am in California (check your local newspaper for your local sunrise time). Find a comfortable seat that faces east, and sit and watch the horizon until the Sun emerges. Let go of all superfluous thoughts, just watch and contemplate. As the Sun comes into full view, close your eyes and visualize the red circle of light within yourself. Now let it descend into the center of your chest. Your chest will tend to puff out now that the Sun is inside—do not be concerned. Watch as the Sun changes from a red circle to a ball of white light. This will echo the external light that is now filtering through your eyelids. As it does this, contemplate this thought:

> All evil vanishes from life
> for those who keep the
> Sun in their heart.

Hold this thought for four or five minutes. At times during the day return to the thought and to the Sun that is in your heart. Let it linger, and repeat the sentence.

Robert Place

Notes:

July 7
Monday

 2nd ♎

☽ → ♏ 11:43 pm

Color of the day: White
Incense of the day: Myrrh

July Cloud Scrying Spell

This activity works best on a warm summer day. To start, you need a mostly clear sky with a few fluffy clouds. Lie on your back someplace outdoors, such as in your back yard or a nearby park. Place a blanket or mat under you, and get as comfortable as possible. Pick a section of the sky that is away from the Sun, and has a few clouds in it. Concentrate on the clouds. What do the shapes suggest to you? This technique will often let you find out what is in your unconscious mind; it will also help you let go of conscious judgment that stands in the way of your general psychic awareness.

Magenta Griffith

Notes:

Let my courage appear.
Let my courage soar.

Keep the crystal with you during the task you are performing. If you feel your courage waning, touch the crystal to renew it.

Jenna Tigerheart

Notes:

July 8
Tuesday

 2nd ♏

Color of the day: Red
Incense of the day: Evergreen

Spell to Find Courage

Lapis lazuli crystals carry the vibration of the planet Uranus. This planet's energy affects the mind and imagination. Those who need to find courage to perform a difficult task or to overcome a phobia frequently use lapis lazuli. You can use a loose crystal or one that is set in a piece of jewelry. To do so, hold the lapis lazuli crystal in your hand and repeat these words in a clear and steady voice:

Lapis lazuli,
You calm my fears.
The power of mind is
yours.

July 9
Wednesday

2nd ♏

Color of the day: Brown
Incense of the day: Cedar

A Vacation Spell

For a change of magical pace, you might try using some magic today to decide your vacation destination. To do this, you will need a pendulum that you have already used. It should be fully charged with your energy. Also, you will need to obtain a map. After you've narrowed your choices to between three to five possible vacation destinations, spread the map in front of you. Hold the pendulum over each site. Ask aloud or silently if this would be a good place to spend your vacation. The pendulum will swing, giving you a "yes" or "no." If the pendulum stands still or vibrates wildly, avoid that location. Move the pendulum to the next place and repeat until it moves in a soft and graceful movement over a place. Have a great trip.

James Kambos

Notes:

some to the change in your wallet and any other place you stash money. Make some up into sachets and tuck into drawers or add to baskets where you keep your mail and bills. Be creative in how you use the powder, and money will find you in creative ways.

Laurel Reufner

Notes:

July 10
Thursday
Lady Godiva's Ride

 2nd ♏

☽ → ♐ 1:48 am

Color of the day: Violet
Incense of the day: Musk

herbal Prosperity Powder

Herbal powders have long been used to improve the quality of a person's life. Here is one herbal potion that will make you prosperous. Take equal amounts of ground cloves, cinnamon, mustard seed, and ginger and grind in a mortar and pestle to a fine powder. Visualize the mixture drawing wealth to you as you work. Sprinkle some of the powder around your home. Toss it in corners. Add

Historical notes: Lady Godiva's original name was Godgifu, meaning "God-given." She was a Saxon noblewoman who was outraged at a tax levied on the people of Coventry by her mischievous husband Leofric. He offered a deal, though: He would cancel the tax if she rode through the town naked. Godgifu's ride has been commemorated by the grateful townspeople of Coventry for many years on this date with whimsical parades and a festival.

July 11
Friday

 2nd ♐

Color of the day: Peach
Incense of the day: Ylang-ylang

Gentle Friendship Spell

Friday belongs to gentle Venus, the goddess-planet who rules over love and relationships and other such things. This spell can help bring more friendship into your life on Venus' day. All you need is a pink ribbon. First, meditate on the qualities you admire in a friend—such as loyalty, or sense of fun, or whatever. Then think about what you offer as a friend. Tie the ribbon around your wrist as a reminder of all of these traits. Now, take advantage of the lovely summer weather to get outside and meet new people. Do not be shy. Walk in the park, visit a street fair, or go window-shopping with one eye peeled on passing humanity. All it takes sometimes is a smile or a warm greeting to folks that pass by. Some will be attracted by your good cheer and obvious peace and contentment. You may end up making arrangements to meet again. Remember: friendships can start small, and often do, but they make a big difference.

Elizabeth Barrette

Notes:

July 12
Saturday

2nd ♐
☽ → ♑ 3:21 am

Color of the day: Blue
Incense of the day: Pine

Sweeten One's Disposition Spell

As summer heats up, tempers often flare. Even the most placid among us may feel irritated by July's heat and humidity. Create a soothing spell to sweeten the disposition of you and others. Start by gathering a fresh jar of local honey and several sprigs of lavender and lemon balm. Gently wash and dry the herbs and place them in the honey. Seal tightly and, if possible, set the jar out in the moonlight. After one week, make a fresh pitcher of home-brewed iced tea or real lemonade, using the honey to sweeten the drink. Serve it to a cranky loved one with plenty of ice, along with a gentle kiss and soft smile. If you need the pick-me-up, add mint leaves, and go put your feet up. Sip slowly.

Karri Allrich

Notes:

July 13
Sunday

 2nd ♑
Full Moon 2:21 pm

Color of the day: Gold
Incense of the day: Clove

Spell to Find a Sacred Stone

One of my favorite activities is searching for magical stones. Magical stones do not need to be precious or valuable, they only need to catch the eye and remind us of the beauty of the place we found them. These stones can be placed on our altar or in a special place. Stones are magical because they help us feel grounded and more down-to-earth. To do this, you need only walk out into a natural setting on the Full Moon. Be sure it's a place where you feel particularly peaceful and spiritually uplifted. As you walk along your trail, allow your eyes to soften their focus as you begin to look from side to side. As you walk, ask the spirits of the land to help you find a special stone that you can keep. Listen to the voice of the place—it may feel silent but there are many tree, plant, and stone spirits that can communicate with you. Listen to the land attentively and then keep your eyes peeled. You may be asked to walk off the path a short ways. Or you may be led to a part of the land you have never seen before. As you

open up your heart to receive communication, you may encounter a small rock that sings out to you. This is the powerful rock that can help teach you the magic of the land you're walking on. Give thanks and take the stone back to your home. Honor it and the land it came from by placing it in a special place in your house.

Jonathan Keyes

Notes:

July 14
Monday
Bastille Day

 3rd ♑
☽ → ♒ 5:38 am

Color of the day: Gray
Incense of the day: Rose

Bastille Day Liberty Spell

In honor of the French holiday, we celebrate liberty and freedom from oppression. To start, on a candle carve these words:

Liberty
Equality
Kinship.

Anoint the candle with sandalwood oil or with the ashes from sandalwood incense and visualize all the world's people living in freedom and harmony with each other and with the natural world. As you light the candle, chant:

Liberty
Equality
Kinship.

Watch the light from your candle spread into the world and join with other such lights. Take concrete action some time during the day to promote these values in your community.

Kristin Madden

Notes:

powerful protection herb—elder flower. To ensure the safety and health of your pet, make an incense of hyssop and elder flowers. Once the incense has begun to burn, allow the smoke to surround the animal and visualize any illness or potential harmful events being carried away from the pet with the smoke. Once the smoke dissipates, you can place small silver bells or other items that represent protection on their collar. Remember that many animals fear smoke and you should try to keep your animal relaxed during this ceremony.

Sheri Richerson

Notes:

July 15
Tuesday

 3rd ≈

Color of the day: Black
Incense of the day: Sage

hyssop Purification Rite

hyssop flowers and leaves are often used in purification rights, but in addition this herb has also been used in protection ceremonies and for healing along with another very

July 16
Wednesday

 3rd ≈
☽ → ♓ 10:14 am

Color of the day: White
Incense of the day: Maple

Attracting Money Spell

To attract some extra money to your business, prepare a special envelope or bag for holding the daily money for deposit. Inscribe this envelope with feoh (Υ), the rune of earned income. Dress this envelope with cinnamon and, if you choose, bergamot oil. As you add the money, state these or similar words:

> Money earned,
> Money gained,
> Our path to prosperity is sustained.

Karen Follett

Notes:

and Horus. This has caused modern UFO enthusiasts to postulate that the Egyptian trinity were at one time living beings, possibly from another planet. Whatever the case, have a look tonight at brightly shining Sirius, and petition Isis for boons and rewards.

Denise Dumars

Notes:

July 17
Thursday

3rd ♓

Color of the day: Green
Incense of the day: Jasmine

Isis and Sirius Ritual

These are the dog days, named for Sirius, the dog star, which is prominent in the heavens this time of year. There are many correlations between Isis and the star Sirius. In ancient Egypt, festivals were held in the name of the goddess Isis Sothis, or "Isis of Sirius." The Sirius star system is also considered sacred to other gods in the Egyptian ennead, including Osiris

July 18
Friday

3rd ♓
☽ → ♈ 6:20 pm

Color of the day: Rose
Incense of the day: Nutmeg

Farewell Ritual

When a good friend is moving away, use this ritual to send him or her off with a blessing and to assure an occasional return visit. Start by inviting the guest of honor and his or her closest acquaintances. With the guest in the middle of a circle, invite each attendee to share a story about the subject with the group. Have the subject and a circle elder each braid three stalks of wheat together. Tie the two ends with a green ribbon to form a circle or wreath. Have the subject and the elder exchange wreaths upon completion. In this way the energy in the circle is given to each person, and each are left with part of the other.

Jenna Tigerheart

Notes:

Search your heart for any anger you harbor toward any other faith or religious system. Say:

> hatred is banished,
> May love now reside.

Feel a new tolerance growing within you. Exhale that feeling out into the world.

Lily Gardner-Butts

Notes:

July 19
Saturday

 3rd ♈

Color of the day: Indigo
Incense of the day: Lavender

Spell for Religious Tolerance

July 19 marks the anniversary of the death of Rebecca Nurse, Sarah Good, and Susanna Martin—all found guilty of witchcraft in 1692. Today is a good day to focus on all working together to halt religious intolerance. Place on your altar as many images of the god and goddess as you can. Light a new purple candle. As the candle flickers, gaze at the gods and goddesses. Meditate on how different civilizations have imagined different images of the divine in so many diverse representations.

July 20
Sunday

3rd ♈

Color of the day: Orange
Incense of the day: Basil

household Shield Spell

Today is the traditional day in Bulgaria for setting up household shields to protect the home from storms and lightning. To provide some protection from storms for your house gather four pennies. Hold the pennies in your hands and envision a blue light connecting the pennies together. Continue envisioning the blue light while you plant one penny in each of the cardinal directions around the outside of the house.

When the final penny is in the ground, envision the blue lights that connect the pennies spreading above and below the house, becoming a blue web that protects the house. If you want to follow the Bulgarian tradition, finish the spell by leaving a cup of wine in an open window as a thank you to St. Elijah, the protector.

Therese Francis

Notes:

oliday Lore: On this day in Bulgaria an enormous chariot is driven across the sky by Elijah, a Pagan god who threatened humans with murderous weather. Christianity transformed the figure into a saint, but scholars trace Elijah back to ancient Sun god figures. Ask Elijah for good weather on this day.

Lazy Introspection Spell

onight begins the last quarter of the Moon, a time of introspection. The tide goes out now, even while it is the hottest time of the year. The heat makes everything slow and lazy, yet summer's peak is already past. Take some time for yourself today, just to rest and watch the clouds float by. If possible, find a place where you can lie on your back in the grass, and say this rhyme:

> Give me the peace
> Of the clouds in the sky
> Like fluffy white sheep
> Ambling by.
> From north to south,
> Into east from the west
> They go softly,
> And bring me sweet rest.

Elizabeth Barrette

Notes:

July 21
Monday

3rd ♈
Fourth Quarter 2:01 am

☽ → ♉ 5:48 am

Color of the day: Black
Incense of the day: Poplar

July 22
Tuesday

St. Mary Magdalene's Day

4th ♉

Color of the day: Gray
Incense of the day: Musk

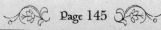

Protection and Good Luck Charm

In olde England, family shoes were often buried in the walls of houses and hidden behind chimney bricks and floorboards. This charm would bring prosperity to the house and the shoe's owner. To ensure prosperity and the safety of a loved one, keep an old shoe that the owner has worn and loved. Fill it with sprigs of rosemary for protection, cinnamon sticks for luck, and bay leaves for good fortune. Tuck the shoe into a secret place where it will be safe from harm—under a floorboard, a cellar or attic hiding place, or even simply beneath a bed. As you hide the shoe, envision your loved one surrounded with protection from harm, wherever he or she may travel in life.

Karri Allrich

Notes:

Holiday Lore: Ever since the Middle Ages, pilgrims have marked this day as the feast of Mary Magdalene's death, who was said to have settled in France after the death of Christ along with her brother, Lazarus, and sister, St. Martha. Mary was ever ashamed of her earlier life of sin, and she settled in a cave grotto, fasting, and praying. When she died many years later after much penance, her soul took the form of a dove and flew away.

July 23
Wednesday

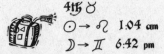

4th ♉
☉ → ♌ 1:04 am
☽ → ♊ 6:42 pm

Color of the day: Peach
Incense of the day: Pine

Protection from Nightmares

The word *mare* is Old English for "demon." In olden days, people believed that troubled sleep was caused by a demon who rode you like a horse while you slept. The terrible things you dreamt were the experiences from the ride. To protect yourself from nightmares and interrupted sleep, find a sacred holey stone. Thread a string through the hole and hang it by your bed. Repeat this old German charm:

> I lay me here
> to sleep;
> No nightmare shall
> plague me;
> Until they swim all the
> waters;
> That flow upon the
> earth;

And count all the stars;
That appear in the firmament!
As I will, so mote it be.

Lily Gardner-Butts

Notes:

July 24
Thursday

 4th ♊

Color of the day: White
Incense of the day: Chrysanthemum

Summer Prosperity Spell

At this time of year, late in July, the butterflies are hovering almost constantly over the coneflowers, and hummingbirds are flashing about the monarda and salvias. In late afternoon, the thunder spirit rumbles, promising needed rain. The richness of July makes this a potent time to work prosperity magic. As the Sun sets, smudge your altar with sage. Deck the altar with red and purple flowers. Two candles should be placed on the altar: one green, the other purple. Light the candles, and speak this charm:

Green of life,
Purple of the vine,
Money and wealth are mine.

Money come to me,
Only my share,
Anymore would not be fair.
And with harm to none.

This spell is even stronger if it should rain and storm as you're working it.

James Kambos

Notes:

July 25
Friday

4th ♊

Color of the day: Pink
Incense of the day: Ginger

July Success Spell

Originally there were ten months in the Roman calendar, which is why the last month is named December, derived from the Latin word for "ten." Eventually, two more months were added, and during the reign of Julius Caesar further reforms were made to make the calendar more accurate. Julius also changed the name of the month Quintilis to July after himself. During his month games were held in his honor, called Ludi Victoriae Caesaris, or "Games of Victoria and Caesar." Victoria is the name of the goddess of victory, who was associated with Caesar. The games were held July 20 to 30. This is a good time to call on the goddess Victoria to assure success. It is also a time to participate in sports and any outdoor activities that should draw you. It is through the development of the virtue strength, or fortitude, that Victoria's assistance is obtained in our regular daily life.

Robert Place

Notes:

Dandelion Spell

If it's not your birthday, and you don't have candles to wish on, you can choose to wish on a dandelion on this day. To do this, pick a dandelion that has turned white and is ready to be blown away. Make a wish, and try to blow away all the seeds with one breath, like you would birthday candles. If you can blow all the seeds away in one breath, you will get your wish! Another version of this spell goes: If you can blow all the seeds away in one breath, your wish will come true immediately. If seeds remain, count them; the number of seeds is equal to the number of days until you will get your wish.

Magenta Griffith

Notes:

July 26
Saturday

 4th ♊
)) → ♋ 6:23 am

Color of the day: Gray
Incense of the day: Violet

July 27
Sunday

 4th ♋

Color of the day: Peach
Incense of the day: Coriander

Warmth of the Sun Ritual

Summer is at its height right now. It is a perfect time to

take advantage of the deep heat of the Sun for magical ritual. Go outside today and turn your face, with your eyes closed, to the Sun. Feel the warmth, and see the light passing through your eyelids. Visualize the light flowing down into your body. As it fills you to overflowing, it brings health and vitality to your every cell. See this light flow into the land around you. Visualize a small Sun beginning to form in the center of your body. Feel this expand and glow as the warmth and energy of the Sun in the sky merges with your personal energy. The radiance extends out beyond your body in a protective oval of light. You are connected to all things. Repeat this ritual any time you feel drained, depressed, or ill.

Kristin Madden

Notes:

home Protection and Removal of Negativity Spell

If you are feeling too much negativity in your life now, inscribe the backs of four small mirrors with the runes eolh (ᛦ) and is (ᛁ). This will charge your mirrors to deflect negativity. You can invoke the divine protection of your magic mirrors whenever you need it. To effect this spell, place one mirror at each compass or directional point in your home with its reflective side facing outward. In a spray bottle, prepare a mixture of distilled water and small amounts of patchouli and lavender oils (five or six drops each). Now, extend your hands over the mixture, forming a magcial protective triangle with your thumbs and forefingers. Visualize a divine beam infusing this mixture with purifying and protective energy. Begin misting the air around the mirror you have placed at the northern point of the compass in your house. Continue misting while moving in a deosil direction toward each compass point until you have completed your circle of purification and protection.

James Kambos

Notes:

July 28
Monday

4th ♋

☽ → ♌ 3:17 pm

Color of the day: Silver
Incense of the day: Peony

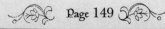

July 29
Tuesday

 4th ♌
New Moon 1:53 am

Color of the day: Red
Incense of the day: Gardenia

Find Romance Spell

Leo is associated with playfulness and flirting, and also with romance. Leo New Moons are therefore a good time to open yourself to love and new romantic connections. Or, if you are already with a partner, this is a good time to rekindle the love that is already there. To prepare for this spell, you will need some essential oils of jasmine and rose, as well as a piece of red clothing such as a shirt or a scarf. To begin, simply take a bath and place a few drops of each essence in the tub with you. As you bathe and cleanse yourself, say these words several times while you stir the bath.

> Stir in jasmine
> Stir in rose,
> I cleanse myself from
> head to toe.
>
> Bring me love
> And bring me heat;
> Passion, romance come
> to me.

Once you have finished bathing, put on your clothes and wear something red when you go out—the scarf or shirt. You don't need to overdo it, just a bit of red will do. Then, try going out dancing or go to a party where you don't know many people. Be open to possibilities. Or, if you are already with a partner, go out on a fun date such as dinner at a new and fancy restaurant. See what kind of magic can happen.

Jonathan Keyes

Notes:

Holiday Lore: St. Martha traveled with her sister Mary Magdalene to France after the death of Christ, and there she encountered, on the banks of the Rhone river, a vicious half-lizard, half-dragon called the Tarasque. Martha, it is said, managed to subdue the monster, thus saving the people of Provence, and she tied it up with her belt. Today, this event is commemorated in the region with a festival in which a mock Tarasque rushes about, stamping and roaring and belching smoke until finally a little girl arrives to subdue the beast. This is likely one of the earliest examples of the Beauty and

the Beast tale later popularized by the Grimm brothers and by Walt Disney Studios.

July 30
Wednesday

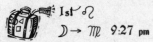
1st ♌
☽ → ♍ 9:27 pm

Color of the day: Yellow
Incense of the day: Neroli

Prosperity herb Spell

To work up some prosperity magic, place a handful of dirt in a bowl. Mix in three tablespoons of your favorite prosperity herbs. Hold the bowl in your cupped hands, and charge the dirt mixture with your needs. Place a cleansed stone atop the dirt, and let it sit untouched in a quiet spot in your home or room for a week. Afterward, place the stone somewhere on your desk, or carry it with you when conducting business matters. To recharge the stone, place it back in the dirt for a few days. You can keep the dirt stored in a glass jar or plastic bag until you need it.

Laurel Reufner

Notes:

July 31
Thursday

1st ♍

Color of the day: Violet
Incense of the day: Evergreen

Jupiter Bounty Spell

Ruled by Jupiter, the most generous of the planets, Thursday brings wealth to all who seek it on this day. And as late summer sees the beginning of the harvest, especially the corn harvest, this money spell takes advantage of the energies that exist now. To start, using your favorite recipe, bake a batch of cornbread muffins. If you can find one of those nifty molds that turns out Sun-faced muffins, that will be an extra bonus; but plain round muffin molds will do, too. After baking, let your muffins cool enough to handle, then hold some of the warm cakes and say out loud:

> harvest time is near at hand.
> Bring me bounty from the land.
>
> Like these corn-cakes round and gold,
> Bring me wealth that I can hold.

Now divide the cornbread: keep half for yourself, and give the other half to a friend. This generosity will help spread the wealth that you seek. What you give returns to you three times over.

Elizabeth Barrette

Notes:

Notes:

August

August is the eighth month of the year and named for Augustus Caesar. Its astrological sign is Leo, the lion (July 21-Aug 20), a fixed fire sign ruled by the Sun. August begins with Lammas, the celebration of the first harvest, especially the grain harvest of corn, rice, millet, rye, barley, oats, and wheat, brought in from the fields in sheaves. In the past, such grains were associated with gods and goddesses of death and resurrection—Tammuz in ancient Sumeria, Adonis in Babylon, Demeter in Greece, Ceres in Rome. Small figurines representing these goddesses were buried with the dead to ensure their resurrection into the afterlife. Baking bread is celebrated now, in all of its steps: grinding the grain, moistening the grain with water, shaping it into a loaf, and baking it. In some Mediterranean countries, women ritually sprout grain seed in dishes or pots to be given as offerings, either thrown in rivers or left at churches, to harvest gods. By midmonth, we begin to transition from the high heat of summer. The harvest is over and signs of the coming fall and winter begin to appear for the first time. Birds have begun to vanish from the trees, cooler air has moved in. The August Full Moon is called the Barley Moon, a time to contemplate the eternity of life evident in the grain of the fields.

August 1

Friday

Lammas

 1st ♏

Color of the day: White
Incense of the day: Parsley

Lammas Bounty Spell

Lammas is also called Lughnasadh; it is a celebration of plenty and optimism, and of nature's infinite bounty. It is the time of the first harvests, and it marks midsummer's joyous and fanciful energy. This spirit is celebrated, too, in Shakespeare's *A Mid-Summer's Night Dream*. To tap into this energy, gather a small bundle of long grass or reeds to braid, and light a white candle. Braid the grass as you speak this verse:

> Fairies prancing in the meadow,
> Spirits in the corn;
> Green Man is flourishing everywhere
> On this Midsummer morn.
>
> Grains begin to ripen,
> All things bear fruit.
> Summer glistens with possibility,
> Blossoms take root.
>
> Fairies whisper secrets,
> Powerful blessings to see.
> Cycles move and all around,
> they share their gifts with me.
>
> Air to fire,
> Fire to water,
> Water to earth,
> Earth to air.
>
> Elements feed spirit,
> And the circle glows.
> At Lammas, day and night,
> We witness Nature's awesome might.
>
> Growing full
> And blessing all,
> Tis Earth's celebration
> Before the chill of fall.
>
> Now braiding this grass,
> I mark this day
> Protect my hearth,
> With the abundance of grain.
>
> The blessings of the Goddess come again;
> Place the braid above my door.
> Hunger be banished now and then.
>
> Blessings be drawn to this place,
> Summer's energy fill this space.
> Air, fire, water, earth unite,
> And bless us all this day.

Abby Willowroot

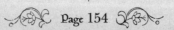

Notes:

Holiday lore: Lammas is a bittersweet agricultural holiday, mingling joy at the current high season's harvest with the knowledge that summer is soon at an end. Many cultures have "first fruit" rights on this day—the Celt's version called Lughnasadh; the Anglo-Saxon version called *hlafmasse*. In the Middle Ages, the holiday became set at August 1, taking its current form for the most part, with sheaves of wheat and corn blessed on this day.

August 2
Saturday

 1st ♍

☽ → ♎ 1:48 am

Color of the day: Gray
Incense of the day: Cedar

Virgo Moon Meditation

Here is an effective meditation on the position of Virgo—in the heavens and in the zodiac. Currently, you should take time to meditate on how Virgo affects your Sun and Moon signs today as you speak this verse:

how chaste the virgin,
Yet how fertile,
Fecund, parthenogenetic
Spiller of milk and
wheaten
Shafts from the stars

To the earth.
No wonder we
Aquarians regard you
cautiously.
Our water
Is clear as crystal.

The Taurus bull
Might be upon you,
horns of stars,
And Scorpio might give
up
And sting himself
Before your very eyes.

The brittle Archer
follows,
Bellowing to the skies,
O Virgo, o Venus
hymenata,
Pliny called you Isis
The great mother,
Begetter of sons
from dead gods.

You sit in Cassiopeia's
great chair
Paired with unlikely
Aquarius
In the great zodiac
of the Cathedral of
Notre Dame.

Jointly, then, we launch
Our boat of a million
years,
So many pails of milk
Or water,
And oh, so little time.

Denise Dumars

Notes:

from your creativity. I
am requesting eloquence,
self-control, and guid-
ance to wisely use these
powers. Expand my
mind with your great
power. For these gifts, I
graciously thank you.

Sheri Richerson

Notes:

August 3
Sunday

1st ♎

Color of the day: Yellow
Incense of the day: Poplar

Spiritual Growth Spell

This is a great time to receive the powers of creativity and spiritual growth. Find a private spot near a lake or stream. If this is not possible, you may use any body of water you can find—a sink or tub full of water, or even a puddle. Sit in quiet medi-tation, visualizing the spirit connect-ing with you. You may stay in this state as long as you wish, but when you return to consciousness, say this:

healing, knowledge, and
mental powers all come

August 4
Monday

1st ♎
☽→ ♏ 5:12 am

Color of the day: White
Incense of the day: Lavender

Dance of Fireflies Spell

With the dreamy heat of late summer and the soft shadows of the warm twilight comes one of the most magical sights of the year: the dance of the fireflies. These insects inhabit the border between magic and reality; scientists still don't understand the secrets of their cool light. Do you remember chasing them as a child? Go outside tonight and watch them again. You may wish to greet them with something like this:

> Firefly flicker,
> Firefly glow,
> Light up the sky and the
> world below.
>
> here on the shadowed
> stage you must play;
> Your light is invisible by
> day.
>
> In this you teach us to
> see,
> That dark brings beauty
> with its mystery.

Elizabeth Barrette

Notes:

August 5
Tuesday

 1st ♏
Second Quarter 2:28 am

Color of the day: Black
Incense of the day: Ginger

A harvest Meditation

As the seasons turn, we begin in August to reap what we have figuratively sown earlier during the agricultural cycle of planting, growth, fruition, and decline. Now is a good time to reflect upon the last eight months of this year's calendar, and to observe your life's efforts. Ask yourself what projects have you nurtured into being? What goals have you met? What unexpected challenges were you able to surmount? Take the time now to contemplate the fruit of all your labors. As a symbol of your allegiance to the cycles of nature, eat a piece of ripe fruit or a fresh vegetable today, and be conscious of living in the moment and savoring every bite. When you are finished, take the seeds, pit, stem, or core, and return all of these to the earth. Consider starting a compost pile to symbolize your connection to the cycles of life, death, and rebirth. Embrace life's inevitable decline by returning the energies of today's food to the earth. This is at the core of this season's lessons: Nothing is wasted in nature.

Karri Allrich

Notes:

August 6
Wednesday

 2nd ♏

☽ → ♐ 8:11 am

Color of the day: Brown
Incense of the day: Coriander

Reap the harvest Spell

When we find ourselves repeatedly in situations that yield a grim emotional, spiritual, or physical harvest, we need to look inward to ascertain if the seeds that we are sowing will grow the crops that we desire. To do this, light a green or brown candle. Place malachite in front of the candle representing your heartfelt desire for change. Focusing on the candle, ask for guidance from your higher self in discovering your heart's desires and ambitions. Script these desires in a visual present tense. State these or similar words:

> The universe unfolds her
> abundant path for me.
> her fruitful harvest is
> mine,
> So mote it be.

Focus the stream of your visualizations on the malachite. That is, visualize the malachite lending vibrations to your vision as it sends your energy out to the universe. Afterward, extinguish the candle. Hold onto the malachite as a reminder of your heart's harvest.

Karen Follett

Notes:

Historical fact: Today commemorates the day that atomic bomb Little Boy fell, in 1945, on the city of Hiroshima in Japan. Within a few minutes, some 75,000 people perished in the shock waves and fires that swept though the city. Tens of thousands more died of radiation sickness afterward. In Japan, on this day, the people of Hiroshima celebrate a peace ceremony in memory of the dead. You may also take today to offer a silent prayer vigil, chanting: "Never again, never again."

August 7
Thursday

 2nd ♐

Color of the day: Turquoise
Incense of the day: Dill

Prosperity Spell for Coming Fall

Today is a good day to meditate on what you want or need in the coming year. To do so, write your desires on dried bay leaves. Meditate on what needs to happen for each desire to manifest. Grind the bay leaves with a mortar and pestle, and add to an incense including rosemary, benzoin, blessed thistle, and nutmeg. Burn the incense while meditating on your desires. After the incense has burned out, write down your desires on nice stationary in the form of affirmations. Fold the paper and seal it with green wax. Keep it on your altar for the coming year. Once a month on the New Moon, open it and reexamine your desires and how you are achieving them. Always reseal it with green wax when you are done.

Jenna Tigerheart

Notes:

brush or quill pen. You can also draw a picture of the problem if you wish. Pokeberry is unusual in that there isn't a fixative known that will set the color. It always fades. And as the ink fades, so will the problem. Be careful handling the berry juice, as pokeberry is poisonous if ingested. Thoroughly wash your hands and any dishes used in this spell afterward.

Laurel Reufner

Notes:

August 8
Friday
Dog Days (Japanese and other)

 2nd ♐
☽ → ♑ 11:02 am

Color of the day: Pink
Incense of the day: Rose

Pokeberry Banishing Spell
This spell is great for banishing a problem or unwanted habit from your life. To start, write what you wish to get rid of on a piece of paper in pokeberry ink using a small paint-

August 9
Saturday

 2nd ♑

Color of the day: Brown
Incense of the day: Patchouli

Sensuous Bath for a Date
If you've got a hot date coming up, take a shower to get clean, then run a hot bath. Add one or two cups of Epsom salts and ten drops each of rosemary and eucalyptus essential oil to the water while it's running. Soak in the water for thirteen minutes. Think of as many pleasant things as you can remember or imagine, from running in a summer breeze to eating

your favorite food. Just before getting out, sink down so your whole body is under water for a few seconds. Imagine the oils energizing your body. Get out and briskly rub yourself dry with a favorite towel. Enjoy the date.

Therese Francis

Notes:

energy go out through the top of your head. Feel the energy fall back to earth like the rain, and move through the earth back up through your legs in a endless cycle or loop. Let the energy flow for a little while until you begin to feel restored, then focus your attention elsewhere.

Magenta Griffith

Notes:

August 10
Sunday

 2nd ♑
☽ → ♒ 2:23 pm

Color of the day: Peach
Incense of the day: Cinnamon

Earth Energy Spell

Here's an exercise to do when you have low energy. It is especially effective for when you are away from home. Sit in a chair, with your feet flat on the floor and your hands flat on your thighs. Become aware that below your feet, if you go deep enough, no matter where you are, is the earth. Feel the energy coming up from the earth, up through your feet and legs into your body. Feel the energy travel up through your hands and arms, and up to your head. Let the

August 11
Monday
Puck Fair

 2nd ♒
Full Moon 11:48 pm

Color of the day: Gray
Incense of the day: Maple

Strengthen the Nervous System and Offset Anxiety Spell

Sometimes we can get stressed out or feel overwhelmed in our lives. At these times we may feel increasing anxiety and nervousness. To offset any anxiety we may feel around the Full Moon, it can be helpful to do some magical work. For this, simply go outside to a natural setting where it is quiet and you will be undisturbed.

Stand tall with your knees slightly bent. Close your eyes and take several slow, deep breaths into your belly. As you do this, visualize drawing in a clear flow of energy through your nose and down into your lungs and belly. When you reach the end of your inhalation, hold your breath briefly for about two or three seconds, and visualize energy coursing through your body. Then gently exhale and release any negative energy and stress out through your breath. Continue to take in deep breaths of pure and clean energy, and exhale all anxiety and stress. After five minutes, you will feel rested and rejuvenated.

Jonathan Keyes

Notes:

Holiday lore: King Puck is a virile old goat who presides over the fair in Killorglin in Ireland. He watches the proceedings from a platform built in town, wearing a shiny gold crown and purple robes. Among the activities: gathering day, which includes a parade; fair day itself, and the buying and selling of livestock; and scattering day, when the goat is disrobed, dethroned, and sent back into the fields at sunset.

August 12
Tuesday

 3rd ♒
☽ → ♓ 7:19 pm

Color of the day: White
Incense of the day: Juniper

Venus Victrix Ritual

Today is the day ancient Romans celebrated a festival to Venus called Venus Victrix, or "Venus Victorious." Venus is the well-known goddess of love and beauty, and on this day love and beauty should reign. Today would be an excellent day for a tarot reading about relationships. Lay out three cards left to right on your left to represent yourself. Skip a space, and, continuing left to right, lay out three more to represent the other person in this relationship. Now lay three more above the two groups and in the center to form a bridge. This represents the interaction between both of you. After you have used this reading to analyze the strengths and weakness of your relationship, end with three more cards of advice.

Robert Place

Notes:

August 13
Wednesday

 3rd ♓

Color of the day: Peach
Incense of the day: Sandalwood

More Wisdom Spell

This day honors Hecate, goddess of wisdom and crone goddess of the waning Moon. Light a new black candle, and bake a Hecate cake—a round chocolate cake—to represent the dark Moon. As you prepare the cake, repeat this mantra:

> Hecate,
> Most lovely one,
> Beloved grandmother,
> Show me a sign.

Pause for a moment at some point to ask what messages come to you as you recite this mantra. Write what comes to you in your magic book, and use the message to inspire further meditation. When the cake has cooled, leave it for Hecate at a crossroads. This has been the custom for Hecate worshippers for centuries.

Lily Gardner-Butts

Notes:

August 14
Thursday

 3rd ♓

Color of the day: Violet
Incense of the day: Carnation

Dame Abonde's Abundance Ritual

Here is a fun ritual for abundance that calls on Dame Abonde, the French prosperity goddess. Dress in your best professional or evening wear. Put on pearls or any jewelry with precious gems. On your altar place a royal purple candle and lavender or rose incense. Offer Beaujolais or other French wine, a baguette, and Brie to the goddess. Go all out and dress a Barbie doll as Dame Abonde if you wish. Light the candle and incense, and meditate on abundance and prosperity and how you will go about getting it. Write your intentions and place them beneath the candleholder. Think and act "rich" for the rest of the day. Burn the petition once the candle burns down.

Denise Dumars

Notes:

August 15
Friday

 3rd ♓

☽→ ♈ 3:00 am

Color of the day: Rose
Incense of the day: Thyme

God Incarnate Spell

The divine is all around us. To tap into the spirit of the divine in your daily life, gather together two pink candles, some jasmine or gardenia oil, some fresh rosemary, a mirror, and a pink cloth that is large enough to cover the mirror. Sit before the mirror with eyes closed, and breathe in the energy of earth and sky. Feel yourself fill with light. Open your eyes and see yourself filled with light. As you anoint the outline of your face with the oil, speak the following verse three times:

> I am the God (Goddess) Incarnate.
> I am filled with light And connected to all things.
>
> I am beautiful. I am loved.

Cover the mirror with the pink cloth. Repeat the verse any time you are feeling lonely, down on yourself, or simply unloved.

Kristin Madden

Notes:

August 16
Saturday

 3rd ♈

Color of the day: Blue
Incense of the day: Lilac

A Purification Ritual

On most mornings, I take a walk along the river near my home. By the time mid-August arrives, I begin to see signs that summer is fading. For instance, wild geese can be spotted flying along the river toward their southern winter homes. And over the river on these mornings, I see the mist rising from the cooling ground. Old timers call this "river smoke"; and indeed, it is a thick and curling white color as it lifts into the morning air. Beautiful and mysterious, river smoke reminds me of the purification rituals I perform to cleanse new magical tools. When-ever I obtain a new ritual tool, I cleanse them in the following manner: In a heat-proof dish, combine dried lavender, wormwood, and a pinch of sage. Ignite these items, and let them smolder awhile. As the smoke curls about you, say:

> Smoke rise,
> Let me be wise.
> This (name of item) is
> cleansed.
> I will use it only for
> good.

Your item is now ready to use.

James Kambos

Notes:

fragrant hair rinse to stimulate the scalp and revitalize your sun-damaged tresses. Take a rosemary-infused bath to calm itchy sun-exposed skin. Splash and smooth the chilled tea on skin before an evening outdoors; rosemary also acts as a natural insect repellent. Applied to stings and bites, rosemary helps quell the itching and inflammation. No wonder rosemary is cherished as an herb of powerful protective energies.

Karri Allrich

Notes:

August 17
Sunday

 3rd ♈
☽ → ♉ 1:52 pm

Color of the day: Orange
Incense of the day: Sage

Rosemary Herbal Soothing Rinse

The last dog days of summer may exact their toll on hair and skin. Both can be soothed and revitalized by a simple infusion of rosemary in spring water. To do this, make a strong rosemary tea by steeping the herb in boiled spring water. Store the tea in a sterile covered jar, and keep chilled. Use as a wonderfully

August 18
Monday

 3rd ♉

Color of the day: Silver
Incense of the day: Chrysanthemum

Mental Flexibility Spell

The skill of visualization forms a cornerstone of magic. Many spells incorporate this practice. Visualization basically means imagining something intensely enough in your mind to manifest it into reality in some form. Here is an exercise to enhance your mental flexibility for future visualization.

Start by sitting or lying still, and visualizing yourself descending a spiral staircase. Keep your hand on the outer wall as you go. You may find it helpful to imagine that twelve steps take you all the way around the inner pole, just as twelve hours complete the circle of a clock face. Most people find it very challenging to visualize spiraling like this in their mind while their body remains motionless. If you can't get it right the first time, don't despair. Practice brings improvement.

Elizabeth Barrette

Notes:

the number of windows in the house. Small cosmetic mirrors are available in drugstores. Place one mirror on each window in the house to reflect any energy sent your way. As you put the mirrors up, repeat these words:

> Unwanted energy,
> Right back you go.
> You shall reap just as you sow.
> From my safe haven,
> Pure and clear,
> Keep out dark intents and fear.

Jenna Tigerheart

Notes:

August 19
Tuesday

 3rd ♉
Fourth Quarter 7:48 pm

Color of the day: Gray
Incense of the day: Honeysuckle

Reflective Protection Spell

This is a powerful spell to deflect unwanted energy from your home. Use this spell when you are being bothered by unwanted attention. You need a set of small mirrors equaling

August 20
Wednesday

 4th ♉
☽ → ♊ 2:41 am

Color of the day: Brown
Incense of the day: Eucalyptus

Protection from Road Rage

Road rage seems ever more common on our highways and roadways today. To protect yourself from an outbreak of road rage—either

from another, or in yourself—prepare (or purchase) a small, white drawstring pouch. Place hematite, bloodstone, and crushed rue in a small bowl. Extend your hands over the bowl and form a triangle with your thumbs and fore-fingers. Visualize a protective beam of energy descending into your crown. Focus this beam through the triangle to the bowl, and say:

> Let the rage of others
> and the rage of my own,
> Become harmlessly
> grounded by herb and by
> stone.

Empty the contents of the bowl into the pouch, and place them in your car.

Karen Follett

Notes:

spell to attract money is to place the fresh green leaves in your wallet or purse. You can also rub the leaves over any area where money is kept while visualizing your money increasing. In addition to these options you may place mint on a green candle that you are burning to draw money. You can also grow mint in or around your home for its money attracting properties. In addition to drawing money, mint is useful for protection, healing, and travel.

Sheri Richerson

Notes:

August 22
Friday

4th ♊
☽ → ♋ 2:44 pm

Color of the day: Peach
Incense of the day: Sandalwood

Paint a Spell

If it's in your heart, bring it into your life with art! For this spell, you'll need an artist's brush with a wooded handle and natural bristles, some acrylic paint, and a blank canvas—the size is up to you. Begin this

August 21
Thursday

4th ♊

Color of the day: White
Incense of the day: Geranium

Mint Money Spell

Mint and money have long been associated with each other. A very simple way to use mint in a

spell during a waxing Moon. After deciding on your goal, sketch your desire on the canvas with a pencil. Do you want a new house? A car? A new love? The only limit is your imagination. Before you begin to paint, though, repeat this charm several times:

> I work with the Moon and Sun.
> With the first stroke, this spell has begun.
> As the paint flows, my power grows.
> The wish in my heart, Is coming alive in my art.

When your painting is finished, frame it or hide it, as you wish.

James Kambos

Notes:

Organizing Spell

Your place looks a mess, and you don't know where to start in cleaning up. Take a deck of ordinary playing cards and stand in the middle of your living room or bedroom—wherever you spend the most time. Toss the deck of cards in the air and let them fall where they will. Pick them up, and as you do, put them in order—ace, two, three, and so on up to the king, each suit one by one (the order of suits is up to you). The act of arranging something neatly will work as sympathetic magic to help you pick up and arrange the rest of the room. Start your tidying up immediately after picking up the cards.

Magenta Griffith

Notes:

August 23
Saturday

4th ♋
☉ → ♍ 8:08 am

Color of the day: Indigo
Incense of the day: Juniper

August 24
Sunday

4th ♋
☽ → ♌ 11:48 pm

Color of the day: Gold
Incense of the day: Clove

Wellness Energy Spell

Energy flows where attention goes. If you worry about a potential health problem, you should give it more energy. You can do this by taking any anxious energy you may have and converting it to wholeness and wellness energy. On a piece of paper, draw a black-and-white sketch that represents the potential health problem. Place this paper inside a box, and place the box on your altar. Take a different piece of paper and crayons or colored pencils. Draw a picture that represents your body as whole and healthy. Make it vibrant with color. Place this picture on the top of your altar or hang it on the wall over your altar so you can see it every day.

Therese Francis

Notes:

Pomona Honoring Ritual

Today is the Opisconsivia, a day dedicated to the goddess Pomona and to Gaia. You can use today's energy to welcome the wealth of Pomona and the earthy bounty of Gaia to your hearth and home. Honor the goddesses by placing a bowl filled with fruit on your table or altar, being sure to include some apples, Pomona's special fruit. Sometime during the day, take some of the fruit and leave it outside in an area with trees—fruit trees if possible. Give Gaia equal honor by placing a small bowl of rich earth on your altar. Remember to return it to Gaia when you are finished with it.

Laurel Reufner

Notes:

August 26
Tuesday

 4♄ ♌

Color of the day: Red
Incense of the day: Evergreen

Bring Order to Your Life Spell

Today is the feast day of Ilmater, the Finnish goddess who created the world from chaos. This spell

August 25
Monday

 4♄ ♌

Color of the day: Lavender
Incense of the day: Frankincense

will bring more organization to your life. To start, you will need a plastic sorter similar to the kind used to sort beads. Fill each compartment of your sorter with amethyst, flourite, and smoky quartz. Light a yellow candle and say:

> Ilmater, Ilmater,
> hear my plea.
> Bring order and struc—
> ture unto me.
>
> Where there was chaos,
> Now there's a code;
> What was disorder now
> has a road.

Commit at least ten minutes every day to an organization project. When you have completed a project, write some details about it down on a piece of paper. Replace one of the stones from your sorter with the piece of paper. Continue this until all the stones are gone.

Lily Gardner-Butts

Notes:

August 27
Wednesday

4th ♌
☽ → ♍ 5:27 am

New Moon 12:26 pm

Color of the day: White
Incense of the day: Cedar

Cleanse and Purify Your Aura Spell
The sign of Virgo has to do with the process of cleansing and purification. By cleansing our physical body and the energy sheath around it, we can help ourselves become more effective in our magical workings. To prepare for this, purchase some fragrant soap, a candle, and a smudge bundle (sage or cedar are both great for this). Begin by taking a bath or a shower using the fragrant soap; you will want to have a pleasant scent afterward. Then put on some fresh clothes and come to your altar. Light a candle and take your smudge bundle and burn some of it. Blow on the smudge and move it along the length of your body from head to toe. Ask that your spirit and body be blessed and puri-fied. Then bring your smudge to your belly and visualize golden yellow light invigorating this area. Then move the smudge to your heart and visualize an emerald forest emanating from your heart. Then bring the smudge to between your brow (third eye), and visualize a violet light emanating from

there. Continue this process for a minute in each center and then give thanks.

Jonathan Keyes

Notes:

May my wishes wing
their way to the gods.
May Jupiter bless me
with good fortune.

Roll this paper up, and tie it with some twine. Keep it in a safe place and revisit your ratings in six months.

Kristin Madden

Notes:

August 28
Thursday

 1st ♍

Color of the day: Green
Incense of the day: Musk

Jupiter Goals Spell

To achieve your goals on this day, write down your wishes on a piece of paper, particularly if these wishes are associated with money. Rate each goal from high to low according to how they will contribute to your personal growth and how they will contribute to a better world. Next, list your regular activities and rate them according to how well they impact your goals. Now, using green or gold ink on lavender paper, write down all those goals and activities that rated high. Holding the paper in both hands say:

May my goals grow with
the Moon.

August 29
Friday

 1st ♍
☽ → ♎ 8:41 am

Color of the day: White
Incense of the day: Ylang-ylang

Salt Spilling Rituals

Folklore says much about salt. It brings luck, prosperity, and protection in many cultures around the world. People warn against borrowing it, as it means borrowing trouble; or lending it, which means giving away one's luck—quite a contradictory bit of advice. Far more elaborate are the warnings and rituals involved in dealing with the spilling of salt, and what to do in such a case. Given the many uses of this element in spells, however, I find that in a magical household, the spilling of salt most often signifies nothing more dire than a hint to strengthen the wards protecting the place. If you happen to spill salt, don't worry; just speak a charm such as this:

> Spill salt, spill luck!
> Sprinkle a bit around the room,
> And that will lift the coming gloom.

Then suit actions to words, visualizing a bright shield over all.

Elizabeth Barrette

Notes:

legend, Osiris was slain by his brother Set and dismembered. Only through her perseverance and magic was Isis able to find him and restore him. Now the mythic lovers are rejoined, and all is well with the world. If you are in a relationship yourself, forget all the worries and troubles of the past, and spend this day together contemplating your unique bond.

Robert Place

Notes:

August 31
Sunday

 1st ♎
☽ → ♏ 11:00 am

Color of the day: Yellow
Incense of the day: Basil

Goldenrod Good health Spell

In the fields just outside of town, on this late August day, grand plumes of goldenrod rise above the dried grasses of summer. They glow as bright as the summer Sun and have long been thought to contain

August 30
Saturday

 1st ♎

Color of the day: Gray
Incense of the day: Pine

Reunion Spell

On the eve of this day in ancient Egypt the reunion of Isis and Osiris was celebrated. According to

the health-giving qualities of the Sun as a healing plant. Say farewell to summer with this goldenrod spell that will protect your health before winter comes.

> Go into a field
> beneath the summer Sun,
> And gather up some
> goldenrod,
> Both stem and plume.
>
> During the solar hour,
> high noon,
> hang it and let it dry
> before scarlet leaves
> begin to fly.
>
> Place the dried
> goldenrod
> in jar or vase,
> Or on your door,
> to protect your sacred
> space.
>
> Keep them until next
> summer's end;
> If you wish, repeat this
> fair spell again.
>
> James Kambos

Notes:

Notes:

September

September is the ninth month of the year. Its name is derived from the
Latin word *septum,* which means "seventh," as it was the seventh month
of the Roman calendar. Its astrological sign is Virgo, the maiden (Aug 21–
Sept 20), a mutable earth sign ruled by Mercury. Though September after-
noons are warm, the days quickly shorten. Meadow grasses dry up as birds
and monarch butterflies migrate southward. Leaves begin to fall from trees
and bushes now, and though most of the harvests have been taken in, clus-
ters of grapes hang dark and heavy on the vine. The wine harvest is most
important now; it is best to begin this process by pouring a ritual libation
into the soil, and praying at an altar decorated with images of Bacchus
and Dionysus. In ancient Germany, wine was considered sacred and placed
into special stoneware jugs. Because wine is such a sacred fluid, the Full
Moon of September was called the Wine Moon, though it is more commonly known as the Harvest Moon today. A ritual for this time involves
dancing in a circle around some white wine in a silver cup with the Moon
shining overhead. Corn, gourds, and squash play a part of the Autumnal
Equinox celebrations, or Mabon. This celebration marks the time of the waning Sun, and the harvesting and storage of food for the coming winter.

September 1
Monday
Labor Day – Greek New Year's Day

 1st ♏

Color of the day: Gray
Incense of the day: Myrrh

Family Prosperity Spell

On this day which honors workers, do this spell so that members of your immediate and extended family will feel secure in their jobs, or will find a job if they need one. To start, light a green candle, and anoint it with Money, Prosperity, or Success oil. Write on a piece of paper with green ink the names of each family member who wants to work. Fold the paper into a small square, and anoint the paper. Sprinkle some green herbs—basil, parsley, thyme, and so on—around the candle. Place the petition and some of the herbs in a small, green-felt bag. Ask the universe for financial security, and carry the charm with you. After Labor Day, give the charm to the person in the family who most needs job security. As his or her financial lot improves, so will the rest of the family's.

Denise Dumars

Notes:

Holiday lore: Many Greeks consider this their New Year's Day, based on the agricultural traditions of the region. This day marks the beginning of the sowing season, a time of promise and hope. People fashion wreaths of pomegranates, grapes, quinces, and garlic bulbs—all traditional symbols of abundance—on this day. Just before dawn on September 1, children submerge the wreaths in the ocean waters for luck. They carry seawater and pebbles home with them in small jars to serve as protection in the coming year. Tradition calls for exactly forty pebbles and water from exactly forty waves.

September 2
Tuesday

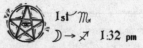 1st ♏
☽ → ♐ 1:32 pm

Color of the day: Black
Incense of the day: Sage

Change in Luck Spell

Luck, or the lack thereof, is primarily self-created. However, with some practice you can influence the universal energies and so tip the scales of luck your favor. For a fast change of luck you will need a gold candle, and to attract a more sustained change in luck you will need a small piece of fluorite. Start by lighting the gold candle. Focus on the changes that you would like to manifest. Focus these changes in the present tense to the fluorite. Visualize your energy melding with the fluorite. State these or similar words:

> Changing energies,
> Universal luck,
> Weighted my way—
> Fortunate door opening,
> Beginning this day.

Visualize the release of energy to the universe. Extinguish the candle. Keep the fluorite with you as a reminder to be alert for opportunity.

Karen Follett

Notes:

September 3
Wednesday

 1st ♐
Second Quarter 7:34 am

Color of the day: Peach
Incense of the day: Maple

Daily Positive Direction Blessing
This is a daily blessing that can be said or sung at the beginning of your day to help focus your thoughts in a positive direction.

> Lady of mystery,
> Goddess of life,

> Won't you bring one day,
> Just one without strife?

> Help me to listen
> To my own heart,
> To hold myself close
> And not tear it apart.

> Turn all of my sorrow
> To motives for change.
> Help me move on,
> Grow and rearrange.

> Lady of Mystery,
> Mother of me,
> Help me to heal,
> Help me be free.

When you say these words each morning, they will help even the worst of days look a little better.

Jenna Tigerheart

Notes:

September 4
Thursday

 2nd ♐
☽ → ♑ 4:51 pm

Color of the day: Turquoise
Incense of the day: Jasmine

Ease Transitions Spell

Today is the festival of the Apache goddess, Changing Woman. This spell helps us to embrace and learn from the changes that come into our life. To start, decorate your sacred space with potted plants. Place on your altar pictures of yourself from all stages of your life. Light a new green candle and ask Changing Woman to help you grow and change. Look at the photos of yourself when you were a baby, a young child, a teenager, and so forth. Realize as you study the pictures that although you've changed radically from your early childhood, you are still fundamentally the same person. Pray to Changing Woman to help you make any changes for the better that may be necessary in your life.

Lily Gardner-Butts

Notes:

Ready for harvest Season Spell

The bittersweet time of year is upon us. Gather the fruits of the season now: pumpkins, gourds, cranberries, and corn. Light candles of yellow for health, orange for sharing the harvest, and purple for deepening spiritual awareness. Hang a braid of garlic for protection from the coming winter. Make a simple grapevine wreath for your door, and entwine it with bittersweet stems. Fashion a new broom, or buy one from your favorite broom-maker, and place it outside your front door. On a clear breezy day, make a clean sweep of the house in a widdershins direction. Open windows and hang out rugs and blankets. Gather fresh air energy into your space. Burn sprigs of rosemary for preservation and longevity. Clear out stagnant forces, and rededicate your home to peace.

Karri Allrich

Notes:

September 5
Friday
The First Labor Day

 2nd ♑

Color of the day: Rose
Incense of the day: Almond

September 6
Saturday

 2nd ♑
☽→ ♒ 9:15 pm

Color of the day: Turquoise
Incense of the day: Carnation

Dill Protection Spell

Dill is a very versatile herb that can be used for protection, to dispel negative energy, or to attract money. The smell of dill is often enough to stimulate lust and other such feelings. Eating or bathing in dill can make you irresistible to those you desire. To promote this, while you visualize yourself as irresistible to the object of your desire, create bath salts by combining a half-cup of Epsom salts with a half-cup of dill weed and a half-cup of orange peel. Run your bath water; pour the bath salt and herb combination into a bowl, and pour approximately two cups of steaming water into the bowl. Place a towel over your head and carefully inhale the steam from the bowl for approximately ten minutes while you continue to visualize yourself being irresistible. Visualize your desired love object being overcome by your beauty and charms. Once the time is up, pour the contents into your bath water and soak while continuing to visualize. Put this energy into effect as soon as possible by seeking out the attentions of the target of your desire.

Sheri Richerson

Notes:

September 7
Sunday

 2nd ♒

Color of the day: Orange
Incense of the day: Coriander

Communicate with a Loved One Spell

Today is a good day to count your blessings, literally. To do so, make a small blessing altar. This can be a space on top of a dresser or a small table. Make a list of everything you are thankful for—including your family, friends, job, good health, home, and so on. Make the list as long and specific as possible, and list everyone and everything by name. Then take a large clear jar or vase and fill it with small objects, such as pebbles or marbles, one for each item on the list. Place a few pictures of specific blessings, such as pictures of your mate, your children, and so on, in front of the jar. Place a white candle on this altar, and light it every day for a few minutes while you give thanks for your many blessings.

Magenta Griffith

Notes:

carry on magical tradition. Remember: Much of the magical lore we use today was passed down to us in orally told stories.

James Kambos

Notes:

September 8
Monday

2nd ♒

Color of the day: Silver
Incense of the day: Rose

The Magic of Storytelling

When I was a boy living on my grandparent's farm, each day my family would gather near the orchard after the day's work was done. This was story time, and as dusk settled over the fields, my grandmother spun her tale. Perhaps it would be about the spirit that lived in the pumpkin patch, or the bluebirds living in the fencepost—the subject didn't matter. I was always mesmerized. As summer ends, and our activities turn toward hearth and home, storytelling is a wonderful family activity we can use to practice togetherness. Create stories that aren't scary, but do include friendly magical beings in your tales. With each tale you tell, you

September 9
Tuesday

2nd ♒

☽ → ♓ 3:07 am

Color of the day: White
Incense of the day: Musk

Night Sky Magic

As we look into the night sky in North America in the early evening at this time of year, we can see a triangle of three bright stars located at the top of the dome of the sky. These are called Deneb, Altair, and Vega—together the Summer Triangle. Deneb is the one closest to the center of the sky. It is a bright star at the head of a cross formed of six stars. The cross is Cygnus the swan, and Cygnus' head is facing the other way, making Deneb the tail (this is what Deneb means in Arabic). At the southwest point of the triangle is Altair, which forms the head of the eagle Aquila. At the northwest is the brightest of the three, Vega, which forms the corner of the constellation Lyra, the lyre. The oldest mystery religion in the West is the Orphic Mystery. Orpheus, its mythical founder, was a fabulous musician who could charm humans, animals, trees, and rocks with his songs. He played a seven-stringed lyre called a kithara. It had one string for each of the seven planets, and it could capture the "music of the spheres." The songs Orpheus played had prophetic and healing power. When his wife, Eurydice, died, he used the persuasive power of his lyre to win permission for Eurydice to leave the underworld, but he lost her again because, contrary to the admonitions of Hades, he looked back at her before she emerged into the sunlight. The only time he failed to conquer with his music is when he tried to tame the maenads of Dionysus. They tore him to pieces, and afterward Orpheus's lyre became the constellation Lyra. Through the centuries, Lyra has maintained its magical powers, and it waits in the sky to play for those who can truly listen.

Robert Place

Notes:

September 10
Wednesday

2nd ♓
Full Moon 11:36 am

Color of the day: Yellow
Incense of the day: Pine

Increase Your Serenity Spell

Today calls for a bath spell, as Pisces Moons are good times to increase relaxation and serenity by connecting to the water element. To prepare for such a bath, collect a half-ounce of lemon balm and licorice, the essential oil of jasmine, and some soothing music. On the Full Moon, make yourself a delicious cup of lemon balm and licorice tea by first placing a pint of water on the stove and adding the licorice. Bring the water to a boil, and reduce it to a simmer. Without removing the licorice, simmer the water for fifteen minutes. Then turn off the heat and add the lemon balm. Steep this for an additional ten minutes while you draw a bath. Place four drops, one for each element, of jasmine in the water, and then play the music on a stereo in your bathroom. Sink into the bath with your cup of tea, and then relax and let your worries drift away. Sip the tea and feel your entire system unwind and calm down. While you bathe, visualize any stress you have as dark knotty energy. As you relax, allow these knots to slowly untie and unwind. You may find yourself able to understand and solve problems that you couldn't when you were so stressed out.

Jonathan Keyes

Notes:

September 11
Thursday

 3rd ♓
☽ → ♈ 11:09 am

Color of the day: Green
Incense of the day: Chrysanthemum

Day of Infamy Ritual

Two years have passed now since the tragic events of September 11, 2001, when terrorists conspired to crash several airplanes into buildings on American soil. This is a day that will go down in history as a "day of infamy," much like like December 7, 1941, which marks the Japanese attack on Pearl Harbor. Yet the first heat of anger and grief will not last forever. We must, in time, allow history to become history—to move out constant thought and into memory. To help with this, consider: Traditional cultures set aside a mourning period for family members after someone dies, the most common length being one year. For such a great tragedy, it seems proper to add another year. Today thus marks the end of immediate mourning for this event. Now we can observe this occasion as a healing ritual that will move this date into history. To do so, set up your altar with images that are appropriate to you, including the photographs of anyone you may have lost. Light four black candles to honor the dead, and in the middle, one white candle for hope. If you can find it, myrrh is a perfect incense for both memorial ceremonies and healing rituals. When you are ready, say several times:

Let there be justice,
Let there be peace,
Let there be healing,
And then release.

Meditate for a time. You may wish to add prayers of protection for the living or the dead, for travelers, for your loved ones, and so forth. Contemplate the world being at peace and at rest. Allow the candles to burn out.

Elizabeth Barrette

Notes:

September 12
Friday

 3rd ♈

Color of the day: Pink
Incense of the day: Nutmeg

Passion Flower Relationship Spell

Consider a relationship that is in conflict. Today, brew yourself a tea of passion flower and vervain. Just before drinking, hold the cup in both hands and ask for spirit guidance. Hold it before your heart and say:

> My heart is open to a path of healing and friendship.

Hold it up to your forehead and say:

> Wise ones, help me to see how I can bring healing to this relationship.

As you drink the tea, consider how you contribute to the conflict and how you might change your responses. When you expect to be with this person, be sure to carry a small amount of dried vervain in your pocket or purse.

Kristin Madden

Notes:

September 13
Saturday

 3rd ♈
☽ → ♉ 9:50 pm

Color of the day: Indigo
Incense of the day: Jasmine

Giving a Power-Punch Speech Spell

Just before you have to give a speech or presentation, rub your hands together until they tingle. Then place them over your solar plexus. Feel the energy enter your third chakra, giving you more presence and energy than you generally project. Breathe the energy in for several slow, deep breaths. If you end up feeling butterflies in your stomach, acknowledge them as a manifestation of how excited and eager you are about sharing this information. They do not mean that you are anxious.

Therese Francis

Notes:

September 14
Sunday

 3rd ♉

Color of the day: Gold
Incense of the day: Parsley

A healing Ray Spell

The human body can heal and maintain healthy balance using its intrinsic gifts and gifts provided by the universe. For this to happen, there needs to be balance between natural health and technical health practices. Here are some tips for activating the natural healing potential of the body: During meditation, focus on any body areas where a need is perceived. Connect with your higher self, and state these or similar words:

> Spirit guides make me
> an open channel to
> receive the healing ray of
> the universe.

Visualize a healing ray of energy flowing through your crown and down through your body. Thank the universe for sending this healing ray, and afterward return to the universe any excess energy you do not need.

Karen Follett

Notes:

September 15
Monday
Respect for the Aged Day

 3rd ♉

Color of the day: Lavender
Incense of the day: Daffodil

Car Seat Charm

This charm was created when my husband and I were going out of town and leaving our daughters with my grandmother. Cleanse the following ingredients in whatever manner you wish—myrrh, rose petals, powdered ginger, lavender, bay, a rose quartz, hematite, an aquamarine, and a blue-cloth drawstring bag. Holding them in your cupped hands, charge them with the sole purpose of keeping your little ones safe while they are in the car. Place everything in the drawstring bag, and pull it tightly closed. Tuck the charm either under the car seat or into some small nook.

Laurel Reufner

Notes:

oliday lore: The Japanese have a marked respect for the aged, and this national holiday is part of this tradition. In a country where the lifespan is the world's longest, Respect for the Aged Day, or *Keiro no Hi,* thanks the aged for their wise service to society. On this day, schools, civic organizations, and the media all offer programs that emphasize the great value of elderly people to family and to community.

September 16
Tuesday
Mexican Independence Day

3rd ♉
☽ → ♊ 10:32 am
Color of the day: Gray
Incense of the day: Gardenia

Spell for Increased Passion

oday is St. Ninian's Day. His plant was the herb southernwood, a form of wormwood. Also known as "Lad's Love," this plant is believed to fan the flames of passion. This spell best done on St. Ninian's Day or when the Moon is waxing. Start by drawing a bath. Place a muslin bag holding the leaves of the southernwood into the water. Light a new red candle somewhere near the tub, and next to it place a ruby, a red jasper, and a garnet. Allow the powers of the herb and the stones, and

the red energy of the candle to enter into every cell of you. Repeat this ritual as often as you wish during a waxing Moon.

Lily Gardner-Butts

Notes:

September 17
Wednesday

3rd ♊
Color of the day: White
Incense of the day: Neroli

Moon Position Divination

hroughout history the Moon has been associated with psychic ability as well as divination. A sure sign of the coming weather can be discovered by examining the position of the Moon. During the first or last quarter of the Moon, if the orb lies in a horizontal position with the top horn pointing directly up this means that the weather will be good for the next month. If the Moon is in any other position, this means poor weather will be coming shortly. Travelers, farmers, or anyone else who relies on what the upcoming weather holds in store

will find that this is a great way
to predict what lies ahead.

Sheri Richerson

Notes:

for flavor. Drink the tea each morning until the next Full Moon.

Jenna Tigerheart

Notes:

September 18
Thursday

3rd ♊
Fourth Quarter 2:03 pm
☽ → ♋ 11:07 pm

Color of the day: Violet
Incense of the day: Evergreen

Prosperity and Promotion Spell

Use this spell to help find a job or
get a promotion. Start by using
your mortar and pestle to grind up
one part rosemary for mental clarity
and protection, one part ginger for
money and success, and two parts
lavender for happiness and protection.
Combine all three herbs and burn
them on your incense burner. Meanwhile, write down on slips of paper
what you need to achieve your goals
at work. When you have written
them all down, burn each slip of paper
in your cauldron. To remain focused
in the days to come, use these same
herbs to make a tea, adding some mint

September 19
Friday

4th ♋

Color of the day: Peach
Incense of the day: Ginger

Change Your Luck Spell

If you wish to change your luck
and bring good fortune, the
Psalms may be of help. Get out of
bed before sunrise on any day and,
facing east, repeat the following
prayer, which contains the holy name
Jiheje, or "he is and will be":

> May it please thee,
> O holy Jiheje,
> To bring prosperity to
> my travels and endeavors.
> For the sake of thy great
> name,
> Grant that my wishes
> and desires be fulfilled.
> Amen.

Now, thinking of Jiheje, read psalm
number 4 three times. Contemplate

the sunrise, and afterward go about your day with confidence and peace.

Robert Place

Notes:

tantly, and open your observations to your intuition. Invite the flame to impart images. Write down your insights, and carefully date your interpretation for future reference.

Karri Allrich

Notes:

September 20
Saturday

 4ℏ ☾

Color of the day: Blue
Incense of the day: Violet

Fire Scrying

As the power of the Sun fades, we embrace the harvest season and the decline of the fire element. This is a perfect time, as we approach the introspective tide of winter, to scry with flame. On a night close to the New Moon, cast a circle of protection, and light a purple candle. Sit silently and breathe deeply, allowing your conscious mind to grow quiet. Gaze at the candle flame and permit your thoughts to drift by without judgment. Soften your focus and relax your vision. Concentrate only on the flame. Ask a question. Observe the flame expec-

September 21
Sunday

 4ℏ ☾
☽ → ♌ 9:02 pm

Color of the day: Peach
Incense of the day: Poplar

Health and Vitality Spell

To create some extra vitality and promote good health as the weather begins to change for the dark of the year, cut a circle from a piece of white or yellow paper. Write on the paper the words Health and Vitality. Add any specific health issues you wish to deal with, and in the center of the paper place one bay leaf, a small amount of cinnamon, and three grains of rice. Fold the paper into a packet to hold the ingredients. Take the packet in hand for a moment and concentrate on your healing intentions, sending that energy into the package. Place the paper in a fireproof container, and light it on fire. As it burns, say:

> Sacred fire,
> I pray to thee,
> Release all bonds
> And set this free—
>
> That health and vitality
> might come to me.

Kristin Madden

Notes:

of Bilbo's 111th birthday, and Frodo's 33rd. The epic then follows Frodo on his quest to dispose of a very powerful, very dangerous magic ring which has come into his possession. A band of individuals—hobbits, elves, dwarves, and men—join him on his mission. If possible, have all three books available before you start, since the first and second end in cliffhangers.

Magenta Griffith

Notes:

September 22
Monday

 4th ♌

Color of the day: White
Incense of the day: Peony

Hobbit's Birthday

Today marks the birthday of both Bilbo and Frodo Baggins, of *Hobbit* and *Lord of the Rings* fame. If you have never read *The Lord of the Rings*, this is the perfect day to start. The first book in the trilogy, *The Fellowship of the Ring*, opens on September 22, at the party in honor

---

September 23
Tuesday
Mabon – Fall Equinox

 4th ♌
☽ → ♍ 3:04 pm
☉ → ♎ 5:47 pm

Color of the day: Red
Incense of the day: Pine

Autumn Blessing

On this day of balance—between hot and cold, light and dark— we can find balance in an autumnal blessing. Use a white and a black candle, placed side by side, for this ritual. Breathe in the glow that comes from the equal balance of day and night. Decorate your sacred space with fruits and grain and harvest leaves, as you slowly speak this verse:

> Protection covers me
> and mine,
> Abundant gifts grow
> from Nature divine.
>
> Mabon comes with
> balance dear,
> The second such time of
> the year.
>
> Second harvest abun-
> dance flows,
> Through our labor the
> storehouse grows.
>
> We fill our stores
> through harvest Moon,
> For winter's cold is
> coming soon.
>
> Harvest brings both
> hope and fear,
> Harder times are draw-
> ing near.
>
> Bless this house with
> abundance clear,
> And bless all who are
> dwelling here.
>
> Strength of the cycles
> For all to see,
> Bringing color to land
> and tree.

> Red, yellow, brown, and
> amber,
> Dress the forests,
> preparing for slumber.
>
> My spirit embrace the
> dwindling light,
> I am ready now for the
> longer night.
>
> Protection and safety
> there will be,
> As the wheel of the year
> turns, blessed be.
>
> The balance now is
> perfect and right,
> Preparations made for
> Demeter's night.
>
> Searching she goes and
> searching she will be,
> Till Kore's return to you
> and me.
>
> Mabon's magic dances in
> me,
> Autumn blessings to all,
> So mote it be.

Abby Willowroot

Notes:

oliday lore: Equinoxes are the bridges between seasons; part of this is physical—the Sun passes across the equator today, and day and night are therefore equal. But even more there is a metaphysical and spiritual bridge crossed today. Buddhists thought this was the day the dead crossed the waters between the worlds. As a result, today the Japanese visit the graves of their ancestors.

September 24
Wednesday

 4th ♏

Color of the day: Brown
Incense of the day: Coriander

Greek Initiates Mystery Spell

It is difficult to determine with any precision the dates on our Gregorian calendar that correspond to dates on the ancient Greek calendar—or calendars, because each Greek city-state had their own version. However, our best reckoning tells us September 24 or 25 corresponds to the 19th day of the Greek month of Boedromion, when the cry went out in Athens:

Initiates to the sea!

This marked the start of preparations for the Eleusinian Mysteries, a celebration of the beginning of the dark half of the year. Upon hearing the cry, participants purified themselves by bathing in the sea. At this time,

we would all profit by purifying ourselves through fasting and a hot bath. It is a good day for introspection. Devote time now to examining what aspects of your soul need development. Tarot is an excellent tool for this.

Robert Place

Notes:

September 25
Thursday

4th ♏
☽ → ♎ 5:49 pm
New Moon 10:09 pm

Color of the day: White
Incense of the day: Dill

Finding Balance in Life Spell

Sometimes it can be difficult to create peace and harmony. We have so many different obligations and responsibilities to fulfill that we become unbalanced and stressed out. We may find ourselves focusing too strongly on one area of our lives (such as work) and avoiding other areas (our relationships or health). We can create more harmony with spellwork to help rebalance our lives.

To prepare, set aside a space in your room or home where you can make a small altar. Gather a special rock, a feather, a red candle, and a bowl of water. For the spellwork, place the four objects in the four directions on your altar. For the northern earth element, place the stone. For the western water element, place the bowl of water. For the southern fire element, place the candle. And for the eastern air element, place the feather. Light the candle and honor each of the directions in your life. Water is associated with emotional health. Earth is associated with work and health; air with relationships and mental states; and fire with creativity, sexuality, and the spiritual. With your prayers ask for balance in all four areas of your life.

Jonathan Keyes

Notes:

A Bittersweet Love Spell

Use woody nightshade, or bittersweet vine, to attract love today. Collect a sprig of bittersweet berries, one dried yarrow flower, and one blanched, crushed almond. Place these in the center of a piece of red fabric, and around them draw a heart. Tie up the bundle with three feet of pink ribbon. Lay the bundle on a table, grasp the ribbon, and slowly pull the bundle toward you, saying:

> Bittersweet, yarrow,
> and almond dust, the love
> I want is coming to me.
> This is a must!

When the bundle is in your hands, clutch it to your chest and whisper:

> Bittersweet, yarrow,
> and almond ground fine,
> the love I want is mine.

Hide your bundle and tell no one.

James Kambos

Notes:

September 26
Friday

 1st ♎

Color of the day: Brown
Incense of the day: Cedar

September 27
Saturday
Rosh hashanah

 1st ♎
☽ → ♏ 6:52 pm

Color of the day: Gray
Incense of the day: Cedar

Abundance for the Future Ritual

Today marks the Jewish holiday of Rosh Hashanah, for the Jewish year 5764. This day is also celebrated as the birthday of Adam and Eve. For an abundance ritual today, you will need a yellow candle, an apple, a carrot, honey, and if possible some raisins and a pomegranate and symbols of peace and prosperity such as a dove, a rainbow, or the peace symbol. Gather the items on your altar, light the candle, and say:

By the light of this
candle all are warmed,
Just as the yellow Sun
brings forth life.
New realities are drawn
from the glowing energy
of this sacred flame.

I am the creator, I am
the creation, I am the
universe, I am a minute
speck of dust.
I am part of all things,
and they are part of me.
I am at peace.

Touch the fruit and symbols, and say:

Ancient fruits of wisdom,
I relish your goodness
and embrace your truths.
I celebrate your abun—
dant essences.
Bless my body and spirit,
And nourish me.

I am the creator, I am
the creation, I am the
universe, I am a fruit of
the Earth.
I am part of all these,
and they are a part of me.
This abundance is
always with me.
So mote it be.

Abby Willowroot

Notes:

September 28
Sunday

 1st ♏

Color of the day: Yellow
Incense of the day: Cinnamon

Elemental Elixir

Recharge your health and energy with the warmth of the Sun.

Place a small carnelian stone in a clear glass bowl, pouring some spring water over top of it. Move a clean feather gently above the water's surface in a spiral pattern, visualizing the air cleansing the water and blowing the gunk away. Let the water sit in sunlight for three hours, and then make it into some green tea. Remember to remove the carnelian from the water before you boil it. As you drink the tea down, feel the power of the Sun, as well as the elements, healing and recharging your body and mind.

Laurel Reufner

Notes:

it through the house, making sure to wave the smoke over all windows and doors. Imagine your home as a place of perfect safety, and say:

> Stern is the mountain
> that touches the sky,
> Bright is the tower that
> guards the palace.
> Sweet is the wine that
> runs from the chalice.
> Deep is the wellspring
> that never runs dry.
> Broad is the river that
> never narrows;
>
> Safe is this house against
> all harm come nigh.

Finally, bury the stub of the incense in your yard.

Elizabeth Barrette

Notes:

September 29
Monday

 1st ♏
☽ → ♐ 7:57 pm

Color of the day: Silver
Incense of the day: Lavender

home Protection Ritual

Watched over by the Moon, Monday is the day of home and family. For a spell to protect your home, light a stick of sage incense and carry

September 30
Tuesday

 1st ♐

Color of the day: Black
Incense of the day: Juniper

Going to the Dentist Ritual

On the day before going to the dentist's office, take a small stone that you can hold in your hand or place on a necklace. Imagine yourself surrounded by white, healing light. Feel the warm light throughout your body. This light helps you breath deeply and easily, while keeping your awareness of pain at a minimum. Imagine the white light folding itself into the stone. Take this stone with you to the dentist appointment. While waiting for the dentist to arrive, imagine the white light unfolding from the stone and surrounding you for the duration of your appointment. After your appointment is over, thank the stone for holding this light for you.

Therese Francis

Notes:

Notes:

October

October is the tenth month of the year, its name derived from the Latin word *octo,* meaning "eight," as it was the eighth month of the Roman calendar. Its astrological sign is Libra, the scales (Sept 21–Oct 20), a cardinal air sign ruled by Venus. Colors are everywhere now, as trees burst into masses of red, orange, and yellow leaves. Our bodies begin to change in metabolism at this time of year, and our consciousness shifts from an active mental state to a more psychically receptive state appropriate to the dark half of the year. The biggest celebration of October, and one of the most magical nights of the year, is Samhain (or Halloween, which is used interchangeably today). It is a time to decorate with signs symbolizing the outward manifestation of inward changes. Gourds and pumpkins decorate the porch or stoop; bundles of dried cornstalks sit by the front steps. As the day nears, the pumpkins change to jack-o'-lanterns that stare from the windows. Blood is common in Halloween costumes, and the Full Moon of October is known as the Blood Moon. Samhain is a celebration of death and is marked by several traditions—such as the Dumb Supper, in which dinner is served with places set for the dead; and the Samhain Circle, in which the living attempt to contact the dead to gain spiritual knowledge.

October 1
Wednesday
The Godless Month

 1st ♐

☽ → ♑ 10:21 pm

Color of the day: Peach
Incense of the day: Sandalwood

Eliminate Office Politics Spell

This potent spell will eliminate negativity and negative office politics from your place to work. To start, gather a half-cup of fresh lemon verbena flowers and a pint of boiled water. Let the water cool to just under boiling. Add the lemon verbena, and stir and meditate on this herb's pleasant scent and its power to purify. Steep it for thirty minutes, and strain the water into a spritzer or atomizer. Spritz the office, especially the corners and doors, and afterward, keep the magic alive by beginning each day with a spritz of the infusion. For an added boost, make yourself a tea of lemon verbena once a week. This will remind you to be pleasant and not engage in negative office politics.

                          Jenna Tigerheart

Notes:

Holiday lore: According to Shinto belief, during the month of October the gods gather to hold their annual convention. All of the *kami* converge on the great temple of Isumo in western Honshu, and there they relax, compare notes on crucial god business, and make decisions about humankind. At the end of this month, all over Japan, people make visits to their local Shinto shrines to welcome the regular resident gods back home. But until then, all through the month, the gods are missing—as a Japanese poet once wrote:

> The god is absent;
> The dead leaves are piling up,
> And all is deserted.

October 2
Thursday
Old Man's Day

 1st ♑

Second Quarter 2:09 pm

Color of the day: Violet
Incense of the day: Carnation

Guadian Angels Spell

Today is the feast day of the guardian angels. In common Catholic religious belief, each person is assigned an angel of his or her own, who protects the person's body and spirit. Although the Church never made the belief part of their official dogma, in 1608 the Pope named October 2 as the day the angels would be honored. The concept of an individual angelic protector is common to Judaism and Islam as well. It can be traced back to the beliefs of the ancient Greeks, Egyptians, and Persians. In Santeria, the guardian angel is associated with the orisha (god) Osun. Osun is the protector of the home. His symbol is a small silver cup with a rooster on top and bells suspended from the rim. The cup is placed in the home for protection, usually at the top of a closet or some place where it cannot be disturbed. If the cup falls over, it is considered a very bad omen.

Robert Place

Notes:

ℌoliday lore: On this day during the reign of Queen Victoria, in Hertfordshire, the local villagers gathered for the funeral of Matthew Wall, a local farmer. Pallbearers, carrying the casket, slipped on some fallen autumn leaves, and the casket crashed to the ground and broke apart. The villagers no doubt were rather surprised when Wall dazedly rose up from the casket; he had not been dead after all, just comatose, and the fall had revived him. He lived for many years afterward, and in his will provided for an annual holiday in the village. Pall-bearers who repeat the steps of that fateful day receive a few pence from Wall's estate, and so the villagers gather still to celebrate the life of the Old Man.

October 3
Friday

 2nd ♑

Color of the day: White
Incense of the day: Ylang-ylang

Freyja's Love Ritual

𝔒ne of the greatest and perhaps the most well-known of all the goddesses of the Norse pantheon is Freyja. Her name can mean "to make love" or "to court," so she is an important figure for those petitioning for love. Friday is Freyja's day, and green is her color. Today wear gold jewelry, especially a gold necklace, which evokes the power of Brisingamen, her magical necklace. Since Freyja is a solar goddess, the following ritual should take place during daylight, but before you go outdoors. Start the ritual by burning both a green and a pink candle, and asking Freyja to show you a sign that love will come your way soon. Offer her a cup of mead or beer, or some suitably festive beverage. Meditate on Freyja for a time, then, when you leave the house, keep an eye open for a sign from her. If you see a cat that is the color of one of Freyja's cats (gray or white), you know that Freyja has heard your prayer. Greet and pet the cat if at all possible. If no cat appears today, try this spell on another Friday.

Denise Dumars

Notes:

from you and going down the drain. See the water turn to red light. As it flows over you, your root chakra is energized. The water gradually becomes orange, then yellow, green, indigo, and violet, in turn energizing each of your chakras as it changes colors. In the end the water becomes white once more, balancing and harmonizing your energy field.

Kristin Madden

Notes:

October 4
Saturday

 2nd ♑
☽→ ♒ 2:45 am

Color of the day: Brown
Incense of the day: Patchouli

Shower Balancing Spell
As you shower today, take a little extra time to clear and balance your energy field. If you don't shower, use this opportunity to perform a visualization exercise. First, stand under the water spray and see it wash you clean of negative influences. See the water as white light, cleansing you of all tensions, fears, or pains. Then, visualize these things spiraling away

October 5
Sunday

 2nd ♒

Color of the day: Yellow
Incense of the day: Sage

A Past Life Dream Spell
In October, the door to the other-world opens. Our dreams serve now as doors to other realms. You can use your dreams to recall former lives, and then use this information to help you deal with problems in your current life. Perform this spell at bedtime when you aren't overly tired. To start, you'll need a smooth

and polished amethyst stone. Sitting on a bed, hold the amethyst and say:

> I call on the power of
> perfect memory to enable
> me to see a past life I've
> lived; it shall be revealed
> in my dreams. I'll see
> only what I should see.
> So mote it be.

Place the amethyst beneath your pillow and go to sleep. When you awake, record any images you recall. Repeat this spell over many nights.

James Kambos

Notes:

October 6
Monday
Yom Kippur

2nd ♒

☽ → ♓ 9:20 am

Color of the day: Silver
Incense of the day: Maple

Atonement Ritual

Rituals of release and cleansing are traditionally practiced by observant Jews on this Day of Atonement (Yom Kippur). It is thought to be a time of judgment and new beginnings. In the spirit of starting fresh and preparing for the winter days of reflection and release, you can honor the traditions of Yom Kippur with this spell. To start, place three candle holders with white candles on a cloth that represents your hopes and dreams for the coming year. Open a window, so that the energies will easily depart from you, and light the first candle, saying:

> I light this white candle
> to free me of all vows,
> oaths, and promises that
> I have made, but have
> been unable to fulfill in
> the past year.

> May all these pass into
> the universe as simple
> wishes for a better time.
> May they be released and
> cleansed.

Light the second candle, and say:

> I light this white candle
> to burn away these com-
> mitments. May these
> vows, oaths, and promises
> melt on the wind as if
> they were never uttered.
> May this release my
> spirit from any obliga-
> tions that may have been
> drawn to me.

Light the third candle, and say:

I light this white candle to begin anew, to dedicate myself to the finest that is in me. May the universe be blessed by my presence within it. My spirit is true.

Abby Willowroot

Notes:

Holiday lore: Yom Kippur is the most important holiday of the Jewish year. On this day, Jews refrain from working, and they fast and attend synagogue. Yom Kippur means "Day of Atonement," and this pretty much explains what the holiday is. It is a day to atone for the sins of the past year and to make amends. It is customary to wear white on the holiday, which symbolizes purity. Traditionally, some people toss bread into a river on this day to symbolize the cleansing of their sins.

October 7
Tuesday

2nd ♓

Color of the day: Black
Incense of the day: Honeysuckle

Opening and Closing Ritual

Today is a great time for clearing negative energy from your home. To start you will need to choose four gray candles that will remain lit for five to seven days. Light the first candle and move throughout your home carrying the candle banishing the negative energies. Arrange your walk throughout your home so that you end up at a door. Open the door and request that any negative entities leave. Once you begin to sense that they are gone, invite good entities into your home through the open door. You should continue this ritual for the next three days, being sure each time to invite good energy into your home to replace the negativity you are chasing away. Do not manually extinguish the candles.

Sheri Richerson

Notes:

October 8
Wednesday

2nd ♓

☽ → ♈ 6:07 pm

Color of the day: Brown
Incense of the day: Eucalyptus

Keeping a Plane Safe Spell

After getting comfortable in your airline seat, close your eyes and imagine a ball of white light in front of you. See the ball get bigger and bigger, until it is large enough to hold the whole plane inside it. See the wings, tail, and nose of the plane completely surrounded in white light, giving strength to the physical structure of the plane and clarity to all of the crew members. Open your eyes and enjoy your flight, knowing that everything is safe.

Therese Francis

Notes:

October 9
Thursday

2nd ♈

Color of the day: Turquoise
Incense of the day: Geranium

Fast Cash Spell for Bills

While obviously it's always a good idea to plan in advance, occasionally the unexpected occurs. Usually this means a bill you did not expect arriving just as the time your bank account is as empty as a lumberjack's back pocket. This spell, coupled with the forthcoming Full Moon in Aries (tomorrow) gives rise to the quick and strong energy needed for finding quick cash. This spell is not intended to create a lasting cash flow. Light a green and a gold candle. Place the bill and your checkbook in front of you, saying:

> Money needed,
> To pay this bill.

> Full Moon light;
> Money sources reveal.

Focus on the money being in your account, and the check being written to cover the bill. Release the energy and be alert to any surprise sources of money that might be unveiled in the next few days.

Karen Follett

Notes:

October 10
Friday

2nd ♈
Full Moon 2:27 am

Color of the day: Peach
Incense of the day: Almond

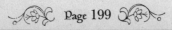

Developing Your Inner Warrior Spell

The sign of Aries is associated with the planet Mars and with its deep warrior energy. Today, on the Full Moon in Aries, is a good time to work on developing warrior strength and building a solid base of internal spiritual fortitude. Though we often need to learn compromise and skills of negotiation in modern society, there are times when we also need to develop and use the ability to defend and empower ourselves when we feel weak or low in confidence. To prepare for this spell, gather a cushion, a red candle, and a small pouch with several small garnet, ruby, or carnelian stones. In view of the rising Full Moon, sit comfortably on the cushion and light the red candle, placing it several feet in front of you. Gaze into the red candle light, and visualize yourself as strong, upright, and full of confidence and power. Tell yourself, too, that this is not a power that you intend to abuse, but it is a strength that will help you direct your will in a good way. Meditate in this way for ten minutes each day until the next Full Moon. As you meditate each day, handle the red stones that you have placed in the pouch. Also, carry the pouch around your neck and near your heart each day until you have finished the sequence of meditations running

from Full Moon to Full Moon. This pouch will remind you of the strength you are building.

Jonathan Keyes

Notes:

October 11
Saturday
Sukkot begins

 3rd ♈
☽ → ♉ 5:05 am

Color of the day: Blue
Incense of the day: Lilac

Send Trouble Rushing Spell

Need to get rid of some really bothersome negative energy? Try this spell: Place a black candle in a small bowl of dirt. Light the candle, and as it burns visualize your troubles burning to near nothingness in the flame. Allow the candle to burn completely down, then take the bowl and the remains of the candle to a flowing stream, river, or creek. Slowly pour the contents into the water. The current will take the last of the negative energy away with it. Wait until you can no longer see your troubles. Return home without looking back at the rushing waters.

Laurel Reufner

Notes:

 oliday lore: The Jewish festival of Sukkot begins five days after Yom Kippur and lasts seven days. The holiday commemorates the forty years the Jews wandered in the desert. In honor of this wandering, people dwell in or eat their meals in a temporary shelter called a *sukkah*. The sukkah has three sides and a partially open roof covered with greenery, and it is decorated with fruits and vegetables.

October 12
Sunday

3rd ♉
Color of the day: Gold
Incense of the day: Clove

Casting an Easy Circle

This is an easy way to cast a circle in a small or medium-sized group. Once everyone is standing or sitting in a circle, start by holding out your hand to the person on your left, and saying:

hand to hand, the circle
is cast.

The person on your left should take your hand in his or her right hand, then hold out his or her left hand to the person on their left, and repeat:

hand to hand, the circle
is cast.

This continues around the circle until it returns to you. When the circle is complete, all should say:

hand to hand, the circle
is cast,
May it hold fast.

Magenta Griffith

Notes:

October 13
Monday
Columbus Day (observed)

 3rd ♉
☽ → ♊ 5:45 pm
Color of the day: Silver
Incense of the day: Chrysanthemum

The Tension of Opposites Spell

Many people equate the sign of Libra with balance. But for

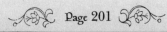 Page 201

many Witches its lesson is closer to psychologist Marion Woodman's concept of "holding the tension of opposites." Of course, this is difficult in a culture where duality reigns supreme. You are either good or evil, light or dark, one of us, or one of them. Yet, in identifying completely with one side and rejecting its opposite, we create an empty space where compassion should dwell. We waste vital energy in defending our position and sustaining our self-identification with one thing. We become rigid and unchangeable. As Witches, it is part of our duty to recognize our unknown self, to embrace our inner shadow, and live with the tension of opposites. Witches should learn to dance the eternal shadow dance, and know:

I am that, too.

Karri Allrich

Notes:

White Buffalo Woman Peace and Protection Spell

Since the end of the twentieth century, more than one white buffalo calf has been born. The white buffalo has long been a symbol in Native American lore of peace and the arrival of a new era. The goddess called White Buffalo Woman, meanwhile, is a goddess of peace. Invoke her to protect your home and keep it peaceful. To do so, find a picture, figurine, or plush toy white buffalo. Place the white buffalo along with any other Native American motifs you may have (a dream catcher, a kachina, and so on) on your altar with an offering of spring water and tobacco. Ask White Buffalo Woman for protection and peace, then smudge each room three times with a bunch of white sage, asking negative energies to leave. Afterward, thank her, and place the artifacts where they will do the most good (dream catcher in the bedroom window, for example.) Smudge the home once a month.

Denise Dumars

Notes:

October 14
Tuesday

 3rd ♊

Color of the day: White
Incense of the day: Evergreen

October 15
Wednesday

3rd ♊

Color of the day: Yellow
Incense of the day: Cedar

Autumn Balancing Spell

Autumn is a time of balance, when light and dark are equal. The sign of Libra also governs balance, along with matters of cooperation. Remember that every story has two sides. When you find yourself confronted with a controversial issue, or when you get into an argument with a friend, Libra energy can help. One thing you can do to tap into this energy at this time is make a talisman that will focus this power. Start by lighting two candles—one blue and one yellow. Hold a coin between them, spinning it in your fingers so light from each candle falls on it. Then say:

> Planet of judgment,
> Balance the scales;
> Bring a compromise
> That never fails.

Carry the coin when you need help seeing another's viewpoint.

Elizabeth Barrette

Notes:

October 16
Thursday

3rd ♊
☽ → ♋ 6:41 am

Color of the day: White
Incense of the day: Musk

Extra Thanksgiving Ritual

Consider having an extra Thanksgiving dinner this year, a little earlier than usual. After all, turkey is available year round, and think of all those special foods that are too good to only eat once a year: sweet potatoes, pumpkin pie, cranberry sauce, and so on. You know you want to, so go ahead; and get started with my stuffing recipe

> 1 or 2 small onions
> 2 to 3 stalks of celery
> 2 tblsps canola oil
> 1 peeled, cored and finely chopped apple
> 2 tblsps powdered sage
> 2 tsps thyme
> Salt and pepper to taste
> 4 cups of cubed, stale bread

Chop the onions and stalks of celery, and saute them in the oil. When they are soft, add the apple. Add the sage, thyme, and salt and pepper to taste, and saute a few minutes longer. Add the cubed stale bread, and stuff the whole into a twelve-pound turkey.

Magenta Griffith

October 17
Friday

 3rd ♋

Color of the day: Pink
Incense of the day: Nutmeg

Gratitude Spell

The Shinto religion celebrates a god-tasting ceremony today, whereby they honor their gods and offer them gifts of food from their recent harvest. Today you might consider what you have harvested in the past year. For this spell adorn your altar with harvest colors of orange and gold. Place upon the altar items that represent the work you have accomplished this year. This can take the form of annual reports, poems you've written, report cards, reviews, items that you've made, and so on. Light a new orange candle, and give thanks to the Goddess for all you've done. Be proud of your accomplishments, and grateful for the health, the time, and all the other conditions that enabled you to complete your work.

Lily Gardner-Butts

October 18
Saturday

 3rd ♋
Fourth Quarter 7:31 am
☽ → ♌ 5:42 pm

Color of the day: Indigo
Incense of the day: Juniper

Pet Memorial Ritual

To hold a memorial for a special pet who has passed on, place a picture of your pet (preferably taken when it was in its prime) on your altar. Light directional candles, and place them around the picture. Light a black candle, and place it next to or on top of the picture. Meditate on your pet's life and the joy it brought you. Look at the picture and speak words of peace for your pet's soul:

Like the wind, soar free
through the heavens.
Like a flame, warm the
hearts of those who
think of you.

Like water, let your
spirit flow ever onward,

Like the earth, be
steadfast awaiting
rebirth.

As the wheel turns, may
you find as much joy in
your next life as you gave
in this life.

                    Jenna Tigerheart

Notes:

to continue until you see the last bit
of light leave your feet and return to
the earth. You are now an open channel that will allow only pure light
and energy to flow. You are ready to
receive divine inspiration and guidance.

                    Sheri Richerson

Notes:

October 19
Sunday

 4th ♌

Color of the day: Peach
Incense of the day: Basil

Chakra Blockage Spell

To remove stress or any chakra
blockages that may be undermin-
ing your health, sit with your eyes
closed in a relaxed state. Breathe
deeply several times, and then begin
to visualize a brilliant white light
flowing through your body. As this
light moves through each of your
seven chakras, see each area expanding,
clearing, and becoming more radiant.
Visualize each chakra spinning clockwise at a perfect speed. Allow this

October 20
Monday

4th ♌

Color of the day: Lavender
Incense of the day: Frankincense

Angel of Dreams Assistance Spell

Monday is sacred to the Moon
and to the goddess Diana.
Diana is the protector of women and
animals and the goddess of the hunt,
but she is also the goddess of night—
the time of rest, sleep, and dreams.
In the Qabalah, the Moon is referred
to as the Angel of Dreams. This
would be a good night to make use
of the magical power of dreams
through a dream incubation spell. To
start, first determine what problem
you would like Diana to help you
with. Write the problem or question

on a piece of paper, and read it several times during the day. At night when you retire to bed, put the paper under your pillow and say the following words softly to yourself:

> Artemis, Diana,
> Goddess of Night,
> Angel of Dreams,
> I have brought to you my question,
> And I await your instruction.

During the night, you will receive instruction on how to mend the problem. If this does not happen on the first night, do not be discouraged. Try again as many nights in a row as you need to until you get a result. To make use of the information, it is essential to recall your dream when you wake up in the morning. If this is difficult for you, then do not get up or open your eyes quickly when you wake up. Lie in bed for a few more minutes. Return your body to the same position that you were in while you were dreaming. Your body has memory. Keep a pad by the bed and write down the dream as soon as you remember it.

Robert Place

Notes:

October 21
Tuesday

 4th ♌
☽ → ♍ 1:01 am

Color of the day: Red
Incense of the day: Sage

housecleaning Spell

Give your house a good sweeping and dusting today—the energies and time of year are perfect for it. Start by moving what furniture you can. Then, clear out the cobwebs gathering in corners and along the ceiling. Actually move items off the shelves to dust under, as well as around, them. As you clean, visualize all of the negative energy gunk swirling up into the billowing dust along with everything else. Feel the dirt squirming with negative energy as you sweep it all up into the dustpan. See it scattering out of the house while you dust. (You might want to dust first, so you can sweep up the residue.) Make sure to deposit all dirt, dust, and vacuum cleaner bags outside immediately.

Laurel Reufner

Notes:

October 22
Wednesday

 4th ♏

Color of the day: Brown
Incense of the day: Maple

Meteor Shower Spell

Since few of us will be awake to see the Orionid meteor shower last this night, we can set up a wish spell to receive visions of it while we dream. Just before falling asleep, when you are relaxed and sleepy, count down from ten to one and enter a deeper, more relaxed state. Visualize Halley's comet passing the Earth. See its tail leaving debris in its wake. Now picture this debris streaking through our atmosphere as meteors—hundreds of shooting stars light up the early morning sky. Tell yourself, with strong intent, that your astral body will watch the meteor showers tonight. Whisper your wish and state that your spirit will take this wish to the stars as you sleep. Then allow yourself to fall to sleep.

Kristin Madden

Notes:

October 23
Thursday
Swallows depart

 4th ♏
☽ → ♎ 4:27 am
☉ → ♏ 3:08 pm

Color of the day: Violet
Incense of the day: Jasmine

A Maple Leaf Prosperity Spell

In the Fall when I was a child, I remember walking past the stately old homes in my neighborhood. Above them towered ancient maple trees, blazing with color. Back then I did not realize that the maple was significant in magic. Ruled by Jupiter, maple leaves are appropriate to use in prosperity magic. To work this beautiful spell, collect three colored maple leaves of different colors—yellow, red, and gold. Upon each, using a marker, draw wealth symbols such as dollar signs, Sun shapes, or the rune feoh (ᚠ), and speak this charm:

> Leaves of magic,
> Leaves of maple,
> Yellow, red, and gold—
> Bring to me wealth to
> hold.

To release the spell, place the leaves on the ground near your home. Let the autumn wind carry them, and your wish, to the divine.

James Kambos

Notes:

Lore for an October day: Maples are among the most stunning trees in nature, often very brightly orange and red. In October, trees are in their full glory and natural beauty (as the green of chlorophyll fades from tree leaves, only the natural color of the leaves remains). Cadmium-colored sumac gathers on roadsides and riverbanks, and provides contrast to the still-green grass and clear blue skies. The first fires have now been kindled inside to fight the coming chill at night, and days suddenly seem very short. Quilts have been pulled from cupboards to warm cold beds; our bodies begin to change in metabolism at this time of year, and our consciousness shifts from an actively mental state to a psychically receptive state appropriate to the dark half of the year. This is the time of the apple harvest; and apples fill fruit bowls or are stored in the root cellar. The house is scented with applesauce laced with cinnamon. Apples have always been magically important—playing a key role in the "wassailing" ceremonies meant to ensure a bountiful harvest in the coming year. Wassail was traditionally made with hard cider heated with spices and fruit—and a ritual imbibing of this drink was likely performed at Halloween and Samhain, and at Yule. Candy apples are a modern treat celebrating the magic of the apple harvest—these treats are eaten often at Halloween even today. Bobbing for apples, too, has a long tradition as a celebratory ritual. Apples have ancient associations with healing (thus the phrase, "An apple a day. . ."), and were said to be useful for curing warts. This may be because the interior of an apple, if sliced horizontally, reveals a five-pointed star. The final harvest of the year is the hazelnut harvest; these nuts are gathered in wickerwork baskets to cure until they can be stored properly. The hazel tree was long sacred, and is symbolic of wisdom, secret knowledge, and divination. Forked hazel rods are useful for dowsing for sources of water or underground minerals, and hazel is a traditional wood for magical wands.

October 24
Friday
United Nations Day

 4th ♎

Color of the day: Pink

Incense of the day: Ginger

All My Relations Spell

Put a drumming tape on today, and sit or lie in a darkened room. Listen to the drums for several minutes, then listen for the space between the drum sounds. Move your awareness into this space as though you are entering a tunnel. On the other side of the tunnel is a wilderness. It might be a garden, lake, or cave. As you look around, allow an animal to approach you with a message. Listen carefully and then move further into the space, and allow another animal to approach you, give you a message, and receive your thanks. Do this until you have acquired all the messages that you are supposed to. Follow the drum sound back out the tunnel.

Therese Francis

Notes:

Releasing Intense Emotions Spell

Sometimes in our daily routine we can build up a lot of intense emotional energy. The Scorpio New Moon is a good time to attempt to release this energy. By ridding ourselves of this excess emotional energy, we allow our minds and bodies to stay healthy. To prepare for this, take a piece of unlined paper, a pen, a black candle, and a bowl of pure water and sea salt. Light the candle and write down any concerns, fears, or frustrations you may be feeling right now. Allow the words to come flowing out from your pen. Do not hold back. You may even feel like saying the words aloud as you write them to allow them to move from inside you to the outside world. Once you have finished writing, burn the paper in the candle flame. After burning the paper, dip your fingers in the water and sprinkle yourself with it while saying:

> I release these words,
> I release this tension.
>
> I release this negativity
> from my life.

Jonathan Keyes

Notes:

October 25
Saturday

 4th ♎︎
☽ → ♏︎ 5:08 am
New Moon 7:50 am

Color of the day: Gray
Incense of the day: Pine

October 26
Sunday
Daylight Saving Time ends 2 am

 1st ♏

Color of the day: Orange
Incense of the day: Coriander

Kali Worship Spell

Kalipuja, the great festival of Kali, the Hindu Dark Mother goddess, is today. Her mantra goes:

> Maha Kali aum jaya.

Translated as "Victory to great Kali," it is repeated over and over again by worshippers on this day. Worship is performed by standing or sitting in front of a statue or picture of Kali, and moving a small oil lamp in the air in front of you. With the lamp write the word *aum* in Sanskrit, while chanting her mantra over and over. You can make an oil lamp by twisting a bit of cotton into a wick, and placing it in a small heatproof bowl. Pout a little olive oil on it, and light it. Pictures of Kali and calligraphic versions of Hindu chants are available on the Internet, or in any store with imported items from India.

Magenta Griffith

Notes:

October 27
Monday
Ramadan begins

 1st ♏

☽ → ♐ 4:45 am

Color of the day: Gray
Incense of the day: Myrrh

Deep Values Spell

Muslims believe Muhammad received the Holy Quran on this night, and also that now is the time when God determines the course of the world for the coming year. For a spell to promote deep values and ethics through the year, place a green candle on your left, a blue candle on your right, and a white candle in front of you. Set out two small bowls, one of salt and one of water, and light the green candle, saying:

> By the power of the
> earth, the forests, the
> plants that make life—
> giving oxygen, I celebrate
> and honor all life this day.

Sprinkle a bit of salt onto the candle flame. Light the blue candle and say:

> By the power of the
> oceans, the rivers, the
> rain and the air that
> carries lifegiving oxygen,
> I celebrate and honor all
> life this day.

Sprinkle water into the second candle flame. Light the white candle and say:

> By the power of spirit,
> by the divine within me,
> by the spirits of my
> ancestors and my
> descendants yet to be, I
> celebrate and honor all
> life this day.

Pour the remaining salt into the water, and stir clockwise with your right index finger, saying:

> By all that is holy and
> all that is divine, I
> dedicate my powers
> to the earth and to her
> creatures this day.

Abby Willowroot

Notes:

Attunement with Divination

Hecate is most active during this time of year. This goddess, usually associated with the dark Moon, can be called upon to lend her guidance in the understanding of and the use of divination tools. To call on her, light purple and black candles. Lay your divination tools in front of you. Speak these, or similar words:

> Great hecate,
> Goddess of prophesy,
> Let these tools speak
> clearly to me.
> Let me precisely per—
> ceive their messages.
> In your honor,
> So mote it be.

Thank Hecate for her presence and her guidance. Please note that Hecate is a powerful goddess. When she speaks to you, she expects you to listen and follow her advice.

Karen Follett

Notes:

October 28
Tuesday

 1st ♐

Color of the day: Black
Incense of the day: Musk

October 29
Wednesday
Lost-in-the-Dark Bells

 1st ♐
☽ → ♑ 5:37 am

Color of the day: Peach
Incense of the day: Neroli

Scorpio Meditation with Persephone

Cast a protective circle, and light candles of blue, violet, and black. Close your eyes and relax your body into the gentle rhythm of your breath. Invite Persephone to guide you into the depths of your own underworld. Visualize her holding your hand as you wind your way down through dark ancient passageways. As images arise, keep breathing. These energies exist in your own shadow self, wherein reside aspects of your rejected identity—projected fears, attachments, addictions, and so on. Ask Persephone to help you heal that which needs healing. Be proactive in your meditation; visualize it happening. When you are ready to resurface, thank Persephone for her guidance, and slowly bring yourself back to consciousness.

Karri Allrich

Notes:

Holiday lore: Many villages in the English countryside share the tradition of "lost-in-the-dark bells." Legend tells of a person lost in the dark or fog, and heading for disaster, who at the last moment was guided to safety by the sound of church bells. The lucky and grateful survivor always leaves money in his or her will for the preservation of the bells. This day commemorates one particular such case, a man named Pecket in the village of Kidderminster, in Worcestershire, who was saved from plummeting over a ravine by the bells of the local church of St. Mary's. In honor of this event, the bells still ring every October 29.

October 30
Thursday

 1st ♑
Color of the day: Green
Incense of the day: Carnation

Angelitos Day Ritual

Today begins a weeklong celebration in Mexico honoring departed loved ones. The first of these days is called Angelitos, or "little angels," Day, as it honors children who have passed on. These holidays are not sad ones in Mexico—rather, the holidays are designed to remember departed loved ones and to welcome their spirits into the home. Some

Mexicans make a path from the cemetery to their homes with hard candies intended to guide the Angelitos home. At home, there are *calavera,* or skeleton, decorations and pictures of the children, toys, and traditional refreshments. Tonight the *jimaninos,* or spirits of children who do not realize they have passed on, also come out, and Mexican Witches may call them in during a ritual. These spirits are said to be playful and not dangerous, and they will dissipate on their own after November 2, the Mexican Day of the Dead.

Denise Dumars

Notes:

October 31
Friday
halloween – Samhain

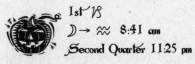 1st ♑

☽ → ♒ 8:41 am

Second Quarter 11:25 pm

Color of the day: Rose
Incense of the day: Parsley

Samhain Ritual

Today is a day for piercing the veil and accessing wisdom from those who have passed on, or are yet to be. With joy and delight, carve a pumpkin for casting spells this special night. Light it with a votive candle, and say:

> Night of nights
> with magic at every
> turn,
> Everywhere pumpkins
> glow and candles burn.
>
> The veil is thin,
> Giving access to powers
> deep within.
> Spirits roam and take
> flight,
> Seeking solace on this
> night.
>
> The year is ending,
> the wheel does turn and
> creak;
> Moments between time
> Give mortals a tiny peek
> Into the realms of those
> who have gone before.
>
> Ancient spirits appear in
> the woods and at the
> door.
> We leave food at cross-
> roads to feed those who
> wander.
> Searching for contact
> Or a place of rest here or
> yonder.

honor the dead
And the living, too,
Samhain spirits depend
on you.
Place the pumpkin
for all to see.
Invite all to feast
And blessed be.

Abby Willowroot

Notes:

Notes:

November

November is the eleventh month of the year, its name derived from the Latin word *novem*, meaning "nine," as it was the ninth month of the Roman calendar. Its astrological sign is Scorpio, the scorpion (Oct 21-Nov 20), a fixed water sign ruled by Pluto. The golden and ruddy leaves of October now lie brown on the ground, and bare tree branches stand out against a bleak gray sky. It is cold outside, and dark, and home hearths glow now with warmth. This is the time of year for psychic, as opposed to physical, activity, and for quiet. Use candles of various magical colors inscribed with runes for magical purposes at this time. It is a good time for nurturing your shamanistic instincts, or for consulting a shaman. As the first snows begin to dust the ground, there are many indoor chores to be done. Celebrate your circle of fire now, knowing that the dark months of the year are what lie ahead. Be thankful for the warmth of your oven, bulging with turkey, pheasant, mincemeat and pumpkin pie. The main holiday of November, Thanksgiving, was originally designed to celebrate the first harvest of Indian corn by the Pilgrims in 1621. The original holiday was not much different from ours today—a large feast, games and contests, with all the community gathered around to look forward to winter months.

November 1
Saturday
Day of the Dead – All Saints' Day

 2nd ♒

Color of the day: Gray
Incense of the day: Lavender

Wisdom of our Ancestors

You can find guidance to deal with difficult situations by accessing the wisdom of our ancestors. To do so, write out your perception of the situation on a piece of paper. Light white, black, and red candles, and cut an apple crosswise to reveal the five-pointed star created by the seeds. State these or similar words:

> I send my voice across
> the veil
> To my ancestors who
> know me well.
>
> Guidance needed,
> Wisdom bequest;
> Answers given to aid my
> quest.

Quiet your mind, and receive guidance. It may arrive immediately or over several days. Thank your ancestors, and offer the apple to them.

Karen Follett

Notes:

Holiday lore: The time between sundown on Samhain to sundown today, the Day of the Dead, was considered a transition time, or "thin place," in Celtic lore. It was a time between-the-worlds where deep insights could pass more easily to those open to them. Through the portals could also pass beings of wisdom, of play, and of fun. And while in time these beings took on a feeling of otherness and evil, as our modern relationship between the realms has been muddled, today can be a day to tap into the magic and wonder of other worlds.

November 2
Sunday
All Souls Day

 2nd ♒
☽ → ♓ 2:52 pm

Color of the day: Yellow
Incense of the day: Poplar

El Día de los Muertos Ritual

El Día de los Muertos, the Mexican Day of the Dead, is celebrated on this day, also called All Souls Day by the Catholic Church. The day is not one of mourning; rather, it is a celebration of the lives of those who have died. Why not celebrate the way Mexicans do on this day? Put a black cloth on your altar, as well as black, orange, and yellow candles, and photos of beloved dead. Marigolds are the preferred flowers; they should be placed on loved ones' graves as well. Invite the ancestors in by setting places for them and leaving a glass of milk and some *pan de muertos,* or "bread of the dead," outside the door. Recipes for pan de muertos and Mexican hot chocolate—traditional refreshments for this holiday—are easy to find in cookbooks, and in the Southwest many Mexican bakeries make these items.

Denise Dumars

Notes:

Holiday lore: Mexico's *Día de los Muertos* calls for day-long picnics beside the graves of dead relatives. And on this day, the cemetary is crowded and filled with colors of flowers and bright cloth. People bring their loved ones' favorite foods and drinks, their photographs, and any other memoribilia that will bring their joy of life alive. Shops and markets too are stocked with death-themed toys: wooden skeletons, toy coffins, sugar skulls, and *pan de muertos,* or bread of the dead scented with anise and shaped to look like people and animals.

November 3
Monday

2nd ♓

Color of the day: Lavender
Incense of the day: Rose

Dream Journal Spell

As the Crone beckons us into the shadows at this dark time of the year, pay attention to your dreams and keep a journal and pen by the bed—otherwise you may miss a chance to take a deep inward journey. The Sun in Scorpio supports our soul's journey toward authenticity and integration, and this time of year is in fact perfect for exploring any mysteries that call to you. Honor the complexity and insight of your inner shadow. Allow your shadow-self to teach you what secrets it may. This season of thinning veils provides an ideal opportunity to develop your instinctive nature. Start this by writing down your dreams and by honoring your personal intuition and insight. Through the process of dreaming, our shadow helps initiate us into deep archetypal mysteries. Immediately upon awakening, write down all you can remember from your dream. This is important; avoid any usual patterns of behavior—such as rushing off to work or to the bathroom. Work to contain and control your inner mind by recording its images. Later, you will begin to work with the images symbolically to discover meaning.

Karri Allrich

Notes:

November 4
Tuesday
Mischief Night – Election Day

 2nd ♓

Color of the day: Gray
Incense of the day: Gardenia

Dome of the Sky Spell

Tonight, as we look up into the center of the dome of the sky, we can find a group of constellations that commemorate the main characters from the myth of Perseus. Near the pole star, if we cast our glance on a circular course, we can find Cepheus and Cassiopeia, the king and queen of Ethiopia. South of them is Andromeda, their beautiful daughter, chained to a rock and waiting to be sacrificed to the sea monster Cetus, who can be found further south. If we look to our left from Andromeda, we will find the hero Perseus, who is on his way to save Andromeda, having just com-

pleted his first heroic task, the slaying of Medusa. Medusa's severed head can be found in Perseus' left hand. In the book *The Origins of the Mithraic Mysteries*, author David Ulansey makes the case that the constellation of Perseus was worshiped by the members of the Mithraic religion as an image of Mithras himself, who slayed Taurus the bull, found just below him to the south. Whichever myth we assign to Perseus, it is clear that he is a venerated ancient hero. Like other heroes, he can be called on for help and protection.

Robert Place

Notes:

November 5
Wednesday

 2nd ♓
☽ → ♈ 12:02 am

Color of the day: Peach
Incense of the day: Coriander

A Bonfire Night Divination

In Britain on this night in 1605, Guy Fawkes' plot to blow up the Houses of Parliament failed. Today known as Bonfire Night in

England, this is a holiday for bonfires and fireworks to commemorate the thwarted Gunpowder Plot. The fire meditation that follows is a very suitable form of magic for this night. Find a quiet spot and intone these words while following their directions:

> When you feel the need
> to inquire,
> Sit before the winter
> fire.
> Upon the flames, sprinkle yarrow, thyme, and
> marigold.
> With these, your answer
> will be told.
>
> Hold your eyes steady as
> you gaze
> Deeply into the dancing
> blaze;
> In the yellow flames, in
> the orange flames,
> Do you see an image, a
> face, or name?

If the flames fail to speak, try again—but wait a week.

James Kambos

Notes:

November 6
Thursday

 2nd ♈

Color of the day: Turquoise
Incense of the day: Sandalwood

Toast to Thor for Prosperity

Today is Thor's day. Pour yourself a glass of grape juice, wine, or beer, and sprinkle it with some ground nutmeg. Hold the glass in both hands and visualize yourself with all that you need. See yourself happily paying bills and looking at a very healthy bank statement. Call to mind an image of Thor, the Norse thunder god, and his wife, Sif of the Golden Hair. Ask them to bless you with a large financial harvest and a fruitful life. Before you drink, toast the sky and earth, then pour a small amount on the ground as you say:

> Hail Thor,
> Link between Heaven
> and Earth,
> Bringer of fertility and
> vitality,
> I thank you.
>
> Hail.
>
> Hail Sif,
> Golden-haired goddess
> of the ripening grain.
> I thank you.
> Hail.

Kristin Madden

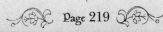

Notes:

Remember to carry your new free attitude with you wherever you go.

Laurel Reufner

Notes:

November 7
Friday

 2nd ♈
☽ → ♉ 11:59 am

Color of the day: Peach
Incense of the day: Dill

Rope of Negativity Spell

Many times we carry negative ideas or perceptions around with us that can be easily sensed by others, preventing them from getting to know us. Now is the time to start getting rid of them! For this spell, pick three negative perceptions about yourself that you are ready to lose. Taking up a foot-length of cording or thin rope, tie a knot in it about one foot from one end. As you do so, focus on one of the perceptions you selected. Repeat the process at the two- and three-foot marks on the cord. Lay the knots on your altar until after the Full Moon, then take up the rope and slowly untie the knots. Say after you untie each knot:

I am now free of (name of problem).

November 8
Saturday

 2nd ♉
Full Moon 8:13 pm

Color of the day: Brown
Incense of the day: Jasmine

Bringing Yourself Back into Your Body Spell

The sign of Taurus is associated with the earth element, with our physical body, and with the pleasure we derive from our senses. This Full Moon is a perfect time to develop the sexual side of ourselves. If you have been feeling harried, excessively busy, and out of touch with your body, the Taurus Moon can help you relax and remember the joys and sensations of your physical being. For this spell you will need either jasmine or rose essential oil—pick your favorite. You will also need to wear earth-colored clothing of greens, browns, ochres, and maroons. On the Full Moon, anoint your throat and your heart with the essential oil, and then put on your earth-colored clothing. Find a quiet spot outside, or, if the weather does not permit, find a relaxing place in your home. Then sit down firmly on the ground, and touch your hands to the earth. Gently begin to breathe into your belly and then slow your breathing down. Start to enjoy the small sensations you feel. Listen to the sound of the breeze; take in the smell of autumn and allow it to course through your body. Feel the sensation of the air as it caresses your face, hands, and body. Allow your eyes to delight in the colors and textures of the land. Let your fingers dig into the ground and touch and caress the pebbles and dirt in your hands. This practice will help you to be grounded and remember your physical and sensual self.

Jonathan Keyes

Notes:

Make Your Wishes Come True Spell

This magic ritual is performed in Thailand every year on this day. Start by making a small boat from colored paper, choosing the color of the boat to represent your secret wish. If you want to bring love into your life, make a pink boat; to bring more money into your life, make a green boat. Place a small offering such as a crystal, a coin, or a flower into the boat, and breathe into the boat your secret wish. When the time feels right, set the boat adrift in a body of water. Keep your wish secret or it won't come true.

Lily Gardner-Butts

Notes:

November 10
Monday

 3rd ♉
☽ → ♊ 12:14 am

Color of the day: Gray
Incense of the day: Peony

Serious Communication Spell

Is there someone you have quarreled with, and you know you

November 9
Sunday

 3rd ♉
Color of the day: Peach
Incense of the day: Clove

should make up to before the holiday season? Now is the time to do it. Start by asking yourself if you've had any particular communication problems lately. Is there some aspect of your discourse with people that is making you uncomfortable lately? If so, then tackle this problem today. After all, with the Sun in Scorpio, the Moon waning in Gemini, an air sign, and a Moon trine with Uranus, this is a good day for serious communication. Write that letter, make that phone call. Promise yourself a nice bubble bath, an hour of computer games, or a dish of ice cream as a reward.

Magenta Griffith

Notes:

ᚾovember 11
Tuesday
Veterans Day

 3rd ♊

Color of the day: White

Incense of the day: Ginger

Season of Rest Spell

As the year winds down, we come into a season of rest and regen-

eration. The leaves are falling; the dark hours are growing longer, and the light is waning. Earth sleeps now beneath our feet. It is at this time that the Hunter comes. Orion, rising in the eastern sky, strides out of the twilight to stand guard over the slumbering world. You may greet him with words like these:

> See the hunter in the sky,
> Silent watcher drawing nigh.
> Long the vigil he must keep
> As he guards us in our sleep.
>
> Hunter, hear the thanks we sing,
> Till we part again in spring.

This charm also works for instilling courage any time of night during the dark part of the year.

Elizabeth Barrette

Notes:

istorical lore: Veterans Day commemorates the Armistice that ended the Great War in 1918. Oddly enough, this war ended on this day, November 11, at 11 am (the 11th hour of the 11th day of the 11th month). Though Congress changed Veterans Day to another date in October at one point during this century, in 1968 they returned the holiday to November 11, where it stands today. The number 11 is significant. In numerology, it is one of the master numbers that cannot be reduced. The number 11 life path has the connotation of illumination and is associated with spiritual awareness and idealism—particularly regarding humanity. It makes sense then that this collection of 11s commemorates the end of an event that was hoped to be the War to End All Wars. Unfortunately, it wasn't the last such great war, but we can at least set aside this day to ruminate on notions of peace to humankind.

November 12
Wednesday

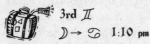

3rd ♊
☽ → ♋ 1:10 pm

Color of the day: Yellow
Incense of the day: Eucalyptus

Travel Time Spell
To prepare for a long car trip, just before starting out smudge the inside and outside of the car with sage or copal smoke. Imagine the smoke penetrating the physical structure of the car, giving it extra strength. Tell the car where you plan to travel, and ask for its assistance in getting there in the safest, simplest manner. If you are open, you will get an "OK" message when it's time to leave.

Therese Francis

Notes:

November 13
Thursday

3rd ♋

Color of the day: Green
Incense of the day: Chrysanthemum

Calm Nervous Energy Spell
Tiger's-eye crystals hold the energy of the higher intellect. The power of this brown-and-gold crystal is to ease distractions and calm nervous energy. Tiger's-eye is frequently used to ease tension, jitters, or nervous and time-wasting activities. To tap into its powers hold the tiger's-eye crystal in your hand and repeat these words several times:

Tiger's-eye,
Clear my mind,
Rid me of distraction.
Calm my nerves and
focus me,
So I can take true
action.

Keep the tiger's-eye crystal with you. Anytime you feel the nervous energy returning, touch the crystal and feel it calm your nerves and clear your mind.

Jenna Tigerheart

Notes:

relations "warming up" as the bread heats up. Know that both people in the relationship are responsible for being receptive to a discussion and better relationship with each other. Once the piece of toast is done, apply butter and visualize it as a healing salve that you are applying to the other person. Then take the piece of toast, bury it in a safe place, and prepare yourself to approach the person so that the healing may begin.

Sheri Richerson

Notes:

November 14
Friday

3rd ♋

Color of the day: Pink
Incense of the day: Thyme

Toothpick Love Spell

If you find yourself having problems in a relationship, try this age-old ritual to get on better terms with your loved one. First, take a piece of bread and use a toothpick or other similar item to inscribe that person's name into the bread. Then place the piece of bread into a toaster or warm oven, visualizing your chilly

November 15
Saturday

3rd ♋
☽ → ♌ 12:48 am

Color of the day: Blue
Incense of the day: Violet

Vamping It up for Saturn's Day!

Today is Saturn's day, and it is also the day you've decided to go out dancing! Wear Saturnine finery by choosing something silver and something black. Add a little patchouli oil to your favorite cologne. Add some basil to something you eat today (or choose an Italian restaurant for dinner if you have a date). If you don't have a date, and want to meet someone, try this: Turn a piece of silver over in your hand at dusk, and say:

> As this silver turns,
> My luck in love returns.

Try a little old-fashioned glamour. Stand in front of the mirror before leaving home, and envision yourself as the most desirable person anyone will see at the club or party you're attending. This may work, but don't be surprised if the person you attract is rather, well, saturnine.

Denise Dumars

Notes:

used medicinally in many cultures to relieve stress and anxiety. Chamomile and lavender are frequently used to calm nerves and relax the body. Clary sage is used to calm and relax the mind. For a good relaxation tea, combine two parts kava, one part chamomile flowers, and one part mint in a cup, and pour hot water over the herbs. While the tea steeps, light a charcoal on your incense burner, and add some lavender and clary sage to the burner. Let the smoke waft over yourself. As you drink your tea and breathe in the incense, feel your stress leaving your body and your mind.

Jenna Tigerheart

Notes:

November 16
Sunday

 3rd ♌
Fourth Quarter 11:15 pm

Color of the day: Orange
Incense of the day: Sage

Stress Relief Spell

To come down after a completely exhausting and stressful day, consult your herbal cabinet. Kava is

November 17
Monday

 4th ♌
☽ → ♍ 9:36 am

Color of the day: Silver
Incense of the day: Lavender

Remove a Ghost from the house Ritual

If you have creeping terrors at night, trying speaking this verse:

This spell is written for
the shadow,
Which moves across the
wall,
And for the unexplained
light
At the end of the hall.

It was written for the
strange scent of jasmine
Wafting in the winter
air,
And for the gauzy mist,
floating above the stairs.

After the dusk has
turned to night.
Light a virgin candle,
tall and white.

Place it before a looking-
glass.
And gaze at it until you
see a spirit from the
past.

When the flame begins to flicker
and sway, gently whisper:

Come, let me guide your
way.

Open your door, carry your candle
into the night, and say:

Come gentle spirit,
Go back,
Follow the light.

In peace you came,
In peace be gone.

For the good of all
And harm to none.

James Kambos

Notes:

November 18
Tuesday

 4th ♍

Color of the day: Black
Incense of the day: Poplar

Chili Pepper Protection Spell

To boost your protective energies
on this day, gather together some
chili pepper and basil. Run your fingers through the herbs, allowing your
energies to attune to them. Say:

I call upon the guardian
powers of chili pepper
and basil. I ask that you
bless my spell with your
protective energies.

In a glass bowl, combine the herbs
with warm water. Hold the bowl in
your left hand and hold your right
hand open over the water. Say:

I call upon the horned
god, protector of all,

charge this liquid with
the powers of the
guardian.

Anoint yourself at each chakra point
with the liquid. Feel yourself surrounded
by the loving protection of the divine.
Take the remaining liquid and sprinkle it at each opening to your home.

Kristin Madden

Notes:

November 19
Wednesday

4th ♏

☽ → ♎ 2:42 pm

Color of the day: Brown
Incense of the day: Cedar

Removing Obstacles to Success Spell

Obstacles are essential elements of growth. They point to our inner learning needs, or to shadow areas of "self-sabotage" in our subconscious. Identifying and addressing obstacles will guide you through the lessons necessary for personal growth in life. Ignoring an obstacle will ensure that it returns later in a more formidable

form. For this spell for overcoming obstacles, light three white candles. Place a cleansed obsidian in front of the candles. State these or similar words:

> By the light of darkest
> night,
> Bring my obstacles into
> sight.
>
> I overcome these barriers
> by my successful might.

Focus on the obsidian. Mentally open yourself to your obstacles. Claim ownership of the obstacles, and trace them back to their roots. Address the shadows or the lessons that these obstacles represent and learn from what they say to you.

Karen Follett

Notes:

November 20
Thursday

4th ♎

Color of the day: White
Incense of the day: Evergreen

Comfort Your Body Spell

As winter's grip begins to tighten, our bodies need sustenance that nurtures, comforts, and boosts our immune system. Kitchen Witches turn now to the wisdom of root vegetables and harvest flavors, restorative spices, and energizing herbs. Slow-cooked stews and lemon-infused dinners, all laced with rosemary, nurture the soul and support the body. Breads and muffins spiked with cinnamon bring luck and fill the house with fragrance. Apple pies and pear crisps honor the Goddess and bring sweetness to the shortening days. Soups and stews brimming with earthy vegetables and warming spices feed not only the body but the spirit as well. Use plenty of ginger, cumin, nutmeg, and chili powder. Rosemary invites protection, and basil stimulates love and desire. Sharpen your Kitchen Witch skills!

Karri Allrich

Notes:

November 21
Friday

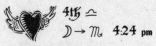

4th ♎
☽ → ♏ 4:24 pm

Color of the day: Rose
Incense of the day: Sandalwood

Creativity Spell

The Mayan god of craftsmen, Kukulcan, is celebrated each year on this date. Pray to him for inspiration and for increased skill in your daily work. Decorate your altar in colors of yellow and orange and with figures of snakes, the totem of Kukulcan. Make a list of what you need to increase your level of creativity. Do you need a private space or a class? Think of one word that summarizes your need, and write it on a length of ribbon. Tie the ribbon onto a feather. Burn a yellow candle, and carefully wave the feather over the flame of the candle. Feel your prayers wafting up to Kukulcan. When you finish, be sure to give thanks to him and leave an offering of food.

Lily Gardner-Butts

Notes:

November 22
Saturday

 4th ♏
☉→ ♐ 12:43 pm

Color of the day: Indigo
Incense of the day: Patchouli

Remembering the Dead Spell

On this day in 1963, President John F. Kennedy was assassinated. What is often forgotten is that two other great men died on the same day—C. S. Lewis and Aldous Huxley. All three of these men were visionaries in the broad sense of the word. They all saw the big picture, and expressed it in ways that were accessible to many people. They shaped the future of our world in sweeping ways. Kennedy proposed we would put a man on the Moon, and we did. Lewis and Huxley wrote books that deepened our understanding of the human condition. By the way, the television show *Doctor Who* also premiered that same day.

Magenta Griffith

Notes:

November 23
Sunday

 4th ♏
☽→ ♐ 4:02 pm
New Moon 5:59 pm

Color of the day: Gold
Incense of the day: Clove

Bringing Adventure into Your Life Spell

Sometimes we get caught walking a treadmill in life. We go through our routines and our schedules, and we start to get bogged down. If this is the case with you now, the Sagittarius Moon can help lift you up and remind you to be playful and a little more spontaneous and adventuresome. To prepare for this spell, you will need a space to dance, a stereo, and a good CD. A few red candles are helpful too. On the night of the New Moon, go to the space and put on some music that helps you to get up and get moving. Turn off any artificial light, and light the red candles around the room. As the music begins to pulse with rhythm, allow your body to flow naturally and spontaneously. Call the fire spirits into your room, and ask for their help to feel invigorated and charged in spirit. Let your arms and legs shake off any old ways of being that are holding you down. Close your eyes and search for an inner spark that will help you to explore life more

creatively and spontaneously. Let the music take you!

Jonathan Keyes

Notes:

These words will need to be written in a spiral manner that covers as much of the paper as possible.

Sheri Richerson

Notes:

November 24
Monday

 1st ♐

Color of the day: White
Incense of the day: Maple

Plain Paper Protection for the home Spell

If you often find yourself battling demons in your home, make a demon trap for them and place it under a rug at each entrance to the inside of your home. To do this you will need a plain piece of white paper. On the paper write:

> All negative spirits that cause disruption, disharmony, or other negative situation in this home, be drawn into this trap. Once you have been drawn into the trap I command you to return to your original domain. So be it.

November 25
Tuesday
Ramadan ends

 1st ♐
☽ → ♑ 3:31 pm

Color of the day: Red
Incense of the day: Pine

Balancing Energy with Stretching Ritual

This stretch helps balance your energy, making your body feel more alive. To start, concentrate on your breathing and how the exercise makes you feel. Assume a kneeling position, feet tucked under your body. Breathing deeply, feel your spine stretch. Raising arms to shoulder level, turn your hands palm up. Bring arms over your head, interlacing your fingers. Slowly stretch to your right side, then left. Lower arms back to your sides, rolling your shoulders slightly. Repeat the stretch, starting with your left side. Return arms to your sides and stretch forward, placing your palms onto the floor and reaching as far as you can. It's a wonderful stretch for balancing energy; do it everyday. Whenever you need to center energy, take a deep breath and recall how it makes you feel.

Laurel Reufner

Notes:

mon good." In explaining magic, Knight makes use of an analogy with mathematics, which is also a construct of the mind yet can have an effect on physical reality. He also points out that Romantic artists and poets believed that to make a work of art was an act of magic. It seems that Lewis Carroll, who under his given name of Charles Dodgson wrote books on math, is part of this tradition, and *Alice's Adventures in Wonderland* certainly fits Knight's definition of white magic. Today would be a good day to make a work of art.

Robert Place

Notes:

November 26
Wednesday

 1st ♋

Color of the day: Yellow
Incense of the day: Neroli

Alice's Adventures Spell

On this day in 1865, *Alice's Adventures in Wonderland* was published. Magician and author Gareth Knight defines white magic in his book *Magic and the Western Mind: Ancient Knowledge and the Transformation of Consciousness* (Llewellyn, 1991), as a technology of the imagination used "to expand consciousness and improve the com-

November 27
Thursday
Thanksgiving

 1st ♐
☽ → ♒ 4:48 pm

Color of the day: Violet
Incense of the day: Dill

Thanksgiving Blessing

Today, of course, is a day to give thanks. Light candles in white or harvest colors, and place them in

front of you. Also surround yourself with images of things you are thankful for. Speak this blessing:

Thank you, Earth,
For your abundant bounty.
I gratefully receive your gifts and blessings.

For the air I breathe,
I thank the plants and trees.

The air, the fire,
The water, and the earth.
Thank you for sustaining my life
And nourishing me.

For the blessings of loved ones, who help me along life's path.
I am thankful.

My life is full to over-flowing
with gifts of ancestors.
Courageous souls who survived,
And made my life possible.

Thank you great spirits of the cosmos,
for the lessons I some-times try to avoid,
But which I need.
And for the joys and pains which open my spirit and expand my heart.

I am grateful for health, abundance, and chal-lenges, each unique.
Thank you all who have touched my life's journey.

Each new day is a gift,
To which I pledge the best of myself.
For the blessings of life's great circle continue in me.

From the cave to the stars,
I have always been and will always be.
I am rich in the things that matter.

With my deepest grati-tude,
I offer my blessings to all on this day.

Abby Willowroot

Notes:

November 28
Friday

 1st ♒

Color of the day: White
Incense of the day: Ylang-ylang

Strengthening a Love Bond Spell

To strengthen your bond with your significant other, use a red wine (or other red beverage) and one wine glass. Pour the wine. Repeat the following words three times while looking your partner in the eyes. First, your partner says the line and drinks, and then passes the glass to you to repeat the line and drinks. Repeat the lines at least three times each.

> I drink to my love
> And my love drinks to me.
> Let the bonds of love keep us through all things,
> Through good times and hard times, eternally.

Jenna Tigerheart

Notes:

Exchanging Klutziness for Gracefulness Spell

When you're feeling klutzy, think of an animal that represents gracefulness to you, such as a butterfly or a gazelle. Sit quietly in a dark room, breathing deeply for a few minutes, then ask the spirit of that animal to join you and to give you some of its gracefulness. Envision the animal spirit entering your aura and remaining with you, and in you, for several minutes. Then thank the spirit for sharing its energy with you and know that your klutziness has vanished.

Therese Francis

Notes:

November 29
Saturday

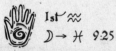 1st ♒
D → ♓ 9:25 pm

Color of the day: Gray
Incense of the day: Lilac

November 30
Sunday

 1st ♓
Second Quarter 12:16 pm

Color of the day: Peach
Incense of the day: Basil

Moon Waxing Energy Spell

Tonight the second quarter Moon brings to us the energy of increase and activity. As the Moon waxes, our power grows. Take advantage of this rising tide to charge up your reserves for the holiday season. Stand outside where you can see the Moon, and say four times:

> In this place and in this hour,
> White Moon fill me with your power!

Visualize yourself brimming with silvery effervescent energy, able to accomplish all your tasks. Whenever you have need, you can repeat this to revitalize yourself:

> In this place and in this hour,
> I call on the white Moon's power.

Elizabeth Barrette

Notes:

Notes:

December

December is the twelfth month of the year, its name derived from the Latin word *decem,* meaning "ten," as it was the tenth month of the Roman calendar. Its astrological sign is Sagittarius, the archer (Nov 21–Dec 20), a mutable fire sign ruled by Jupiter. This month is buried under blankets of snow. In the evenings, holiday lights twinkle for the Yule season. Back porches are stacked with firewood. Ovens bake confections for serving around a decorated table. Sweets have a particularly ancient history at this time; they are made and eaten to ensure that one has "sweetness" in the coming year. The Full Moon of December is the Oak Moon. It is a time when the waxing Sun overcomes the waning Sun, and days begin to grow longer again. In some Pagan traditions, this struggle is symbolized by the Oak King overcoming the Holly King; rebirth triumphing over death. It is no coincidence that Christians chose this month to celebrate the birth of Jesus. The Winter Solstice is a solar festival and is celebrated with fire in the form of the Yule log. New Year's Eve is another important celebration during December. The old dying year is symbolized at this time by an old man with a long white beard carrying a scythe. The new year is seen appropriately as a newborn child.

December 1
Monday

 2nd ♓

Color of the day: Lavender
Incense of the day: Frankincense

Family Lotus Tea

Monday is family day—so why not throw a tea party for your own family today? After everyone has come home from work or school, serve lotus tea (available at specialty tea shops and at some Starbucks), and lotus buns (available at Chinese bakeries). The lotus is sacred to many pantheons. The Egyptian deities revere the lotus, as do the Hindu gods and goddesses. For more traditional Chinese items to add to your tea, include a statue of Kuan Yin along with some water lilies in a bowl of water (true lotuses are hard to find in the U.S.). Burn lotus incense as well. Make it a theme party with appropriate incense and attire and the kids will love it; or make it a romantic evening for just the two of you in kimonos, enjoying the sensuous taste and scent of lotus.

Denise Dumars

Notes:

December 2
Tuesday

 2nd ♓
☽ → ♈ 5:56 am

Color of the day: White
Incense of the day: Juniper

Appalachian Smoke Signal Divination

To the country folk of Appalachia, the ability to predict the weather by watching the rising of chimney smoke was crucial to survival. It is actually very easy to learn how to read these signals. Here are some points to remember to divine the weather from smoke: When smoke rises straight up, even during rain or snow, it means the weather will clear soon. If the smoke hangs low near the roof, precipitation will occur within the next twenty-four hours. If smoke hangs low, but birds are active, the weather will clear soon. And if smoke drifts back down the chimney, the weather is about to change. Watching the weather can enhance certain magical activities, such as fire divination and spirit contact.

James Kambos

Notes:

December 3
Wednesday

 2nd ♈

Color of the day: Yellow
Incense of the day: Coriander

The Clothes-Maker Spell

Spelled clothing is a way of casting a spell by making clothes. The magic works if you can knit or crochet. Begin this spell by picking an easy project, such as a scarf or hat. Choose as a focus an ongoing intention, such as protection or good health, and compose a short affirmation, mantra, or chant that embodies your aim. This can be as simple as:

> May I have all the energy
> I need.

Or else you can use something more complex if you need it. As you start your project, chant your phrase once for each stitch you knit or loop. Work on your project as long as you can keep the intention in mind. It may take you longer to finish the project, but as a result of your sustained magical intentions the item will keep its power for a long time.

Magenta Griffith

Notes:

December 4
Thursday

2nd ♈
☽ → ♉ 5:30 pm

Color of the day: Violet
Incense of the day: Carnation

Pallas Athena Wisdom Spell

The Romans dedicated this day to Pallas Athena, goddess of wisdom and intellect. Honor her by wearing colors such as blue and white, or by playing games of wit and strategy. One of her most famous symbols is the owl. If you don't have an image of Athena herself, you can substitute an owl. Light blue candles on your altar, and welcome her with words such as these:

> Athena,
> Gray-eyed goddess,
> Banish doubt and
> confusion;
> Bring to me the
> illumination of your
> wisdom.
>
> Let me move silently
> And see clearly,
> As your sacred owls.
> Athena, bless me so!

By calling on this goddess, you also ally yourself with strong and intelligent women everywhere. This is true whether you are a man or a woman.

Elizabeth Barrette

Notes:

December 6
Saturday

 2nd ♉

Color of the day: Brown
Incense of the day: Pine

Guidance of Saturn Spell

Seek the guidance of Saturn today by lighting frankincense incense and holding an amethyst crystal in the smoke. Ask that this crystal be purified of all unwanted energies and filled with the ability to effect beneficial change; then sit in meditation with this crystal and call upon the energies of Saturn. Be aware of any feelings that may arise in you at any time during the ritual. Consider how Saturn tends to bring limitations and establish boundaries; consider how such limitations might affect you, and think about how you will likely respond to this type of energy. Ask for the guidance of Saturn in these efforts, that you might grow through these reactions and attain true freedom in the process. Say out loud:

> I accept the challenge to grow. I ask the blessings of amethyst and Saturn on my journey of personal evolution.

Carry the amethyst with you whenever possible.

Kristin Madden

December 5
Friday

 2nd ♉

Color of the day: Pink
Incense of the day: Nutmeg

Stimulating Love Spell

A wonderful way to ensure faithfulness, and to stimulate love and arouse lust, is to make your loved one a cake that has both candied violets and lavender in it. The lavender may be mixed into the batter, icing, or laid on top of the cake as a decoration. The violets should be candied and placed on top of the cake as a decoration. You will need to make sure that your loved one does sample both the lavender and the violets. If you think getting them to eat the violets will pose a problem, you may choose to use violet water in place of regular water in the recipe.

Sheri Richerson

Notes:

Notes:

December 7

Sunday

Burning the Devil

2nd ♉

☽ → ♊ 6:26 am

Color of the day: Gold
Incense of the day: Parsley

Feast of St. Ambrose Spell
Today is the feast day of St. Ambrose. He was the bishop of Milan in the fifth century, and because of his scholarship and writing, he is called one of the four "Doctors of the Church." Much of Ambrose's work was concerned with synthesizing classical Pagan philosophy, particularly the work of Plato, with Christianity. He was particularly involved with the mystical teachings of the classical age known as Neo-platonism. The city of Milan is the most likely birthplace of the tarot, and although Ambrose lived a thousand years before that birth, he made an important contribution to tarot symbolism. St. Ambrose was the first person to refer to the four virtues that had been expounded on by Plato and Aristotle, which he called the Cardinal Virtues—temperance, justice, fortitude, and prudence. The word "cardinal" is derived from the Latin root *cardo,* which refers to the axis of a wheel. "Cardinal" means that which turns the wheel, referring to the four directions and the four constellations of the seasonal changes. St. Ambrose used the term "cardinal" for the virtues to indicate that they were more powerful than time and space. The goddess Fortuna was the ruler of this wheel, and she and her wheel have been assigned a place in the center of the tarot trumps. In fact, wisdom is illustrated on the Marseilles' tarot Fortune card. Here we see the wheel of fate or time with three foolish creatures around it. They represent the three follies that cause the three aspects of suffering that are depicted in the second section of the tarot trumps. The three other cardinal virtues can also be seen in this second section of the tarot trumps. They are numbered in the opposite order from the way they were presented by Pythagoras and Plato. The virtues of the tarot are moving against time and suffering just as St. Ambrose taught.

Robert Place

Notes:

Holiday lore: Cultures around the world have shared throughout history a penchant for the ritual burning of scapegoats, enemies, and devils. There is something primal about the roar of a large bonfire and its ability to bring purging light to a community. Today is such a day in the highland towns of Guatemala. Men dress in devil costumes through the season before Christmas, and children playfully chase the men through the streets. On December 7, people light bonfires in front of their homes, and into the fires they toss garbage and other debris to purify their lives. At night, fireworks fill the air.

December 8
Monday

 2nd ♊
🌕 Full Moon 3:37 pm

Color of the day: White
Incense of the day: Myrrh

Remember Our Inner Self Spell
The sign of Gemini is associated with trickster energy, or with what certain Native Americans associate with coyote medicine. Sometimes trickster energy can jolt us out of our ordinary and mundane routines and help remind us of our path. The trickster energy can help us wake up from the dream of our ordinary life. Gemini is also associated with duality. As we are both physical and spiritual beings, this is a good time to remember the hidden and underlying self we may have forgotten. To prepare for this spell, you will need a bell and a small mirror. On the night of the Full Moon, find a quiet place and stare into the mirror. You may find yourself worrying about small concerns or suddenly critiquing your personality and lifestyle. Every time your mind drifts, ring the bell. This is the bell of awakening, and it will help you to remember to be present right where you are, and alive in the moment. After you have meditated for a time, allow yourself to look deeply into your own eyes and remember that you are beautiful and powerful. Honor the good aspects of yourself. When you start to forget them and drift back into worries or concerns, ring the bell again. Begin to see your inner radiance on a regular basis.

Jonathan Keyes

Notes:

December 9
Tuesday

 3rd ♊
☽ → ♋ 7:11 pm

Color of the day: Gray
Incense of the day: Honeysuckle

Preparing for the Team Spell

To foster a bit of team spirit in yourself today, take a red cloth, string, or piece of clothing that you will be able to carry with you during the sports event. With this item in hand beforehand, light a red candle. Call to Aries, god of sports and competitions, to imbue you with strength, clarity, and focus. Imagine the Aries energy surrounding and penetrating both you and the red object. See the object vibrate with the energy. Just before the the game, hold or wear your red object. Imagine the energy in the object surrounding you, augmenting your, or your team's, own abilities.

Therese Francis

Notes:

December 10
Wednesday

 3rd ♋

Color of the day: Peach
Incense of the day: Sandalwood

Thanksgiving for the Souls of Animals Spell

Inuit hunters begin a five-day purification rite on December 10 for the souls of the animals they've killed that year. To pay thanksgiving to the food that has sustained you through the year, begin with a green altar cloth and two new candles, green and black. Place a cauldron in the center of the altar, and images of the animals and plants that make up your diet. Light the candles and visualize yourself as an animal. Recite this variation of *The Song of Amergin*:

> I am a stag of seven tines,
> I am a flood on a plain,
> I am a wind on the deep waters,
> I am a shining tear of the Sun,
> I am a hawk on a cliff,
> I am a salmon in the pool.
> I am life,
> I am death.
> I am the universal soul.

Lily Gardner-Butts

Notes:

and so finally bringing your spending habits under control.

Jenna Tigerheart

Notes:

December 11
Thursday

 3rd ♋

Color of the day: Green
Incense of the day: Geranium

Eliminate Bad Spending habits

To help eliminate bad or careless spending habits, pull out one basic denomination of paper money (one dollar, one euro, and so on), and place it on your altar. Light a white candle and look into the flame. Meditate on any recent spending habits that need to change. Write these items down, and when the list is full read through it again. Light a green candle, and start reading these items out loud. As you speak, see the habits disappearing into the air and leaving you. Then say:

> Open my eyes,
> Lend clarity.
> I will find just what I
> need.
> What I don't need,
> I will leave.

Visualize yourself spending your money only on those things you need,

December 12
Friday

 3rd ♋
☽→ ♌ 6:40 am

Color of the day: Rose
Incense of the day: Ginger

The Mirror of our Emotions

Our relationship choices are like mirrors. They reflect what we project to the world, and they reflect what we would like to keep hidden. In other words, for good or for bad, relationship choices show us our unconscious needs, wants, and wounds. To contact your hidden emotional needs and wounds (especially if you repeatedly find yourself in abusive or unfulfilling relationships), gaze into your own eyes in a sage-smudged mirror. State these or similar words:

> Mirror, mirror
> on the wall,
> Unveil my compulsions,
> One and all.

Look past your physical features into your unconscious to the needs, the wants, and the wounds that lie behind the surface. Make changes in your life, and in your relationship choices, based on what you learn.

Karen Follett

Notes:

on the winter goddess and her lesson of stillness. Find the cool and clean space she offers, free of clutter and activity. It is the season for centering and grounding ourselves, and for defining who we really are. After the bath, take your journal and write down your goals by candlelight. Contemplate the coming rebirth, and identify which direction you wish to channel your energy and focus your intentions.

Karri Allrich

Notes:

December 13
Saturday

3rd ♌

Color of the day: Blue
Incense of the day: Lavender

Pre-Solstice Ritual Bath

During the Winter Solstice, we often place emphasis on celebrating and sharing this joyous, but often difficult, holiday. For Witches, however, now may also serve as a time to atune to a quiet, internal spirituality. To begin to do so (with the solstice less than ten days away now), prepare a ritual bath with oils of rosemary, pine, and orange. Add a touch of patchouli for grounding. Light gold and green candles, and immerse yourself in watery solitude to refresh your weary holiday spirit. Meditate

December 14
Sunday

3rd ♌
D → ♍ 4:07 pm

Color of the day: Orange
Incense of the day: Poplar

A Walk in the Snow

This is the season of snowstorms, of blustery winds and blizzards and arctic chill. Many of us need to come to terms with the cold and deathly silence of this season. To do so, take a walk in the snow. In actuality, few things are better for the soul, and the body, than a walk outside in a winter wonderland. There's something wonderfully contemplative about the sights and sounds of a world covered in snow. During a light snow storm is a particularly good time to discover the outdoor. When you walk, make sure you are bundled up as warmly as possible—with the whole works: mittens, hat, down parka, and so on—so you can take your time and simply meander. Meanwhile, listen to the sounds of winter as well as to all the inconsequential chatter in your head that you usually ignore. This walk isn't about how fast you get there, but how much you enjoy getting there. After your walk, head indoors for some hot chocolate with lots of marshmallows floating on top like a soft snowbank.

Laurel Reufner

Notes:

Taking in Fairies Ritual

Fairies tend to sleep during the winter months. However, at this time you may invite them into your home so that they may work their magic there. To let them know that they are welcome where you live, set up four candles in your home—a green one in the north, a red one in the south, a blue one in the west, and a yellow one in the east. Place a crystal or other stone beside each candle, and walk to each candle in a circular motion sprinkling ginger as you go. Then stand in the center of your room and call out this greeting:

> Welcome fairies and
> nature spirits.
> I bid you enter, welcome
> all.

Sheri Richerson

Notes:

December 15
Monday

3rd ♏

Color of the day: Gray
Incense of the day: Rose

December 16
Tuesday

 3rd ♍
Fourth Quarter 12:42 pm
☽→ ♎ 10:46 pm

Color of the day: Black
Incense of the day: Evergreen

Norse Rune Divination

The Norse people used runes to record important events, inscribe names on weapons and monuments, and divine the future. As the year-wheel turns, we have an opportunity to glimpse what lies ahead. Runes are especially suited to this kind of work, as this verse explains:

> Rune craft, rune lore,
> Seek to learn a little
> more.
> Rune old, rune true,
> Whisper what it's
> coming to.

To preview the coming year, draw twelve runes (see the back pages of this book for samples), and lay them out in a row. The first rune on the left corresponds to January, and so on down the line. Each one suggests the overall tone for that month.

Elizabeth Barrette

Notes:

December 17
Wednesday
Saturnalia

 4th ♎

Color of the day: White
Incense of the day: Eucalyptus

Remind-Yourself Success Spell

To remind yourself of your own self-worth, take one whole almond and carve the word "success" on it. Hold it as you visualize yourself enjoying a successful business or school career. Take a deep breath and, as you exhale, blow this intent onto the almond. Brew a cup of chamomile tea and soak the almond in it overnight. Allow it to dry and carry it with you throughout the next day. That night, bury the almond in the earth or in a houseplant that ordinarily resides wherever you do your work. Draw a pentacle in the dirt over the almond. Holding your hands out over the pentacle, call up that visualization of success and charge the pentacle with this intent.

Kristin Madden

Notes:

Holiday lore: Saturnalia was Rome's biggest and most beloved festival. Among the many wild and festive activities on this day, masters gave slaves a week of freedom and waited on them. All schools, law courts, shops, and offices were closed on this day; everyone relaxed in leisure activities and ruminated on the "Golden Age" of the past that was embodied by the god Saturn. On December 17, festivities would culminate with a public pig sacrifice and feast. People played games with dice and exchanged gifts (a custom that still survives today in our Christmas gift-giving traditions).

December 18
Thursday

 4♄ ♎

Color of the day: Turquoise
Incense of the day: Musk

Wealth of Turquoise Spell

One of December's most magical symbols is the blue turquoise. For this spell, place a turquoise stone in the center of a piece of paper. To the left of the stone, draw the shape of an anchor; on the right, draw a hand. Holding your power hand above the paper say:

> I am anchored and steady.
> I'm ready to receive abundance and prosperity.

Now hold the turquoise. Breathe on it, then speak:

> Stone of blue,
> Like sky and sea,
> Favor me with wealth.

> It must be.

Lay the stone on the paper, then fold it as you would fold a letter. Place this prosperity packet near where you keep your wallet or purse. Handle the turquoise occasionally, to keep the spell active.

James Kambos

Notes:

December 19
Friday

 4♄ ♎
☽ → ♏ 2:20 am

Color of the day: Peach
Incense of the day: Almond

Do-Unto-Others Spell

Many Witches believe that whatever you do returns to you threefold. So today, practice three random acts of kindness. Pay for the coffee of the stranger behind you at the coffee shop. Let someone go ahead of you in line at the grocery store. Do the dishes, or vacuum the living room when it isn't your turn. Leave the waitress an extra large tip. Shovel snow or mow the lawn for a neighbor. Get in the spirit of the holiday season by being kind to others.

Magenta Griffith

Notes:

December 20

Saturday

hanukkah begins

 4th ♏

Color of the day: White
Incense of the day: Coriander

Golem Lore for the First Day of hanukkah

An interesting myth of Jewish tradition involves the creation of an artificial human through the mysterious magic of the Qabala. The golem is a Frankensteinian creation; however, instead of being merely a reanimated human being or one made of human parts, the golem is altogether artificial and is animated by the use of magical and holy words. The most famous golem legend revolves around Rabbi Loew of Prague. There are several versions of this legend, which is set in the mid-eighteenth century. In most versions, the rabbi creates the golem as a guardian or protector of the Jewish people in the Prague ghetto. But soon the huge creature—built of clay and animated by the secret name of God—runs amok and must be destroyed. In some golem legends it is the Star of David itself that animates the creature, and only the removal of this symbol from the creature's body will cause the havoc to cease. The story of the golem seems to have a moral: that man should not "tamper in God's domain," as the saying goes. It was perhaps meant as a cautionary tale to those who took Qabalistic magic too far from its sacred origins and wished to use it to glorify their own powers. In any case, the golem is a folk legend that spans many centuries, has many versions—including on film, with the silent version from 1915 perhaps the most excellent.

Denise Dumars

Notes:

Holiday lore: Like most December holidays, Hannukah is a festival of lights—a midwinter rite that celebrates the light within in the midst of the surrounding darkness. Its origins are in Jewish lore regarding a king in the second century B.C. who strove to convert the Jews to a Greek polytheism through bloodshed. In the midst of this horror, Jewish guerrillas, led by Judah Maccabee, fought off the king's forces and entered the temple, decreeing that there should be an annual festival celebrating this rout. It is said that when he lit the menorah, or candelabra, its light lasted miraculously for eight days though it had oil enough for only one day. The menorah is today a symbol of the holiday.

in the direction of the smoke each thing you want to eliminate. Watch each negative item drift away from you in the smoke. Make sure you grind enough of the herbs to last through the rite if you intend to eliminate more than a few things. When you have voiced everything, waft the incense toward yourself and cleanse the last negative remnants away.

Jenna Tigerheart

Notes:

December 21
Sunday

 4th ♏
☽ → ♐ 3:16 am

Color of the day: Yellow
Incense of the day: Cinnamon

Purification from Negativity Spell
To purify yourself from negative thoughts, bad habits, or dark experiences, use a potent mix of equal parts bloodroot, thistle, and lemon verbena. Start by grinding the herbs in your mortar and pestle and burning them in your censor. State aloud

December 22
Monday
Yule – Winter Solstice

 4th ♐
☉ → ♑ 2:04 am

Color of the day: Lavender
Incense of the day: Peony

Yule and Solstice Ritual
The solstice is a time for gathering resources out from deep in the subconscious. Surround yourself with candles of red, green, and white, and evergreens and holly, as you say:

> Longest night and
> shortest day,

Magic comes bright.
We gather now on this
longest night,
honoring darkness,
praising light.

Dancers hail the
standing stones,
As growing solar light
returns.

Ancient ones at
Newgrange gathered,
Awaiting dawns first
light.

hidden tombs and
carvings old,
Illuminated by solstice
sunlight bright.
World round, grateful
souls
Celebrate this night of
returning light.

May we see this shaft of
brilliance,
A sign of summer growing.
Cut the evergreen
adornments,
And build the sacred fire
to coax the Sun higher.

Yule log embers and
torches bright,
Warm our dreams this
magical night.
Memories and ancient
secrets

Of the Druids come to
me tonight.

May this increase my
wisdom now,
The ancestors guide my
spirit.
Magnifying brilliance
and promises to come,
Spirals dance in solstice
first light.

Visions planted, now on
this night,
Grow strong and clear
with the light.
holly, mistletoe, ivy,
pine,
Magic be, on this day.

So mote it be.

Abby Willowroot

Notes:

holiday lore: The Yule season is a
festival of lights, and a solar festival, and is celebrated by fire in the
form of the Yule log—a log decorated
with fir needles, yew needles, birch

branches, holly sprigs, and trailing vines of ivy. Back porches are stacked with firewood for burning, and the air is scented with pine and wood smoke. When the Yule Log has burned out, save a piece for use as a powerful amulet of protection through the new year. Now is a good time to light your oven for baking bread and confections for serving around a decorated table; sweets have a particularly ancient history at this time. They are made and eaten to ensure that one would have "sweetness" in the coming year. Mistletoe hangs over doorways, and kissing under the mistletoe is a tradition that comes down from the Druids, who considered the plant sacred. They gathered mistletoe from the high branches of sacred oak with golden sickles. It is no coincidence that Christians chose this month to celebrate the birth of Jesus. Now is the time when the waxing Sun overcomes the waning Sun, and days begin to grow longer again. In some Pagan traditions, this struggle is symbolized by the Oak King overcoming the Holly King; rebirth triumphing over death. And so the holly tree has come to be a symbol of the season, and is used in Yuletide decorations; wreaths are made of holly, the circle of which symbolized the wheel of the year—and the completed cycle. (Yule means "wheel" in old Anglo-Saxon.)

December 23
Tuesday

 4th ♐
☽ → ♑ 2:55 am

Color of the day: Red
Incense of the day: Sage

Strengthening the Foundations of Your Intentions Spell

Capricorn is associated with the earth element and with foundations in our lives. By strengthening our spiritual core and foundations, we help ourselves to be more solid and grounded in our beliefs and our goals. Without a solid core to depend on, our lives are as precarious as any building with a week foundation. To prepare for this spell you will need a few dark rocks such as obsidian, jade, or onyx. You will also need some root herbs such as ginseng and licorice. And you will need a small box no more than a few inches in diameter, and four darkly colored candles. On the night of the New Moon, place the four candles in the four directions and then light them. Ask for assistance in your magical work, and then open up the box before you. Place the roots and the rocks inside the box. As you do this, say aloud your basic beliefs and your core intentions in life. Make these words clear and heartfelt. The roots and stones are symbols of your intentions. As you place them in the box, ask that these foundations may support you on your journey and that positive manifestations will flower from these good intentions. Keep the box on an altar until you feel you need to renew your foundation work.

Jonathan Keyes

Notes:

the cauldron, write its name on a piece of paper. Burn a new red candle dressed with bayberry oil. Focus on the flame and feel the magic vibrating around you. Feel your power coming up from your solar plexus. You can make yourself happy and at peace if you only give yourself the gift. Merry Christmas!

Lily Gardner-Butts

Notes:

December 24
Wednesday

 1st ♑

Color of the day: Brown
Incense of the day: Cedar

Spell for Christmas Eve

For many of us, the holidays seem at odds with an otherwise meditative and quiet time of year. This spell serves as a special gift to yourself. Start by asking yourself what it is you want now. Carve out a piece of time on this day for your spell. Decorate your altar with greenery, a cauldron, and any other decorations that are meaningful to you. Place your gift to yourself inside the cauldron. Or, if it won't fit in

December 25
Thursday
Christmas

 1st ♑
☽ → ♒ 3:13 am

Color of the day: White
Incense of the day: Vanilla

Christmas Magic Spell

Today is a day for candles, white red, and green surrounded by tiny personal treasures that make you smile. This spell is for spreading magic:

Sparking lights and
baubles bright,
hold the magic

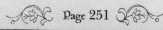

on this night.
hold the magic on the
morrow,
May we never feel true
sorrow.

Spin the magic and let it
glow,
Let your Christmas
cheer grow.
Kindness spread from
heart to heart,
Making living a sharing
art.

Strangers reaching and
forming bonds,
That touches the heart
and beyond.
Angels and spirits laugh
in joy
to see a child smile with
a toy.

Looking around, I do see,
Lives I touch and bless
with glee.
Giving time can grow
my soul,
Being more human is my
goal.

We are messengers of
the light,
We each bring spirit this
day and night.
Christmas cheer is alive
in me,
I find its miracles in all I
see.

A blessing in the world,
So mote it be.

Abby Willowroot

Notes:

December 26
Friday
Kwanzaa begins

 1st ≈

Color of the day: Pink
Incense of the day: Dill

Empowering Your Family's Dreams
To bring your family's dreams to fruition, take a small pottery bowl that everyone likes. Place a burning piece of sage or copal in the center, so that the smoke rises out of the bowl. Let each family member, one at a time, speak a wish into the rising smoke. Then as a group, blow into the bowl, imaging your breaths intermingling with the smoke and going out into the universe to attract your wishes to you.

Therese Francis

Notes:

December 27
Saturday
hanukkah ends

 1st ≈,
☽ → ♓ 6:10 am

Color of the day: Gray
Incense of the day: Violet

The Evangelists Spell

Today is the feast day of St. John the Evangelist. St. John was the youngest of the twelve apostles and the brother of Peter and James. He is said to be the author of the fourth Gospel. Unlike other apostles, John lived into his old age when he had the time and introspection to write about the events that he had witnessed. Because his spirit soars upward in his text, especially when he speaks of Christian love, he is symbolized by the eagle, and his symbol appears on the upper right corner of the World card in the tarot. Once when John was in the company of Emperor Domitian, the emperor ordered him to drink a cup of poisoned wine. When John picked up the cup, the poison departed in the form of a snake and he drank it unharmed. In fact, John lived a long life and died of natural causes. A cup with a snake emerging from it also became his symbol. This symbol was used by alchemists as an illustration of their great work, and they were attempting to transform poisonous mercury into a healing elixir. By praying to St. John, we can obtain the wisdom to transform the destructive aspects of ourselves into our greatest allies. This is the true wisdom of any magical operation.

Robert Place

Notes:

December 28
Sunday

 1st ♓

Color of the day: Peach
Incense of the day: Sage

Superfueled Nutrition

Our mothers are right—good nutrition is a foundation of good health. My mother's favorite

saying was: "A car can't run without gas." So in keeping with the car-as-good-health metaphor, let's say you can increase the octane of your food and drink by tapping into the energies of the universe. To do this on a daily basis, pour yourself a glass of water (preferably spring or purified). Extend your hands over the glass, forming the thumbs and forefingers into a triangle. Visualize a stream of energy passing through the triangle and into the water. Don't worry on the color of this energy; let the universe choose. Enjoy your new smooth-running engine.

Karen Follett

Notes:

buy. This quick spell should get things moving. Start by drawing a picture of your desired home on a piece of paper. If you have an ad for the exact place you want, clip it out and paste it to the drawing. Light a brown candle, saying:

> housing, housing,
> Come to me.

Roll the paper up, place it in a small glass bottle, and seal it. Put the bottle somewhere in the room you consider the heart of your current home. Once the new home is secured, remove the drawing and burn it in the candle flame. If possible, bury what remains of both candle and ashes.

Laurel Reufner

Notes:

December 29
Monday

1st ♓
) → ♈ 1:08 am

Color of the day: Silver
Incense of the day: Chrysanthemum

Find a New House Spell
Need to find new housing in a hurry? Or maybe things have stalled on the house you want to

December 30
Tuesday

1st ♈
Second Quarter 5:03 am

Color of the day: White
Incense of the day: Gardenia

Conjuring a Goal Spell

Our collective focus now turns to the coming year, and to our goals, resolutions, and new beginnings. To strengthen your focus on a new goal, select a card from your favorite tarot deck that symbolizes your desire. If it's an increasing or attracting goal, choose a night during the waxing Moon to cast this spell. If it's a decreasing or releasing intention, choose a night during the waning Moon. Light a white candle. Place your tarot card in front of you. On a clean piece of paper write down your goal three times. Fold the paper three times, and place it in your wallet. Place the tarot card on your altar. When the goal is achieved, burn the paper and return the card to your deck.

Karri Allrich

Notes:

December 31
Wednesday
New Year's Eve

1st ♈

Color of the day: Yellow
Incense of the day: Neroli

New Year's Eve Ritual

The old year is about to pass now. You can use white candles to symbolize this passing. This is a spell for letting go of things which hold you back as we move into the new year.

> Blessed year passing away,
> May your joys with me stay.
>
> Make me lucky, make me wise.
> Magic blessings before these eyes.
>
> Magical time between old and new,
> Yesterday and tomorrow.
> Lessons learned will be due.
> Pass away regret and sorrow.
>
> Magic passing stay with me,
> And I will hold you dear.
> New Year's Eve and New Year's Day,
> Let the spirits of possibility play.
>
> Words that open doors to secrets old and new dear.
> What I reap return to me.

Tomorrow begins
another year.

Notes:

Skills I have to grow
and blossom,
Talents I lack will come
to me.
May lessons learned stay
now with me,
With open eyes I am
free.

Grow powers in me and
vision true,
to clear the past and
grow anew.
None of the past will
cling to me,
I am happy.

So mote it be.

                    Abby Willowroot

Notes:

A Guide to Witches' Spell-A-Day Icons

 New Moon Spells Full Moon Spells

 New Year's Eve, Day Jewish Holidays

 Imbolc Samhain, Halloween

 Valentine's Day Thanksgiving

 Ostara, Easter Yule, Christmas

 April Fool's Day Sunday Health Spells

 Earth Day Monday Home Spells

 Beltane Tuesday Protection Spells

 Mother's Day Wednesday Travel Spells

 Father's Day Thursday Money Spells

 Litha Friday Love Spells

 Lammas Saturday Grab Bag

 Mabon

Daily Magical Influences

Each day is ruled by a planet that possesses specific magical influences:

Monday (Moon): peace, healing, caring, psychic awareness, and purification.

Tuesday (Mars): passion, sex, courage, aggression, and protection.

Wednesday (Mercury): conscious mind, study, travel, divination, and wisdom.

Thursday (Jupiter): expansion, money, prosperity, and generosity.

Friday (Venus): love, friendship, reconciliation, and beauty.

Saturday (Saturn): longevity, exorcism, endings, homes, and houses.

Sunday (Sun): healing, spirituality, success, strength, and protection.

Lunar Phases

The lunar phase is important in determining best times for magic. Times are Eastern Standard Time.

The waxing Moon (from the New Moon to the Full) is the ideal time for magic to draw things toward you.

The Full Moon is the time of greatest power.

The waning Moon (from the Full Moon to the New) is a time for study, meditation, and little magical work (except magic designed to banish harmful energies).

Astrological Symbols

The Sun	☉	Aries	♈
The Moon	☽	Taurus	♉
Mercury	☿	Gemini	♊
Venus	♀	Cancer	♋
Mars	♂	Leo	♌
Jupiter	♃	Virgo	♍
Saturn	♄	Libra	♎
Uranus	♅	Scorpio	♏
Neptune	♆	Sagittarius	♐
Pluto	♇	Capricorn	♑
		Aquarius	♒
		Pisces	♓

The Moon's Sign

The Moon's sign is a traditional consideration for astrologers. The Moon continuously moves through each sign in the zodiac, from Aries to Pisces. The Moon influences the sign it inhabits, creating different energies that affect our daily lives. All times are EST.

Aries: Good for starting things, but lacks staying power. Things occur rapidly, but quickly pass. People tend to be argumentative and assertive.

Taurus: Things begun now do last, tend to increase in value, and become hard to alter. Brings out an appreciation for beauty and sensory experience.

Gemini: Things begun now are easily changed by outside influence. Time for shortcuts, communications, games, and fun.

Cancer: Stimulates emotional rapport between people. Pinpoints need, supports growth and nurturance. Tend to domestic concerns.

Leo: Draws emphasis to the self, to central ideas or institutions, away from connections with others and emotional needs. People tend to be melodramatic.

Virgo: Favors accomplishment of details and commands from higher up. Focus on health, hygiene, and daily schedules.

Libra: Favors cooperation, compromise, social activities, beautification of surroundings, balance, and partnership.

Scorpio: Increases awareness of psychic power. Precipitates psychic crises and ends connections thoroughly. People tend to brood and become secretive under this Moon sign.

Sagittarius: Encourages flights of imagination and confidence. This Moon sign is adventurous, philosophical, and athletic. Favors expansion and growth.

Capricorn: Develops strong structure. Focus on traditions, responsibilities, and obligations. A good time to set boundaries and rules.

Aquarius: Rebellious energy. Time to break habits and make abrupt change. Personal freedom and individuality is the focus.

Pisces: The focus is on dreaming, nostalgia, intuition, and psychic impressions. A good time for spiritual or philanthropic activities.

Glossary of Magical Terms

Altar: a low table that holds magical tools as a focus for spell workings.

Athame: a ritual knife used to direct personal power during workings or to symbolically draw diagrams in a spell. It is rarely, if ever, used for actual physical cutting.

Aura: an invisible energy field surrounding a person. The aura can change color depending upon the state of the individual.

Balefire: a fire lit for magical purposes, usually outdoors.

Casting a circle: the process of drawing a circle around oneself to seal out unfriendly influences and raise magical power. It is the first step in a spell.

Censer: an incense burner. Traditionally, a censer is a metal container, filled with incense, that is swung on the end of a chain.

Censing: the process of burning incense to spiritually cleanse an object.

Centering yourself: to prepare for a magical rite by calming and centering all of your personal energy.

Chakra: one of the seven centers of spiritual energy in the human body, according to the philosophy of yoga.

Charging: to infuse an object with magical power.

Circle of protection: a circle cast to protect oneself from unfriendly influences.

Crystals: quartz or other stones that store cleansing or protective energies.

Deosil: clockwise movement, symbolic of life and positive energies.

Deva: a divine being according to Hindu beliefs; a devil or evil spirit according to Zoroastrianism.

Direct/Retrograde: refers to the motions of the planets when seen from the Earth. A planet is "direct" when it appears to be moving forward from the point of view of a person on the Earth. It is "retrograde" when it appears to be moving backward.

Dowsing: to use a divining rod to search for a thing, usually water or minerals.

Dowsing pendulum: a long cord with a coin or gem at one end. The pattern of its swing is used to predict the future.

Dryad: a tree spirit or forest guardian.

Fey: an archaic term for a magical spirit or a fairylike being.

Gris-gris: a small bag containing charms, herbs, stones, and other items to draw energy, luck, love, or prosperity to the wearer.

Mantra: a sacred chant used in Hindu tradition to embody the divinity invoked; it is said to possess deep magical power.

Needfire: a ceremonial fire kindled at dawn on major Wiccan holidays. It was traditionally used to light all other household fires.

Pentagram: a symbolically protective five-pointed star with one point upward.

Power hand: the dominant hand, the hand used most often.

Scry: to predict the future by gazing at or into an object such as a crystal ball or pool of water.

Second sight: the psychic power or ability to forsee the future.

Sigil: a personal seal or symbol.

Smudge/Smudge stick: to spiritually cleanse an object by waving incense over and around it. A smudge stick is a bundle of several incense sticks.

Wand: a stick or rod used for casting circles and as a focus for magical power.

Widdershins: counterclockwise movement, symbolic of negative magical purposes, and sometimes used to disperse negative energies.

Norse Runes

Feoh — money, wealth ᚠ

Ur — strength, physicality ᚢ

Thorn — destruction, power ᚦ

Os — wisdom, insight ᚩ

Rad — travel, change ᚱ

Ken — energy, creativity, change ᚲ

Gyfu — gift, sacrifice ᚷ

Wynn — joy, harmony ᚹ

Haegl — union, completion ᚻ

Nyd — need, deliverance ᚾ

Is — ice, barrenness ᛁ

Jera — bounty, fruition, reward ᛄ

Eoh — resilience, endurance ᛇ

Peordh — change, evolution ᛈ

Eolh — luck, protection ᛉ

Sigil — success, honor ᛋ

Tyr — courage, victory, justice ᛏ

Beorc — healing, renewal ᛒ

Eh — journeys, work ᛖ

Mann — man, self, intelligence ᛗ

Lagu — healing, protection, life ᛚ

Ing — fertility, energy ᛝ

Daeg — opportunity, change ᛞ

Ethel — land, prosperity, power ᛟ

Call for Submissions

We are looking for magical daily lore for next year's *Witches' Spell-A-Day Almanac*. If you have lore or history to share about a day or holiday, we'd like to hear about it.

Writers: Daily lore descriptions should be 75 to 125 words long, and focus on a topic related to a particular day, holiday, time of year, or season. We are looking for unique and interesting lore that is timely and revealing.

Submissions should be sent to: annualssubmissions@llewellyn.com

or

Witches' Spell-A-Day Submissions
Llewellyn Worldwide
P.O. Box 64383
St. Paul, MN 55164

(Please include your address, phone number, and e-mail address if applicable.)

If you are under the age of 18, you will need parental permission to have your writing published. We are unable to return any submissions. Writers and artists whose submissions are chosen for publication will be published in the 2004 edition of the *Witches' Spell-A-Day Almanac* and will receive a free copy of the book.